THREE ON THE BOARDS

THREE ON THE BOARDS

NEW PLAYS FOR THREE ACTORS

EDITED BY KIT BRENNAN

Cover design by Doowah Design Inc.

We acknowledge the financial assistance of the Manitoba Arts Council and The Canada Council for the Arts for our publishing program.

Printed and bound in Canada by Marquis Book Printing.
Printed on Ancient Forest Friendly stock.

Library and Archives Canada Cataloguing in Publication

Three on the boards / Kit Brennan, editor.

ISBN 978-1-897109-19-9

1. Canadian drama (English)--21st century. I. Brennan, Kit, 1957-

PS8309.O5T48 2007 C812'.608 C2007-906788-3

Signature Editions
P.O. Box 206, RPO Corydon, Winnipeg, MB R3M 3S7
www.signature-editions.com

CONTENTS

FOREWORD

Three people or objects placed at equidistance form a triangle, which is a sharp-cornered, spiky sort of a shape. They don't roll well, they're not curvy. They give off pointed vibes. So, I discovered, do recent Canadian plays for three actors—at least, the ones that I was drawn to for this collection.

Seven plays of various lengths, by writers living in Edmonton, Saskatoon, Toronto, Montreal and St. John's, form a dark and mainly urban picture of Canada in the first decade of this new century and millennium. Some of their themes are not for the faint of heart. Love is variously celebrated and thrown away—as is tolerance, as is hope. There's a lot of substance abuse, as well as other kinds of abuse; many of the characters are running as hard as they can away from themselves. At the same time, they can be endearing, caustic and often extremely funny, because they are very human. Three of the plays have a writer (poet, novelist, screenwriter, journalist) as a character and—especially when considered together—these dramas question what it's like trying to live, stay sane and document the world we've inherited (and created) at this poised, imminent heartbeat in time. Even the two gentler, shorter comedies have dark edges: a young woman mourned by a grieving father, an affection-starved, spooky landlady. In plays for three actors, it seems everyone is fighting their own battle in a sharp-cornered ring, which flings them together and then apart. Oddly, taken as a whole, they become almost uplifting.

The playwrights range from established voices, whose work you may have encountered before, to emerging writers of various ages. Their backgrounds, too, are widely differing and contribute to the ways in which they tell their characters' stories. For each, three actors are required to work in a vibrant ensemble, with all corners fully inhabited.

With these seven plays, I hope the anthology also demonstrates the ever-evolving nature of new writing for the theatre, which is acutely aware of the speed with which we now process image, sound, and even time and space. Scenes and characters morph seamlessly, borrowing from new techniques of film as well as the ancient craft of oral storytelling, while remaining true to the necessities and immediacy of theatre.

I thank the writers whose work appears here, as well as the many other playwrights who submitted their scripts. I hope this collection may spark further productions, and perhaps a few heated discussions about our future, our country, and our theatre.

Kit Brennan
Concordia University
Montreal, Quebec

CURTSY

BRIAN DRADER

Photo: Maxim Coté

BRIAN DRADER

ABOUT THE PLAYWRIGHT

Brian Drader has been working as an actor, playwright and screenwriter for the last twenty years. His stage plays have been produced across Canada and in the United States. Recent awards for his writing include the Herman Voaden National Playwriting Award for *The Norbals*, and the Philadelphia Brick Playhouse New Play Award for *Prok*. *Prok* was also nominated for the 2003 Governor General's award (Canada), the McNally Robinson Book of the Year, and won the Lambda Literary Award for Drama (USA). His play *Liar* was a finalist in the Joyce Dutka Arts Foundation Playwriting Competition, New York, and premiered at Prairie Theatre Exchange in February of 2004. *The Norbals*, *Prok* and *Liar* are all published by Scirocco Drama. A Theatre for Young Audience piece, *To Be Frank*, recently toured high schools in Eastern Canada with Montreal's Geordie Productions.

Brian has also acted in over eighty professional theatre productions across Canada, as well as numerous films, television projects, and radio dramas, and has served as the Associate Artistic Director of Prairie Theatre Exchange in Winnipeg, Manitoba. He is presently the Director of Playwriting at the National Theatre School of Canada in Montreal, Quebec.

PRODUCTION HISTORY

Curtsy was developed over a period of three years with the assistance of The Canada Council, The Manitoba Arts Council, and the Winnipeg Arts Council. Dramaturgical support was provided by Emma Tibaldo (Playwrights' Workshop Montreal) and Iris Turcott (Canadian Stage Company). The play received a one-day workshop with Playwrights' Workshop Montreal in the spring of 2005. The first workshop and public reading of *Curtsy* took place as part of the National Art Centre's On the Verge series, in conjunction with the Magnetic North Theatre Festival, in Ottawa, Ontario, Canada, on June 15, 2005 (under the title of *Dissecting Homo*). It was directed by Emma Tibaldo and stage managed by Tina Goralski, with Julian Doucet (Randolph Gitz), Greg MacArthur (Dillan Smith), and Hubert Proulx (Bart Fidel).

For production rights, contact Signature Editions, Playwrights Guild of Canada or the author at briandrader@sympatico.ca.

CHARACTERS

Randolph Gitz — A professor of Human Studies in his early thirties.

Dillan Smith — A writer in his mid-thirties. Dillan is mosaic, a condition in which the individual has a mixed set of chromosomes, in this case both male and female chromosomes. The condition can result in the individual having both male and female genitalia, as is the case with Dillan.

Bart Fidel — A young male hustler, good-looking but worn out in a beat-up, rough trade, white trash sort of way.

SETTING

Most of the action takes place in Randolph and Dillan's condo, in their living area. The living area includes a couch and a coffee table, and a portable bar located behind the couch. Their front door is stage right, an exit upstage leads to their bedroom, and an exit stage left leads to the kitchen.
Other locations include:
A lecture podium.
A bench outside the university.
A bathhouse.
A hospital waiting area.
A bench outside the rehab centre.

Bart's monologues can take place anywhere.
"/" in the text indicates overlapping dialogue.

ACT I

Light finds Professor Randolph Gitz. He is relatively young for a professor—early thirties. He's good-looking, although rather bookish, wearing a dress shirt and tie. He's standing at a lecture podium, sorting through his notes. He looks up, takes in the audience.

RANDOLPH: Settle, please…

Everyone in the right room? Human Studies 207?

Good.

The first half of any given class will be lecture. I suggest you attend all classes. There is no text book. I've included a bibliography in the course outline. I suggest you read everything.

We'll be starting with an examination of gender and sexuality in contemporary culture.

Case study—Stella Walsh. Born Stanislawa Walasiewiczowna, the only daughter of Polish immigrants, emigrated to the States in the early 1900's when she was two, became a high school sprinting star in Cleveland, and went on to become a world-class athlete, running for her native land of Poland, and winning an Olympic gold and silver medal in the 100-metre dash in 1932 and 1936, respectively. She continued to compete as an amateur until 1954 and was inducted into the U.S. Track and Field Hall of Fame in 1975. Five years later she was killed by a stray bullet at a Cleveland shopping centre during a holdup. An autopsy revealed that Walsh had male as well as female genitals, and both male and female chromosomes—a condition known as mosaicism.

Two questions.

A slow evening light finds Dillan. He is dressed in a long silk robe.

DILLAN: And…fade in.

RANDOLPH: First question—Should Ms. Walsh be stripped of her medals and record standing?

Second question—If the medical option were available to Ms. Walsh's parents, should they have physically corrected their child's condition, either by removing the penis or closing the vagina?

DILLAN: Gypsumville. A scrubbed and polished fairytale-like town in the Manitoba Interlake area.

RANDOLPH: We'll discuss all questions in the second half of the class.

Light fades on Randolph at the lecture podium.

DILLAN: A mining town. Well-ordered on the surface; innocent, scrubbed, polished. Idyllic. On second glance, however, perfection takes on the taint of repression, an anal preoccupation with order that suffocates and chokes, like a fine black leather dress belt that's been pulled two notches too tight. Underneath the mannered exterior of Gypsumville, you see, lies a great chaotic labyrinth of tunnels and caves and shadows, a dark and claustrophobic maze filled with sweaty, toiling beasts. The mines.

Light finds Randolph, sitting on the couch in the living room, listening to Dillan's story.

This is the tit that nurtured our anti-hero, Barblow, through his childhood and into his teen years, when he began to grow restless for adventure.

RANDOLPH: Barblow?

DILLAN: *(excited, selling his story)* Everyone used to call him Bar because that's the only place anyone ever saw him, and so he started using it as his drag name, and then he got into the drugs and he started blowing guys in the bar—under the table, in the john, wherever—so everyone started calling him Barblow.

RANDOLPH: This is the *Heart of Darkness* we're talking about, right?

DILLAN: It's *inspired* by the *Heart of Darkness*, Randolph. It's not a retelling. It's *not Apocalypse Now.*

RANDOLPH: You're calling him Barblow instead of Marlow. Nobody's going to take that seriously.

DILLAN: You could at least show me the courtesy of letting me actually tell you the story before you start ripping it apart. The whole mining town thing is just back story anyway, it's not important,

I'm just setting up a visual metaphor for later, I'll put it all under the opening credits or something, and who cares what his name is, I'll call him…I don't know…Frank or Rupert or something, it doesn't matter. What's important is the first time he meets Curtsy. He's turned his back on the mines. He's a young stallion just coming into his oats and he's restless, so he leaves Gypsumville behind / and sets out for…

RANDOLPH: / Curtsy?

DILLAN: It's her drag name. Curtsy. She's the reigning Empress of the Imperial Sovereign Court of Winnipeg and All of Manitoba. The Queen of the Prairies. It's the drag version of the Imperialism that underpins…that underscores…what's the word I'm looking for…

RANDOLPH: That's "in"?

DILLAN: Yes. Exactly. That's *in* the novel. Get it? And I'm thinking she's constantly surrounded by an entire court of young fags, all beautiful and fabulous but kind of sallow, too, you know? Washed out, used up, almost ghoulish under the harsh light of day, slaves to the Imperial order, but of course they're fabulous in club light, it's a great visual, and Curtsy, she can connect anyone with anything, and everyone worships her and wants to be her friend, because to be the friend of Curtsy is to be at the centre of the Winnipeg Gay Universe. And this is where our story starts. Barblow arrives in Winnipeg.

RANDOLPH: Why Winnipeg?

Silence.

DILLAN: Why not Winnipeg?

RANDOLPH: I don't know. It just seems like an / odd choice.

DILLAN: / I'm trying to tell you my story, it's my *work* for God's sake, I let you talk about your work ad nauseam, would it hurt to just humour me? *Pretend* you're listening?

RANDOLPH: I'm obviously listening. I couldn't be asking you questions if I wasn't listening. It's because I'm listening that I can inquire about specific questionable choices in the story you're telling. Like why Winnipeg.

DILLAN: Because I can't start them in fucking...New York or wherever, because then I don't have anywhere to go, do I? So I start Barblow in Gypsumville, and he goes to Winnipeg and he sees Curtsy win the fucking Empress thing and then Curtsy takes off to Toronto for the National Imperial Duchess of the whatever competition and she disappears. You get it?

Silence.

RANDOLPH: Get what?

Silence.

What?

DILLAN: Curtsy. Disappears. Just like Kurtz in Conrad's thing. Except Curtsy disappears into the *urban* jungle, instead of the Congo or wherever Kurtz ended up. And so the Imperial Court of Manitoba has to send Barblow to find her, and everywhere he goes, the legend of Curtsy grows, just like Kurtz, until it almost breathes by itself, spreading like a virus.

And eventually it leads Barblow to New York, or maybe Vegas, some place trashy and huge, wherever, and he finally catches up with her, with Curtsy, in this dark, dingy steam room in some third-rate, back alley bathhouse, surrounded by wigs on wig forms that look like skulls on sticks. It's a visual echo of the jungle stronghold in the book, get it? And not only that, it kind of looks like the mines underneath Gypsumville where Barblow came from. All dark and dank and filled with dirty, sweaty men. So visually the whole thing comes full circle. Back to where Barblow started as a kid, as a teenager. It's fucking brilliant. And Curtsy's being guarded by all these whorish little fag trolls, the dregs of the homo underworld who have nowhere else to go, and they worship her as a sort of false idol. She's a madam, with a stable of wretched, lice-infested boy prostitutes, and she deals drugs and keeps the lights dimmed to hide her ravaged beauty. We can cake the makeup on really thick so it kind of melts in the steam room, you know? Like her whole face is sliding off. Very Marlon Brando.

Silence.

So? What do you think?

RANDOLPH: That's it?

DILLAN: Of course that's not it. I mean there's the whole big dialogue at the end, in the bathhouse, and I figure Curtsy can die of an overdose, freebasing or something, you know, the horror, the horror. I'll work all that in. I'm talking about in general. What do you think of the basic story? The concept. Do you think it works?

RANDOLPH: Well, it's cinematic. It's visual. That's a good start. I'm just not quite sure about the tone, maybe. Does it know what it wants to be?

DILLAN: Does what know what what wants to be? What kind of a question is that? It wants to be a movie. What the hell else would it want to be? I'm writing a screenplay.

RANDOLPH: I meant the tone, the genre. You talk about it like some big drama, but you've named the central characters Barblow and Curtsy. So it's what? A parody of *Heart of Darkness*? A...homage? A...

DILLAN: Forget the *Heart of Darkness*, okay? I should have never even mentioned it. This is its own story. *The Heart of Darkneth.* Not Darkne*ss*. Darkne*th*.

Silence.

Okay, look, I borrowed some of the plot and I'm playing around with the names a bit. So what? The rest of it's mine.

RANDOLPH: Yeah, but right there, that's what I mean. I don't get it. I don't get what you're trying to do.

DILLAN: I'm trying to tell a fucking story. Why does it have to be more complicated than that?

RANDOLPH: Fine.

DILLAN: No, no, no, not fine. You can't just bail out. I'm asking you for your opinion. / You can't just bail out ...

RANDOLPH: / I'm trying to give you my opinion, but / you won't stop talking...

DILLAN: / bail out because I don't /

RANDOLPH: / long enough to / fucking listen!

DILLAN: / accept that opinion!

Long silence.

This is why I can't write anymore. This is it. Right here. This is why I haven't written anything decent in three fucking years. How am I supposed to work in this kind of environment? I am being smothered with criticism. Drowning in a quagmire of negativity.

RANDOLPH: You can't write because you're stoned.

Silence.

DILLAN: I beg your pardon?

RANDOLPH: You're stoned.

DILLAN: Right. Of course. Divert the blame off of you. Put it on the drugs. It's the booze. It's the dope. But it's certainly not you, is it, Randolph?

Dillan goes to pour himself a drink.

RANDOLPH: You don't have to get defensive. I didn't say it was a bad idea. I just don't think you're going to be able to do anything with it. Who's going to buy it? Who's going to produce it?

DILLAN: Excuse me very fucking much, but it's not like this is the first thing I've ever written. I have a track record. I've got a reputation. I have awards, all right?

RANDOLPH: Fine. You're right. It's perfect. Run with it.

DILLAN: I never said it was perfect. But it's something. It's a start. You could at least acknowledge that.

RANDOLPH: I'm really getting sick and tired of this bullshit, you know that? You ask my opinion, and I give you a straight, sober answer and it's not what you want to hear and you get all bent out of shape. So don't ask, all right? If you don't want to hear what I have to say, then don't ask.

Long silence.

DILLAN: You want a drink?

RANDOLPH: Scotch.

Dillan makes Randolph a drink.

DILLAN: How were your classes?

RANDOLPH: Fine.

Silence.

DILLAN: I've only had a couple of drinks and a little spliff. I haven't done coke in forever. A month, at least.

RANDOLPH: That's not the point.

DILLAN: Of course it's the point. It's always the fucking point.

RANDOLPH: I know you've been laying off it, I know you've been trying, and I'm proud of you. I am. But it's not the point. The point is you're not really working, you're just pretending. You're fooling yourself.

DILLAN: Fuck you, I'm not working. You're not here all day. You don't see what I do.

RANDOLPH: When was the last time you actually wrote something down? You wander around here like some sort of ghost, mumbling about god only knows what, whatever story is crawling through your booze-addled brain, and whatever idea it is always bottoms out and you abandon it and go on to the next one. But you never write anything down.

DILLAN: I'm not an accountant. This isn't paint by numbers. It's a process. It takes time.

RANDOLPH: It used to be a process. You used to write. When was the last time you wrote anything down? You just talk about it.

DILLAN: I wake up thinking about it, and I go to bed thinking about it. I think about it every fucking minute of the day. Just because I don't write it down, just because I haven't found the right…structure for it, or or or the right starting point or the right whatever doesn't mean that I'm not working. I can't believe that after seven years we /

RANDOLPH: / Eight./

DILLAN: / still have to have this conversation. You know what it's like. You know what it takes. And may I remind you that while I'm working AT HOME, I'm keeping this fucking place clean, and buying the fucking groceries and washing your fucking underwear, so don't start lecturing me on not working, all right? I'm working my ass off.

RANDOLPH: When was the last time you wrote anything down?

DILLAN: You're impossible, you know that? You just don't get it.

RANDOLPH: I get it.

DILLAN: No you don't! Lest we forget that I carried your ass for three years of university and then another two years after that because you couldn't find a fucking job, I carried your ass doing exactly what I'm doing right now, the same thing, I was getting paid then and now I'm not. That is the only difference. The work is exactly the same, so don't you turn around and start treating me like I'm some big milestone around your neck, all right? I did my part and I will do my part again, as soon as I've got a solid project to run with, it's just a matter of time, so don't you turn on me now, Randolph. Don't you fucking turn on me now!

RANDOLPH: Are you coked up?

Silence.

DILLAN: Okay, fine. You want me to get a job? Fine. I'll get a fucking job. *(he grabs the newspaper and starts rifling through the classifieds)* For you, Professor Randolph Gitz, I will find a "real" job. That is the sacrifice I will make. My career, my passion, my bliss, the very thing that feeds my soul and my spirit, I will abandon so that I can get a "real" job and make my boyfriend happy. Here. Here's one. The Attention Deficit Disorder Family Resource Centre is looking for a qualified what? What is a...whatever.

RANDOLPH: / Dillan ...

DILLAN: / Excuse me? Randolph? Do you mind? I'm looking for a job? Oh, I know, what is that expression, "Do what you know," that's it, and I do know my booze, don't I, sweetheart? A bartender. It's a natural. What do you think? Do you think I'd make a good bartender? A purveyor of alcoholic beverages? Pitching pints, and trading quips, listening to strangers pour their hearts out, desperate for my sage advice. Actually, this isn't a bad / idea.

RANDOLPH: / You don't have to get a job, Dillan. That's not what I / meant.

DILLAN: / Fuck you. Fuck you and what you meant. I don't care what you meant. I'm going to get a job, and you can't take that away from me, just because all of a sudden you realize that it might be a good idea, that I might actually have a little fun, get out of the cave now and again, make a little money, you all of a sudden realize that this might actually be good for me, so now you want to take it away. Well, fuck you. I'm going to be a bartender, and there's nothing you can do about it. I'm going to have a specialty drink, people will come from all over the city, lining up, waiting / for hours ...

RANDOLPH: / Are you coked up?

Long silence.

DILLAN: I found a little bit in one of my old drug boxes. It's not like I'm rockin' it up. I had a little snort, that's all. It was crap anyway. I barely got a buzz off it.

Silence. Dillan sniffs.

I'll make us some dinner.

RANDOLPH: I'll cook.

Randolph gets up and starts to leave.

DILLAN: I'm sorry, sweetheart. I am. I really am. I'm a big fuckin' waste-of-skin bitch asshole fuck-up, and I'm not working, you're right, I'm not working the way I should be, but I'm trying.

RANDOLPH: I know.

DILLAN: No, no, please, don't do that. You don't know. Don't do that, Randy. Don't bat it away by "agreeing" with me. I want you to listen. I want you to hear me, okay? I am trying. I am trying to write, but it's just not happening right now, okay? That's not my fault, it's not because I'm just lying around doing / nothing...

RANDOLPH: / I know / ...

DILLAN: / No you don't fucking / know!

RANDOLPH: / Can you hear yourself? Do you hear what you're doing? A couple of minutes ago it was "Randolph, I have this issue with you because you're questioning my work habits," and now it's "Randolph, I have this new issue that's about me feeling bad because I had that other issue a few minutes ago." Do you not see the pattern here? You've cut me out of it entirely. I could be a fucking goalpost, it wouldn't matter. You are completely and entirely reacting to your own reaction. You don't even need me here. You could have this argument with yourself.

DILLAN: I am not reacting to my own reaction. I'm reacting to you being an asshole.

Silence.

RANDOLPH: I'll go make us some dinner.

Randolph heads for the kitchen . Dillan watches him go. He sniffs, gives his nose a bit of a flip.

Lights find Bart, standing alone. He is a young, good-looking guy, but prematurely tired and worn. He's dressed rough and casual. He addresses the audience.

BART: One of my boyfriends told me about this guy. Well, he's not really my boyfriend. We've hung out a couple of times. I suck his dick, he gives me money. That kind of boyfriend.

Lights fade on Dillan.

Anyway, he told me about this guy, Danny Boy Kane, who was a Hell's Angel, right? He was just some nobody when he was younger, small-time stuff, but then he met this other guy, Ace Simard, in a hot tub, and they got it on, they sucked each other's dicks. I mean Danny Boy had a wife and kids and all, but that doesn't mean anything, just 'cause ya like chocolate doesn't mean ya can't like strawberries too, ya know what I'm saying? Anyways, they're suckin' each other's dicks, and it turns out Ace does some hit work for the Angels and he pulls Danny Boy in, and Danny Boy just rises up the ranks, you know? And before you know it, he's a bodyguard and a driver for some of the big boys, right? He's a Rocker. This is like the enforcing arm for the Nomads, which is like the most notorious chapter of the Hell's Angels, the Nomads do all their dirty work, so Danny

Boy Kane, this little bi-homo from butt-fuck Quebec, is all of a sudden smack in the middle of the nastiest group of criminals in the whole fuckin' country.

Light finds Dillan, still in his silk robe. He's napping, or possibly passed out, on the couch.

I just think that is so fuckin' wild. I mean think about it. If Danny Boy Rocker Kane was your boyfriend. Nobody would fuck with you.

There is a tapping at the door to Randolph and Dillan's apartment. Dillan doesn't stir.

Lights fade on Bart.

The tapping at the door grows more insistent. Dillan rolls over, sighs, and bellows.

DILLAN: Fuck off!

Silence. Dillan snuggles in to go back to sleep. The tapping at the door returns. Dillan lunges off the couch and heads for the door. He whips it open.

What!

Bart is standing there, a little twitchy, and looking kind of hunky.

BART: Is Randy home?

Silence.

DILLAN: No, he's not. Can I help you with something?

BART: Do you know when he's going to be back?

DILLAN: And you would be…

Silence.

BART: What do you mean?

DILLAN: What do you mean what do I mean? Who are you? How do you know Randy?

BART: What the fuck business is it of yours?

A long silence.

DILLAN: I see. Would you like to wait for him?

BART: I'll come back.

DILLAN: I insist. Come in. Make yourself at home. Please.

Dillan shepherds Bart through the door.

Let me take your coat. Can I get you a drink?

BART: I'll come back later.

DILLAN: Nonsense. Coat, my dear. Come, come.

Dillan waits. Bart takes off his coat. Dillan takes it.

What would you like to drink? A beer? No, wait, let me guess. Rum and coke.

BART: Yeah, sure.

DILLAN: Of course.

Dillan dumps Bart's coat on a chair and makes them drinks.

What's your name, sweetheart?

BART: Bart.

DILLAN: What a strong, burpy sort of name that is. Bart. Halfway between barf and heart.

BART: You sure it's okay if I wait?

DILLAN: It's entirely my pleasure to have you here, Bart. I insist. Make yourself at home. And allow me to provide you with some small diversion in the interim. And you've known Randolph how long?

BART: A couple of months.

DILLAN: Interesting. He's never mentioned you.

BART: You his roommate or somethin'?

DILLAN: Or somethin'. Actually, I'm his life partner. His wife, if you will. His live-in. His lover. He's never mentioned me, I take it?

BART: No. No, we mostly...We work together.

DILLAN: You're a professor?

BART: ...No. I...clean. I'm the janitor. At the university.

DILLAN: There's only one?

BART: One what?

DILLAN: Janitor. You said you're *the* janitor at the university, suggesting at least linguistically that there's just the one of you. My goodness, that must be a big job.

BART: Course there's more than one of me. There's a bunch of us. A hundred, maybe.

DILLAN: A hundred janitors. That makes much more sense. Soda?

BART: What?

DILLAN: Would you like some soda water? In your rum and Coke.

BART: No. Thanks.

DILLAN: I used to be a rum-and-Coke boy myself, in the day, and then as I got older I started throwing in a wee bit of soda to cut the sugar. Have to watch my girlish figure, don't you know. Now I just drink straight rum. Or whatever's handy. Here you go.

Dillan delivers Bart his drink and plunks down beside him.

So. You're Randy's janitor friend from the university. How sweet.

BART: Maybe I better go. I'll come back later.

DILLAN: Oh, silly boy. Don't be afraid of little ol' me. Any friend of Randolph's is a friend of mine. Relax. How's your drink?

BART: Good.

DILLAN: Excellent. You know, I don't think I've properly introduced myself. In fact, I don't think I've introduced myself at all. Dillan Ramsey Delaney Azumu Thunderhoof LeFray Smith. At your service.

He extends his hand to be kissed. Bart shakes it.

BART: That's a lot of names.

DILLAN: It certainly is. My mother raised me alone, a single working gal, died of cancer, years ago. Tragic. She wanted me to remember my rich cultural heritage, and thus the string of pearls that is my name. It represents seven branches of DNA going back four generations. There's an eighth, too, but I don't use it. Cocksworth. Who could possibly take me seriously with a name like Cocksworth? And you? Where do you come from, young man?

BART: Nowhere, I guess.

DILLAN: Oh that's so sad, to come from nowhere. You poor strapping young thing. You don't have a mother? A father? Parental units?

BART: I take care of myself.

DILLAN: As any self-respecting young man should. It must be hard though. What do you do for money? You must have a livelihood.

BART: I told you, I'm a janitor. At the university.

DILLAN: Of course. Sorry. Odd that it should slip my mind so quickly. I should take notes. Avert the danger that I might lose my place entirely. It's happened before. Now I understand the janitors and the professors are quite tight at the university. Practically a club. And why wouldn't they be? They have so much in common.

BART: How long you been with Randy?

DILLAN: And that would be your business because…

BART: Just askin'. Can't be that long. I figure if you guys were tight he'd have said something about you.

DILLAN: One would figure that, wouldn't one? On the other hand, it may be a reflection of how well he knows you, or doesn't know you, as the case may be. Considering that Randolph and I have been together for eight years, solely and completely and monogamously together for eight years, that information would definitely fall into the category of "personal," and as is the nature of personal information, it does tend to be shared only with the inner circle to which perhaps you unfortunately don't belong.

BART: You're pretty fruity.

DILLAN: And you're a lying little piece of trash whore-bait, so shut your face.

Silence.

DILLAN: My goodness. Sorry about that. That's the Thunderhoof in me. Great-grandmother, father's side. Apparently she was a very proud but alarmingly forthright woman.

Bart gets up to leave.

BART: I better go. Tell Randy I dropped by.

DILLAN: Did I offend? I'm so sorry. Is it my "fruitiness" that's bothering you? I could be a bit more vegetable-like, if that would help. Or maybe something from the dairy group?

BART: Are you mad at me?

DILLAN: Mad? Me? Moi? No! Of course not. It's my sense of humour. People just don't get me.

BART: I didn't mean anything, when I said you were fruity. I was just talking out loud. I got lots of fruity friends.

DILLAN: Oh, sweetheart, that is so sweet, that's so lovely, I'm your friend? Sit down. That's so special. A friend. Well I consider you my friend too, even though we hardly know each other. It's funny, isn't it? Some people you can spend your whole life with, and something happens and suddenly you realize you don't know them at all, you don't have a clue what they're up to, and other people, like you for instance, you can meet them and within seconds you know exactly who they are. You can see through them like Saran Wrap. Do you find that? That some people you just know right away?

BART: Yeah, sure.

DILLAN: Eloquently put. Do you work out?

BART: A little. I like to keep in shape.

DILLAN: Mmhm. I've always had a weak spot for the squandered physique. That sort of young "I could be fabulous if I wasn't so fucked up" thing you have going on. The lustfulness of youth in perfect balance with the neediness inherent in the decay of self-abuse. It's good for business, I'm sure. I mean the sanitational engineering business, of course. You have to be in shape to handle that mop and bucket. I'm sure you handle yours with sublime physical mastery.

BART: What do you do?

DILLAN: What do *I* do? My goodness. What a question. I do so many things, really. I swan about, that takes up a good deal of the day, and I must confess I do like my naps—did you know if you time your naps properly you can get drunk and sober up three times in a single day?—it takes discipline, let me tell you. But mostly I write, I suppose.

BART: What do you write?

DILLAN: What don't I write might be the better question. I use whatever medium best serves the story, dear boy, and the stories are flowing continuously. I'm a veritable font. I'm actually a little famous.

BART: Really?

DILLAN: I wrote for a TV series for a few years. Just a little thing on one of the specialty channels. "Strawberry Roads."

BART: Fuck off. You wrote "Strawberry Roads"?

Silence.

DILLAN: You know it?

BART: Sure I do. I used to watch that show all the time. That was the one with the guy who was having the affair with his teacher, right? And there was that whole pink mafia thing going on? Is that the one?

DILLAN: How sweet of you to remember it.

BART: Oh fuck, yeah, I used to stay up late, and I'd sneak downstairs with a couple of the other guys from the home and watch it, it was pretty racy for TV, we'd watch it and diddle each other. It was pretty cool. What was I—thirteen, maybe? That was fuckin' forever / ago.

DILLAN: / Yes, well, how time flies. And look at you now. All grown up.

BART: Hey, you know any stars?

DILLAN: An entire constellation's worth, my dear.

BART: You writing for anything now? Any TV shows, or…

DILLAN: Unfortunately, I am cursed with an auteur's sensibility. I tried to acclimatize to the deadening and lifeless world of commercial television. And film. And radio. And theatre. But I simply couldn't abide the soul-sucking, brain-numbing madness of it all. My path, I'm afraid, is the lonely one. I am an *artiste*, not a craftsman.

Silence.

BART: So you writing for anything now?

Silence.

DILLAN: I'm working on a film.

BART: Who's in it?

DILLAN: Oh, you dear sweet innocent thing. Mel Gibson and Meryl Streep.

BART: Fuck. Off.

DILLAN: I kid you not.

BART: That is so fucking cool!

DILLAN: Once again, eloquently put. Would you like to see my vagina?

Silence.

BART: Pardon?

DILLAN: My vagina, sweetheart. I've got a vagina. Isn't that special? I'm no ordinary mango, my sweet young thing. A little more complicated than that, I'm afraid. I have both. Lucky me. Would you like to see them?

BART: You got both? What do you mean?

DILLAN: *(checking his watch)* I have both a vagina and a penis. Actually the vagina is passive, just a wee thing, and my penis, technically, might be a clitoris. It's quite a mess down there, until you get used to it. And then the possibilities become endless. I can literally fuck myself, on a good day. Do you have any coke left?

BART: What?

DILLAN: Coke. Cocaine. Blow. Do you have any left?

BART: I don't do coke.

DILLAN: Your pupils are the size of dinner plates, and if you don't stop bouncing your knee you're going to drill a fucking hole in my floor. Do you have any left?

Silence.

BART: Yeah.

DILLAN: Let's do a bit, shall we?

BART: I don't have very much.

DILLAN: If you wish to take a personal tour of my unique anatomy, you will produce some cocaine, dear boy. It's not a complicated equation.

Silence.

Bart pulls out a flap, and starts to cut them a couple of lines.

That's my boy. How is your drink?

BART: Good.

DILLAN: *(checking his watch again)* Fabulous. You know, I have to tell you, I simply can't get over how opportune your surprise visit to our humble abode has been. There's so little real drama left in this sad, sorry world we live in. So few surprises. You've made my afternoon. Take off your shirt.

Bart hands Dillan a cut straw.

BART: What?

DILLAN: I'll give you twenty bucks. Take off your shirt.

Dillan leans in and snorts a line off the table while Bart ditches his shirt. Dillan sits up, sucking the coke back. He hands Bart the straw.

My goodness, look at you. The wonders of youth.

BART: Thanks.

The door opens. Randolph enters. He sees Bart, stops. Bart vigorously sucks back his line with one good noisy snort.

DILLAN: And it begins. Randolph. I'm so glad you're home. Right on time, as usual. Boringly predictable, one might say, if one were in a scrappy mood, and one is.

RANDOLPH: What are you doing here?

DILLAN: He's a visitor, my sweet. An unexpected guest. Your young janitor friend from the university. He and I have been chatting and getting to know each other. He already considers me one of his best friends. I'm a little put out that you haven't mentioned him. He's lovely. And I suspect a cock the size of a beer can. I mean, look at the boy.

BART: Hi.

RANDOLPH: What the fuck are you doing here?

DILLAN: Randolph! Is that any way to treat the company? Bart, I'm so sorry, he's like this at the end of the day sometimes. Prickly. Cocktails are in order, I think. Another rum and coke for you, and you, Randolph? A scotch straight up, I suspect. Stiff and to the point. And I think I might have something girlie, maybe an Irish Cream to sooth my cackles. Please, everyone. Make yourself comfortable. Oh, goodness. Almost out of ice. Bart, would you be a dear and fetch some?

Dillan hands Bart the bucket.

The kitchen's that way.

BART: Yeah. Sure.

Bart grabs the bucket and heads off towards the kitchen.

Silence.

RANDOLPH: Where did the coke come from?

DILLAN: Oh my, no. You mustn't start in on the cocaine. There are other, much more pressing issues at hand, wouldn't you agree?

RANDOLPH: What did he tell you?

DILLAN: That is of little consequence, my dear. I'm much more interested in what you have to tell me.

RANDOLPH: It's not what you think, Dillan.

DILLAN: And what is it that you think I am thinking, sweetheart?

RANDOLPH: Let me get rid of him, and we'll talk. All right? I don't know what he's doing here, I didn't invite him, let me just get rid / of him, all right?

DILLAN: / No, no, dumpling, you're overreacting. I'm simply curious, that's all. What do you think I'm thinking, and how could you possibly know? What amazing feat of transcendental mind-melding divination has allowed you to see into this labyrinth perched upon my silken shoulders? Like magic, you've somehow reached into my brain and picked out, like a ripe tick, this "thought" that I'm having, and then you further amaze me by telling me that this "thought" is wrong. "It's not what you think." Fine. Let's simplify. Get rid of the clutter. Let us start with "the thought." What is it that you think I am thinking?

RANDOLPH: I don't know. I don't know, all right? I don't know what you're thinking.

DILLAN: Excellent. Honest, straightforward, and to the point. Superb start. I'm very proud of you, Randolph. And to reward you for that clean, clear, honest answer, I will tell you what I am thinking. I am thinking that the young man who is presently in our kitchen fetching ice is a hustler. It's been a while, but I am pretty sure I can still recognize a fellow professional. So. I believe we now have a "fact" that we can muse over, that we can roll around on our metaphoric palate, taste it, test it with the tongue of our logic. A fact. You, Randolph Gitz, are consorting with a young prostitute. And as is so often the case, this fact is… Yes, yes, I can feel it forming…The fact is leading to a question. And the question is why. Why, Mr. Gitz, are you consorting with said prostitute? There it is. Simple. Clean. Efficient. I would like to know why.

Silence.

You speak now, sweetheart. It's your turn. Go ahead.

RANDOLPH: I paid him for sex, okay? I paid him to have sex with me, and he's been following me around, he showed up at the university, I guess he found out where we live. He's a cokehead, Dillan. He just wants money.

DILLAN: I see.

RANDOLPH: It was only a couple of times. I was horny. That's all. It was just sex.

DILLAN: I see.

RANDOLPH: Come on, Dillan. Stay with me here. Let's just send him on his way, okay? We'll talk.

DILLAN: I'm not entirely sure that's the best thing to do.

Bart appears in the doorway, with the ice bucket.

Ah. The boy du jour has returned. Lovely. Come. Sit. Make yourself at home.

Dillan takes the ice bucket from Bart, and begins preparing cocktails.

RANDOLPH: What are you doing here?

BART: Just dropped in to say hi. Havin' a chat with your wife.

RANDOLPH: Cut the crap.

DILLAN: My oh / my …

RANDOLPH: / What are you doing here?

BART: I came to see you.

RANDOLPH: Why?

BART: 'Cause I thought we had something going on.

RANDOLPH: I paid you for sex. It was a purchase. It was not an invitation into my home.

DILLAN: My god. I'm married to a monster. The poor boy is obviously smitten with you, Randolph. He thought the two of you had "something going on," not just some tawdry exchange of money for blow jobs.

RANDOLPH: Dillan, please, don't. We'll talk, all right? Let me get rid of him and we'll talk.

DILLAN: Randolph! The boy is sitting right there. He can hear you. How can you be so heartless? You can't just "get rid of him." He's not a piece of garbage. He's not disposable. He's a human being, he has feelings, for / God's sake.

RANDOLPH: / Fine, yes, of course, you're right, he's a human being, he has feelings. Fine. Bart, I'm sorry, okay? I'm sorry if you misunderstood my intentions. But I am making them clear now. I paid you for sex. That's what my reality was. I no longer want to continue that relationship with you. Okay? I'm sorry. I would like very much if you would leave now.

Silence.

Please.

Silence.

Oh, for Christ's sake. *(Randolph takes out his wallet)* Here. Here. There's at least fifty bucks there. Call it a closing fee. Now just fuck off, all right?

BART: I was thinkin' maybe I could crash here.

Silence.

RANDOLPH: What?

BART: I don't have anywhere else to go.

RANDOLPH: Are you fucking nuts? You can't / stay here.

DILLAN: / Oh. My. God! This is brilliant! We have to let him stay, Randolph. He's an orphan. Have some compassion. A young, homeless, pitiful, sad little thing shows up on our doorstep needing what, a little comfort, a little shelter, a little love, all things that we have in abundance, my dear, and we're going to turn him away? Nonsense! We are bigger people than that.

RANDOLPH: Dillan, / please …

DILLAN: / We are bigger people than that! Of course we'll take you in, Bart. Of course we'll shelter you. Just think, Randolph, he can be the son we never wanted.

RANDOLPH: Please…

DILLAN: I feel a step closer to heaven already. Perhaps we could comb the streets for other hapless youth. Open a shelter of / sorts.

RANDOLPH: / Shut up!

Silence.

RANDOLPH: Please, just…please don't do this. You're punishing me, I understand that. But nothing good is going to come of it. It's not going to make you feel better.

DILLAN: Au contraire, my dear, quite frankly, it's making me feel fabulous.

RANDOLPH: That's the coke, Dillan. I sure hope it is, anyway. Because if torturing me, if dragging me through the mud for a stupid mistake, a stupid mistake, if that's what's making you feel fabulous, then I guess there's really not much point, is there?

DILLAN: I've never cheated on you. I've done a whole lot of crap in my short life, and I know there's been lots of times when I've treated you like shit, but I've never cheated on you.

BART: I better get going.

DILLAN: Tired of our humble little abode already, my dear? We barely had a chance to get to know you. Ah well. I understand. The restlessness of youth. You must be moving on. Set sail in search of new ports to pillage. Such is a pirate's life. Your clothes.

Bart takes his shirt and his coat from Dillan and heads for the door.

Thank you so much for the visit. Do come again. Call ahead next time, and I'll prep your room.

BART: Bye, Randy.

Randolph doesn't respond.

DILLAN: He's just a little verklempt right now.

Dillan ushers Bart to the door.

It's because he cares. Deeply. Parting is such sweet sorrow. From that hollow pocket comes his silence. I, on the other hand, could give a flying fuck. And if you ever come near him again I'll rip your eyes out and shove them up your ass and you can spend the rest of your miserable little life staring at your own colon. Lovely meeting you.

Dillan closes the door.

And now. To business.

RANDOLPH: I'm not talking to you when you're like this.

DILLAN: When I am like what, sweetheart? Angry? Cuckolded? Betrayed? Cheated upon? Is that what you mean? When I'm like that?

RANDOLPH: You're hopped up on coke, Dillan. We'll talk when you've straightened out.

DILLAN: I've freebased half an ounce in a single session, Mr. Gitz. I assure you that one line has not altered my perception of the tarnished reality I find before me.

RANDOLPH: What do you want me to do? I was horny. I picked up this kid. We had sex. I paid him. That's all it was.

DILLAN: A "couple of times," if I'm not mistaken.

RANDOLPH: Yes, that is correct. It happened twice. So what?

DILLAN: So what? So what? Is it me? Have I lost my fucking mind? You slept with someone else, you asshole! Why wouldn't I be pissed off! I think I'm responding in a very sane and very humane manner, considering the circumstances. I am hurt. I am upset. And you are treating it like you went out for ice cream and didn't bring any back for me.

RANDOLPH: I understand you're upset…

DILLAN: No, you don't! You obviously don't understand that I am upset, because if you understood, you wouldn't be sitting here trying to justify it to me!

RANDOLPH: I am not trying to justify it.

DILLAN: Of course you are! "I was horny." "It didn't mean anything." What do you call that? You are absolutely trying to justify it, and I won't let you! It's / bullshit.

RANDOLPH: / Oh for fuck's sake, you've slept with hundreds of people! Give me a / fucking break.

DILLAN: / Nobody touches me! Nobody. Unless I want them to. You are the only person that has touched me since the day I met you. The only person. I have *never* cheated on / you.

RANDOLPH: / No. No. I'm not going to let you go there. This, *this*, is justification. You were a hustler, Dillan. You used to be a hooker. How can / you possibly…

DILLAN: / I was not a hooker! I was an / entertainer!

RANDOLPH: / You turned tricks for money! And then your writing took off and you met me and you stopped, and then what happened, Dillan? Tell me what happened / then.

DILLAN: / Fuck / you.

RANDOLPH: / Your writing washed up, and you went back to turning tricks. That's what happened. For two fucking years, you filled your head full of coke and you supported your habit by turning tricks. And I sat on the sidelines, hating it, and begging you to / stop,

DILLAN: / Fuck. / You!

RANDOLPH: / begging you to get your act together, begging you to quit treating yourself like shit, begging you to stay home with me, and you ignored me, you pissed on me, you treated our life together like it was an inconvenience, like I was the enemy, you were with hundreds of people, hundreds, Dillan, and I put up with it, I stayed with you, I supported you, I helped you in every way I could, and I do not begrudge that. I don't. I honestly don't. But don't you stand there and tell me you haven't cheated / on me.

DILLAN: / I never let them touch me! Never! I took their money and showed them my messed-up shit, and I spent their money on drugs. I was doing it for the drugs! I never cheated / on you.

RANDOLPH: / You're romanticizing it! You're turning it into some great romantic femme fatale bullshit thing that is completely removed from reality, and you're doing that so you can justify your anger at me. I get it. I get what you're doing, and I accept it, and I will / allow it …

DILLAN: / Don't you play professor / with me!

RANDOLPH: / I will allow it because I love you, and I want to work through / this!

DILLAN: / Don't you fucking dare play professor with me! I'm not some moony-eyed, empty-headed little college boy that's going to hang on your every word, that's going to accept what you say verbatim because it's coming from the oh-so-high-and-fucking-mighty Professor Randolph Gitz! You can't pull your little psychological doublespeak reverse crap with me. So don't even try, all / right?

RANDOLPH: / All I'm trying to do is sort out how you're feeling so we can deal / with this.

DILLAN: / How dare you! How fucking dare you turn around and blame this on me, on my feelings. He's sucking your cock, asshole, / not mine!

RANDOLPH: / That's hardly the / point.

DILLAN: / That is exactly the point! You can twist it around any way you want to. It's not going to change what / you did!

RANDOLPH: / I'm trying to give it a broader context. That's all. I'm trying to look at this in a way that allows us to inform what is going on between *us*. Between you and me. I'm trying to look at it in a way that we might, that we just might be able to get something constructive out of it, but you, in typical fashion, / won't be

DILLAN: / Typical?

RANDOLPH: / happy until you've turned it into a fucking / opera!

DILLAN: / No no no. Fuck you, typical! I will not allow you to categorize me! I will not allow you to put me back in my little box and call it hissy fit number five. I am not your case study. As much as that may be our pattern, as much as you'd like to retain that particular comfort / zone …

RANDOLPH: / You're not making any sense, / Dillan…

DILLAN: / From the day I met you I have been a fucking case study! Your pet project. Your ultimate conclusion. The only reason you started dating me is because I fit your master's / thesis.

RANDOLPH: / That is complete and utter / bullshit!

DILLAN: / It's the fucking truth, and you know it! And whether you can handle that particular truth is of no consequence to me. It doesn't change a thing. It doesn't change now. Right now. We are dealing with right now, Randolph, and right now, in what I would suggest is a very "untypical" fashion, you have been consorting with a young male prostitute, you have had repeated sexual liaisons with said prostitute, and it wasn't to support a drug habit, and you most certainly did have physical contact, and there was certainly something more to it than diddle diddle wham bam thank you ma'am. Am I right? Am I right!

Silence.

I have never cheated on you, Randolph, I have never betrayed you emotionally, and that is now more than you can say to me.

RANDOLPH: Okay, fine. Fine. Let's do it your way. I cheated on you. I'm sorry. What exactly is it you'd like me to do about it?

Long silence.

DILLAN: I could have cheated on you. I've had no shortage of offers over the years, *mon petit tricheur.* And no shortage of desires. But I never did. I've always been faithful to / you.

RANDOLPH: / I know./

DILLAN: / I don't fucking care if you know! You're going to hear it anyway. I have always been faithful to you. From the day I met you, I have been yours. That was a given. And I assumed that you felt the same way about me, and now I find out that you've been seeing someone else. How am I supposed to feel about that?

RANDOLPH: I wasn't "seeing" him. We had sex. It wasn't a / relationship…

DILLAN: / Twice. You had sex twice. That, my dear, is seeing someone.

RANDOLPH: Don't do this. Don't turn this into something bigger than it is. / Please.

DILLAN: / You saw him twice. You went back for more. You were seeing him.

RANDOLPH: Do you remember the last time we made love? Because I don't.

Silence.

Do you remember the last time we made it through a day without fighting? When was the last time it felt like we even liked each other? What the fuck am I supposed to do?

I was lonely, and I was horny, and I was driving home, and he was there. Standing on the side of the road. Waiting. Waiting for someone to pick him up. And I did. And we had sex. In the car, Dillan. We had sex in the car. We didn't even get undressed. I didn't kiss him. I did not kiss him. He blew me, and I paid him, and he left. That was it.

Silence.

DILLAN: And the second time?

Silence.

RANDOLPH: He showed up at the university. I guess…I don't know, I guess I'd told him I was a professor, I don't remember, I don't know how he found me, but he showed up at the university. And I liked it. I liked it when he blew me, okay? It was some sort of contact, some sort of…something, and he showed up at the university and there was no one there and he walked into my office, and I felt good. I felt wanted. I felt like…I was worth / something, like…

DILLAN: / Oh please. What a pile of bullshit. Like you were worth something? What is that supposed / to mean…

RANDOLPH: / I felt like somebody wanted me! Like somebody might actually want to be with me. Like somebody found me attractive, and desirable, and worth something.

DILLAN: You paid him. He's a hustler. And a cokehead. He needed money. So he went back to where he'd received money before. It was not a romantic overture, Randolph.

RANDOLPH: I know perfectly well what it was. But at the time, I needed something, and he showed up. It's that simple. That's all it was, and it's that simple.

Silence.

DILLAN: I see.

RANDOLPH: I'm sorry.

DILLAN: Of course you are. You got caught.

RANDOLPH: No. No. I am not sorry because I got caught. I am sorry because I made a choice that hurt you, and I don't want to hurt you, and I'm sorry for that, Dillan, I truly am, but I can't keep doing whatever this is. I can't keep pretending that you're the same person I fell in love with. You're not. You're not the same person. You used to be fun. You used to be strong, and brave, and ferocious. You used to take on the whole world, and you invited me along for the ride, and I fell in love with you. But you aren't that person anymore, Dillan.

Silence.

DILLAN: I see.

RANDOLPH: Please, Dillan, please listen to me. You're drinking too much, and you can't handle the coke, it owns you, and I know you're trying, I know that, but it's got you, it owns you, and you smoke too much dope, and you aren't dealing with anything, and I think you should get some help.

DILLAN: I see.

Dillan goes to leave the room.

RANDOLPH: Dillan, please...

DILLAN: No, really, I understand. I see the horrible position I've put you in. What a burden I've become. What I've driven you to. I understand you precisely, and I'm truly sorry for any trouble I've caused you, and I thank you sincerely for your concern. I'm so glad we had this opportunity to share.

Dillan leaves the room. Randolph watches after him.

Light finds Bart. He addresses the audience.

BART: There's a million stories about what went down with the police raid.

Lights fade on Randolph.

It was huge, eh? Seventy or maybe eighty towns, all over Quebec and Ontario, the cops just shut down the Angels, and Danny Boy Kane was like the main informant behind the whole thing.

But it was his boyfriend Ace Simard that started it all. Fuckin' Ace snitched on Danny to keep his own sorry ass out of jail. This is his fuckin' boyfriend and he snitches on him. So Danny was forced to talk, he had to protect himself. What else was he going to do? And Danny ends up spilling way more than Simard did and the cops got enough to bring down over a hundred bikers and tons of drugs and weapons and all sorts of shit. 'Cause a couple of fags got in a spat.

Here's the crazy shit, though. Simard, you can't find out anything about him. Sometimes you hear he was murdered and sometimes you hear he's in jail and sometimes it seems like he just disappeared, right? And Danny Boy, they say he killed himself, but the stories are all nuts, they've got holes in 'em all over the place, I mean his own mom has never seen his body. The police wouldn't let her. What does that tell you? It was carbon monoxide poisoning, it wasn't a gun shot to the head or somethin'. Why wouldn't they let her see him? It's got witness protection written all over it. I mean, come on. If you got that kind of action going on, you're not stupid, and if you're not stupid, you get the best deal you can. Danny Boy wasn't stupid. And I think he knew what he wanted. I think he wanted out, and I think he wanted to take his butt buddy with him. And I think he wanted to come out clean, so he works with the cops and the cops make it look like they're both dead.

But I'll bet you a dollar to a fuckin' doughnut they're together somewhere, somewhere warm, with beaches and cocktails, and they're laughin'. They're sittin' in their little fuckin' beach chairs, holding hands, watchin' the sunset, and laughin', 'cause they got away with it.

Lights up on Dillan. He's prepping a line of coke.

Danny Boy Rocker Kane got the government to pay for his early retirement in the Caribbean, and he got to take his fuckin' boy toy with him.

Dillan snorts, with robust vigour.

He is one smart dude.

Lights fade on Bart.

DILLAN: And regroup.

Dillan paces about, focusing.

The long arduous trek through the urban jungle of civilization has drawn to its natural conclusion. Curtsy and Barblow come face to face in the bowels of a third-rate bathhouse in…fuck. Taipei. Why not. Barblow has followed Curtsy to the other side of the world and found him in Taipei.

Why?

Silence.

Fucking asshole. Why?

Okay. So. What? Barblow knows who Curtsy is now. He knows what she's done, the legend she's left behind her, a legend littered with scandal and abuse and human decadence and false worship and delusions of grandeur, and yet he pursues her still. What is it that keeps our dear sweet Barblow so entranced? What is Curtsy's allure, what does he see in her, this decrepit, decaying thing that was once a queen?

Silence.

What does he see in her sallow, melting flesh that still spurs him on, and draws him in, compels him to seek her out, to know her mysteries? What has she managed to keep alive that draws this moth to her flame?

Silence. Lights up on Randolph at his lectern.

What has she got that I haven't got?

Randolph is in mid-lecture.

RANDOLPH: It might be interesting to note at this point that in ethicist and historian Alice Dreger's book, *Hermaphrodites and the Medical Invention of Sex*, she demonstrates that inter-sexed individuals led relatively normal lives up to the late 19th century, at which point they were "discovered" by medicine and deemed "ill and in need of repair."

Lights fade on Dillan.

RANDOLPH: What's fascinating about this is that they were considered ill solely on the basis of the appearance of their external genitalia, with no regard to their psychological well-being. And yet all the available literature of the time indicates that these individuals were psychologically quite healthy and well-adjusted. And now, after a century of the condition being treated as "abnormal," there are myriad character flaws that seem to be consistently inherent in those living in a state of what is now referred to as "gender confusion." Some of the common negative characteristics include an obsession with self and a propensity towards...uh...towards drug and alcohol abuse. It doesn't take a huge leap of empathy to understand the possible origin of these flaws. The inter-sexed, with the dubious assistance of medical science, now grow up in a state of otherness that is infinitely more acute than most of us experience. They perceive from their earliest consciousness that they do not fit in. Of course, we all feel this otherness at times, we all have a glimpse of our lonely plight on this planet, but generally we spend our conscious days blithely accepting our part in the larger world. I am straight. I am gay. I am male. I am female. Broad and basic classifications that provide a group, a place of origin, an identity. For the inter-sexed, of course, those basic classifications aren't available. Thus, the profound sense of otherness that drives the individual inward, resulting in a state of extreme isolation...

Silence.

But... Uh...but it is, of course, possible for the gender-confused, sorry, for the inter-sexed, to lead perfectly happy and productive lives. We need look no further than our first case study, Stella Walsh. It is well documented that she was happily married, and had a long and prosperous career and home life before her accidental death. There are many such documented cases...

Silence.

I'm sorry. I've lost my...let me just check my notes... Yes, yes. My point being is that despite one's gender, despite what one is born with in terms of genitalia, we are all still individuals. There are patterns, commonalities in any given grouping, but these commonalities only lead us back to common experience, and someone with a mosaic, inter-sexed condition does not have to answer to the common traits or experience of a mosaic. The categorization has no significance on a personal level. None of us fit into a category.

Dillan is found, passed out on the couch. Throughout the following, Randolph grows increasingly agitated and angry.

We are individuals, each individual with a uniquely defined sexuality, and a uniquely defined responsibility to one's self within that sexuality. Given that, there is absolutely no reason that being inter-sexed should doom the individual, anymore than being a—a—a "straight" female or a "gay" male should doom that individual, either on a personal level or in terms of sustaining a successful relationship and leading a productive life. A physical condition *does not excuse* the inter-sexed individual from the same basic responsibilities that we all have—a responsibility to ourselves, and a responsibility to our loved ones. We do not have the right to blame someone else for our unhappiness!

There is a knock at the door. Dillan sits straight up, a startled animal. He listens. Nothing.

Randolph is collecting himself, now lost inside his own lecture.

I... uh... I think we've covered enough for one day. If you could make a note of any questions you may have, I'll be happy to address them in our next class. Thank you.

Lights fade on Randolph.

Dillan lies back down.

Another knock at the door.

Dillan bolts upright. Listens. He makes his way stealthily to the door. He looks through the peephole, opens the door. Bart is standing there, shifting his weight back and forth like a young stallion.

BART: Hi.

DILLAN: You have some fucking nerve.

BART: I got some coke.

Silence.

I got some crack, some rock. You want to do it?

Silence.

He's not going to be home for hours. He's teachin'. We can do some rock, have a good time. Whatever you want. Except I need some money, eh? I got it on credit, 'cause I had cash for the first couple of rocks and I know these guys, but I gotta pay 'em, these guys are assholes, I don't want to fuck with them, so if you got some money I'll bring you in on it, we can have a good time, eh? Just you and me. Do some rock, fuck around a bit, you know what I mean?

DILLAN: I know precisely what you mean.

Lights fade slowly as Dillan shepherds Bart into the condo.

End of Act I

ACT II

Lights up on an empty living room.

We hear the sound of someone trying to enter at the front door, and then the door being unlocked. Randolph enters, briefcase in hand.

RANDOLPH: Dillan?

Randolph dumps his briefcase, heads straight for the scotch, pours himself a drink.

You home?

Dillan appears in the hallway leading off to the bedroom. He is dressed in his silk robe, naked underneath.

DILLAN: You're early.

Randolph looks at his watch.

RANDOLPH: It's after four.

DILLAN: Oh. Well. How time flies when one is in the throes of creative fervour.

Throughout the following, Dillan's enunciation is tight, and he attempts surreptitious mouth stretching. He avoids eye contact with Randolph.

RANDOLPH: You were writing?

DILLAN: Mmhm.

RANDOLPH: Good.

Dillan remains in the bedroom doorway, fidgeting. Randolph throws him a glance.

You can go back to it if you want. I'm fine.

DILLAN: I need a few things for dinner. Can you run out for me?

RANDOLPH: What are you making?

DILLAN: A...thing. With chicken. And we're out. Could you? Would you mind?

Dillan attempts nonchalance, avoids eye contact. Randolph notices a coat and shoes by the door.

RANDOLPH: Yeah, sure, in a bit. So you've been writing?

DILLAN: I need it now. I've got everything else on the go. I can't do anything until I have the chicken, and I was wondering if you could just...if you could just pop out to the store for me.

Silence. Randy stares at Dillan. Dillan fidgets.

Okay, is this unfair of me to ask you to take ten minutes out of your precious time to go pick me up a few things so that I might finish making a meal for you?

RANDOLPH: How about I change first?

Randolph heads for the bedroom. Dillan stops him.

DILLAN: You don't have to get... You can, just, finish your drink, for God's sake. You don't need to get all urgent about it. I'm going to put some clothes on. Can I get you anything? Are you okay?

RANDOLPH: Sit down.

DILLAN: I'll be right back. I'm going to get dressed. Four o'clock? My god. Another day peeled off the calendar of our lives, and here I am still in my lounging wear. It's no wonder you don't think I do anything all day. I'll just go throw something on. I'll be right back.

RANDOLPH: You look fine. Sit down. I'll make you a drink.

Randolph proceeds to make Dillan a cocktail.

DILLAN: I'll be right back.

RANDOLPH: Sit down!

DILLAN: Don't yell at me!

Silence.

Please, Randy, don't yell at me. I'm not a child. I'm not some dog that needs to be disciplined. I didn't piss on the carpet, all right? I'm not...I'm just not...I'm not feeling very well, and I'd really appreciate it if you could just cut me a little slack. I'm just going to go get changed, and then if you could go to the… Go to the the store for me, and pick up some…things, then I can make us some dinner. Could you do that? For me? Please?

Silence. Randolph glares at Dillan.

Okay, look, I don't know what you think is going on, Randolph, I don't know what you're insinuating here, with this little silent treatment thing, with this attitude, but I / can assure you…

RANDOLPH: / Look at you. You're as white as a ghost, you're shaking, you're sweating, you think I can't see this?

DILLAN: I told you, I'm not feeling well.

RANDOLPH: Of course you're not feeling well! You're strung out on coke. Why would you be feeling well?

DILLAN: And here we go again. The sanctimonious accusations of the high and mighty. Of course I must be stoned. Of course I must be disappointing you once again. What are the options? I couldn't possibly be legitimately ill, could I? I couldn't possibly be suffering from some bacterial or viral scourge, or maybe, or maybe food poisoning from eating week-old crap because you won't go to the fucking store and get me some fucking chicken!

We hear a crash from the bedroom off. Silence.

Excuse me a moment.

Dillan exits, leaving Randolph standing there.

We hear frantic, pinched whisper-shouting from off.

Silence.

Dillan reappears.

Left the window open. How is your drink? Would you like another?

RANDOLPH: Is that Bart? You have Bart in there? What the fuck are you doing, Dillan!

DILLAN: I told you. It was the wind! I left the wind open!

Silence.

DILLAN: The window. I left the window open. I'll make you another drink. How was your day?

RANDOLPH: This is so completely and utterly unacceptable. You must know that. Whatever state you're in, whatever you're on, whatever you're doing with that little asshole in there, you cannot be so far gone that you can't see how completely out of line this is.

DILLAN: I would tend to characterize it more as payback, sweetheart. Payback and out of line exist in two entirely different arenas of the emotional spectrum, wouldn't you agree?

RANDOLPH: Get out.

DILLAN: I beg your pardon?

RANDOLPH: Get out of my house.

DILLAN: You can't kick me out. I live here.

RANDOLPH: I want you to take that little piece of trash you have holed up in the bedroom, and I want the two of you to leave, and I don't want to see you again until you've gotten / some help.

DILLAN: / Lest we forget, that little piece of trash that I have holed up in the bedroom isn't mine, sweetheart. He's yours. So don't be turning this around and making it my fault. I didn't solicit his services. In fact, if the truth be known, I'm not paying for it. He came to me of his own voition. *(Dillan restretches his mouth)* Volition. Of his own desire. For me, Randolph. He desires me, and he came to me, and who am I to turn away my lover's lover? What kind of a hostess would that make me? What would Martha say?

RANDOLPH: *(yelling off)* Get out here, you little shit!

DILLAN: Oh, I see, I see. It's all right for you to whore around, to get your cock sucked by some little gutter rat, but god forbid that I should have a little fun. God forbid that I should share in the communal trough / of degeneracy.

RANDOLPH: *(yelling off)* / Get your little ass out / here, right now!

DILLAN: / That wouldn't do at all, would it? What's good for the gander is apparently not good for the goose.

RANDOLPH: Shut up, Dillan.

DILLAN: Of course. Lucid and to the point. I would expect nothing less of you, Professor. Years of academic study and liturgical perfection boils down to that most sublime and potent conclusive remark, the denouement of the highly educated. Shut up. Thank you so much for weighing in with that obviously thought-out and considered response.

Randolph slaps Dillan, hard. Dillan is stunned, speechless.

Bart enters, his clothes tossed on. The three stand in silence, looking at each other.

BART: Hi.

DILLAN: You should go now, Bartholemew. Your services are no longer required here.

BART: I don't have anywhere to go.

DILLAN: None of us do. A pity, I'm sure, but that is the lot in life that we must accept. We must go on without a clear destination in mind, without a goal, without an end to the means. We must forge ahead and take the journey as our reward. We must make our own lives. We must "make do." We must not depend on the kindness of strangers. Look what happened to Ms. Dubois.

RANDOLPH: I want you to go with him.

DILLAN: This is my home, too! You can't kick me out. You can't throw me out of my own home. In fact, how about I toss you out? You, Randolph. You are no longer welcome here. Get out. Leave.

BART: *(to Dillan)* Can I just… Can I stay for a bit? I just want to crash for a couple of hours, and then I'll leave, okay? I just wanna get my head together a bit, and then I'll take off, I promise, I won't bug you guys / again.

RANDOLPH: / I think you should leave now.

BART: *(still to Dillan)* Just a couple of hours, okay? I'll just crash out in / the bedroom.

RANDOLPH: / Get. The fuck. Out of my house. NOW!

BART: Hey, fuck you! I don't need your permission. I'm here with him. I don't need your fuckin' permission, all right? So fuck you.

Randolph lunges for Bart, grabbing him by the scruff of the neck and hauling him towards the door.

Hey! Hey! Fuck off, asshole! Get your / fucking hands off me!

DILLAN: / I would suggest you don't struggle, / my dear.

BART: / Let me go, you / fuckin' dipshit!

DILLAN: / The beast has been released, an ugly sight / I'm sure,

BART: / You don't have to go fucking ballistic / on me, all right?

DILLAN: / and not one that you want to / take lightly.

BART: / I didn't do anything!

Randolph opens the front door and tosses Bart out.

(from off) You tore my shirt! It's the only decent shirt I got, and you fuckin' ripped it!

Randolph tosses Bart's shoes out, and his jacket, and slams the front door.

(from behind the door) You fucking asshole! I'm calling the cops! I'm going to call the fucking cops and I'm going to sue your ass off for...for...fuckin'...battery!

Dillan and Randolph stand facing each other, waiting.

I'm going to sue both your asses off! I'll tell them you raped me! I'll tell them you picked me up and drugged me and fuckin' dragged me back to your place and raped my ass! Then we'll see who's Mr. Tough Guy! You fuckin' jerk!

Something heavy hits the door from the outside.

And I want my fuckin' money! You owe me, girlie-boy! You owe me for the fuckin' rock, and I want my money right fuckin' now or I'm callin' the cops!

Silence.

BART: You think you're so fucking smart just because you're a fucking teacher! You paid me to suck your cock, asshole! You know what that makes you? It makes you stupid! Fuckin' old and ugly and stupid! A fucking worthless piece of shit!

Silence.

Assholes!

A long silence.

DILLAN: Another day in paradise. Cocktail?

Randolph makes his way back to the couch, sits, tries to collect himself.

RANDOLPH: I want you out of here. You don't live here anymore. If you lived here, if you honestly shared this house with me, this life with me, you wouldn't be throwing it away like this, like poker chips, upping the ante, seeing how big the pot's going to get before we have to show our cards. Well, I'm all in, Dillan. I've got nothing left. I can't do it anymore. I can't watch you kill yourself. I can't do it.

DILLAN: Sweetheart. I'm not dying. I'm a little fucked up, to be sure, but I'm not dying.

RANDOLPH: Yes, you are. There's no life left in you, in us. It's turned into one long fade to black, the credits are rolling, and quite frankly, I can't wait for it to finish. It hurts too much, Dillan. It hurts too much, and I'm not going to let you take me down with you. I'm sorry. I can't / do it.

DILLAN: / My goodness. Now who's being the femme / fatale?

RANDOLPH: / Jesus. Fucking. Christ! Why? Why do you have to be like this, Dillan? Why? I just want us to be happy. That's all. It's a simple little thing. I just want us to be happy.

DILLAN: My dear sweet naïve little boy. What a gloriously tepid response to all this that you find before you. Of course you want to be happy. We all want to be happy. What's the alternative? And why, why, Randolph, in this great chaos of life, am I always the cause and you are the effect? Why do I have to bear the burden of your happiness? Why is it my fault if you are not content?

Perhaps, just perhaps, it is the great dark smothering cloud of your unhappiness that has driven me away in the first place. Perhaps, my sweet, it is you that are killing me.

RANDOLPH: What am I supposed to say to that? You're blaming me for the drugs. You're blaming me for your weakness. You're drowning, and you're blaming me because I won't go down with you? It's not a rational response. How am I supposed to answer / that?

DILLAN: / Don't. Don't answer it. I'm not looking for an / answer.

RANDOLPH: / Okay. Fine. You want to play this out, I'll play it out. I accept that this is all my fault. I have driven you to this. I have systematically and unequivocally led you down this road of self-destruction and here we are. So tell me, what can I do? What do you want?

Long silence.

DILLAN: Well. There we have it. The ball is back in my court, and I can't seem to find my paddle.

RANDOLPH: It's a racquet.

DILLAN: It certainly is. Beyond a racket, a veritable din, I would say.

RANDOLPH: No, I mean it's a racquet, not a / paddle.

DILLAN: / I know what you meant. I was attempting wit. A little verbal levity to lighten the mood, and once again I fail you. I'm proving to be as useless as tits on a log. Oh. There. Tits. There's something. Perhaps I want tits. A lovely little B cup, I think. Something perky that wouldn't get in the way. Would you like me more if I had tits? Because that's the nub of it, I think. This alien ship, this foreign vessel that I call my home isn't a home at all. It's a prison. I have done my best with it—a nice coat of paint, a room with a view so to speak, but this too too sullied flesh betrays me at every turn. Do I stand up to pee or do I squat? That is the question.

RANDOLPH: I've never wanted you to be anything different, Dillan. I've always loved you, just the way you are.

DILLAN: How very Billy Joel of you.

RANDOLPH: It's true.

DILLAN: My sincerest appreciation for that sentient sentiment, but methinks that perhaps it has never been enough. It can't be, because, you see, if you love what I hate, then we are enemies, aren't we? How can I possibly respect you for loving the thing that I loathe? Do you see it? The high and its oh so potent accompanying crash brings with it a strange gift of lucidity that is proving to be almost worth the price of admission. I suddenly see very clearly the ludicrous impossibility of our personal equation, my dear. I can only love you if you hate what I am, because if you hate what I am, then we have something in common. What a nasty trick God has played on us.

RANDOLPH: You don't believe in God.

DILLAN: I have to blame someone.

A long silence.

Dillan sits down on the couch with Randolph.

I didn't plan this. I didn't plan that it should turn out like this. It just happened. I don't know what's wrong with me. I just want to stop thinking, and I want to be normal, and I want to be here, I want to be here with you, but I can't do it on my own.

Randy puts his arm around Dillan, draws him in.

Long silence.

RANDOLPH: I want you to leave. I'm sorry.

DILLAN: You don't mean that.

RANDOLPH: There's nothing left for me to do, Dillan. I've run out of solutions, I've run out of answers, I don't even know where to start anymore. You have to leave. You have to do it on your own. I'm sorry.

Dillan gets up with great dignity, gathering himself with all the power of a grand dame.

You need to get some help.

DILLAN: Of course. Of course that's your response. Of all the things that you could have said, you chose to offer someone else's help. Not yours. "You need to get some help. You need to go away."

But what you really mean, of course, is that you need to be rid of me. I am a failure, and by extension that makes you a failure, and you can't stand that. So sweep it into the streets, honey. Get rid of it. Get rid of all evidence that you aren't perfect, that you aren't sublime in your mastery of this thing we call life. I am an imperfection, I am not to be tolerated, I am to be discarded, because the going has gotten too tough, and you don't do tough, do you / Randolph?

RANDOLPH: / Do you think I want to do this? Are you that fucked up that you think this gives me some kind of pleasure, some kind of relief? I don't have any fucking choice! Tell me, Dillan, tell me what choice I have. What am I supposed to do? Tell me. Tell me!

Silence.

I want you to leave. Get some help. Get better. I'll wait for you. I promise you that. I will wait for you.

DILLAN: If I do this on my own, I will not come back, Randolph. Why should I? If I can do this on my own, I apparently don't need you. And if I can't? If I fail, if this is the beginning of the end, I want you to mark this moment. I want you to remember every detail, every sound and every smell, remember this shattered shell you see before you in all of its faded glory, remember it all, Randolph, because this is the moment, this is the exact moment, right now and right here, that you killed me. Every minute we have spent together, every lover's embrace, every gentle word, every knowing glance, every weighted touch, it all adds up to right here, and right now. This is what you think of me. Remember that.

Dillan leaves the room.

Lights fade on Randolph, as they come up on Bart. He's agitated, crashing.

He addresses the audience.

BART: That Ace Simard guy? Kane's boyfriend? That fucker Simard? He's going to get his. The Angels are gonna find him, they'll figure it out, and they'll leave Danny Boy alone 'cause he didn't start it, it was Simard that started it and they'll figure it out and find him and they'll come screamin' down on him, their big white wings spread out, they'll come screamin' out of the sky shriekin' like eagles, their big yellow eyes on fire, and they'll rip him apart, they'll rip him apart, and eat him up. And then Danny Boy, he'll be all alone, he'll be all alone and lookin' for someone to keep him company, and I'll show him what a real boyfriend's all about. I'll take care of him. I'll wash him in the tub like a baby, and take care of him and make him feel good. I can do that. I'm a good guy. I'm worth somethin'. I can take care of him, and show him I'm worth somethin', somethin' good. I'm not some piece of garbage you can just throw out, I'm not some piece of crap that's worth fuck all, that you can just flush down the shitter and forget about. I'm worth somethin'. I'm a good guy. I'm a good guy. I'll show him.

Lights come up on Dillan, in the steam room of a bathhouse. He's dressed in his silk bathrobe, now stained with sweat.

Bart looks up, focuses on something in the far distance.

The Angels are coming. Listen.

Bart's light fades, leaving Dillan in the steam room, mumbling to himself. He is wearing heavy make-up and a wig. He is busy setting up wigs on wig forms, which are mounted on the ends of sticks. He places the sticks around the steam room, inserting them in the cracks in the floor, trying to get them to stand upright.

DILLAN: You can hear them. In the distance. *(Dillan makes helicopter noises)* The helicopters are approaching, and the natives are growing restless, and you have no place left to hide. It is the end of the road. The reckoning. The final sunset. You feel it, somewhere down the river, a deep thrumming, pulsing. The smell of burning coal. The taste of night. And you, my dear, are alone. Abandoned. You have followed the dark path through the jungle, machete in hand, beating back nature to reveal an undergrowth thick with cloying despair, clawing at you, pulling at you, and you embrace it. You are one with it. You have become the putrid corner of the human condition that the rest fear.

DILLAN: You are the conclusion. You are what is left when all else is stripped away.

You are consequence. You are the snake in the grass, the thorn behind the rose, the poison dripping from the ivy. You are the angel of death, kept in this necrophagus state to teach the world what it does not want to know. You. Here. Now.

Dillan makes more helicopter noises, and continues with his set-up.

Lights fade on Dillan as they come up on Randolph.

Randolph is sitting on a bench, eating his lunch. He is making notes, prepping for an afternoon lecture.

Bart approaches, watches Randolph.

A long silence. Randolph stays focused on his notes, doesn't look up.

RANDOLPH: What do you want?

BART: You.

RANDOLPH: Give it a fucking rest.

BART: I just wanna talk to ya.

RANDOLPH: You're a hustler. You don't want to talk. You want me to want you. And you'll say and do whatever it takes to make that happen. Because if I want you, then you can control me. You can get what you want from me. Which is what? Money? My condo? Did you have a plan as to how far you were going to go with this? Or are you just making it up as you go along? The latter, I assume. I don't imagine you have the intelligence to actually have a plan.

BART: Fuck you.

RANDOLPH: No, fuck you. You see, I know what your little game is. I know hustlers. I've been living with one for eight years. And I've been living with a good one, not some amateur piece of shit like you.

BART: You don't know me. You think you got me pegged, but you don't know squat about me.

RANDOLPH: And, as luck would have it, I don't want to know you. I don't care who you are. And if you don't leave, I'll drag your sorry ass off campus, and once we are off campus, I will beat the fucking shit out of you again, and then I, *I* will call the cops, and we'll see how you get on with them.

BART: How's Dillan?

Silence.

RANDOLPH: He's fine.

BART: Yeah? You two working things out?

RANDOLPH: It's none of your business.

BART: That's what he said too.

Silence.

RANDOLPH: When did you see him?

BART: He's been hanging around at the bathhouse. We've been spending some time together. Didn't he tell you? Oh, that's right. He's not living with you anymore, is he? Cause you kicked him out, right? You gave him the boot 'cause you couldn't handle him doing a bit of rock? That's what he said, anyways. You know what he does? He sits around the bathhouse and makes money showing off his freaky shit and does more coke than he'd ever do if he was still living / with you.

RANDOLPH: / Stay away from him. If I find out you've been anywhere / near him...

BART: / You can't tell me what to do! You're not the boss / of me.

RANDOLPH: / Stay the fuck away / from him!

BART: / Fuck you! You gave up your right to tell Dillan what he can do, and you never had no right to tell me what I can do.

RANDOLPH: What do you want?

Silence.

BART: Dillan's gone now, I figure maybe you're ready for a new guy. Here I am.

RANDOLPH: Is there something wrong with you? What, in your wildest dreams, would make you think that I want to have anything to do with you? You have been nothing but a huge pain in my ass from the moment you strolled into my life, and now you're standing there telling me you want to be my new boyfriend? Am I missing something here? Am I sending out some sort of signal that means nothing to me but in white-trash-waste-of-skin-boy-hustler language means "I want to marry you"? You are a piece of stupid ignorant garbage of the very lowest order. There is nothing of value in you. Nothing.

You're an idiot with a dick. You've fucked up my life, you've fucked up my partner's life, and you will fuck up your own life and every other life you touch until some act of God mercifully puts you out of your worthless misery. And if that happens today, if it so happens that you get hit by a bus this afternoon or a comet falls from the sky and crushes your fucking skull, or if you die of food poisoning from eating out of a fucking garbage bin, it will not be too soon. We will all be better off for it. Now get. The fuck. Out of my sight!

Silence.

Fuck off!

Silence.

BART: When I came and found you here. You were in your office, remember? And I came and found you, and I peeked through the window. And I saw a dead man. You were dead, leanin' over your desk, all alone, like an old man, just waiting for the Grim Reaper to come and finish you off. And then I walked in. And you recognized me. And you were a kid again. There was life in your eyes like laser beams. I could see your heart start to pump, right through your shirt I could see it. You wanted me, 'cause I made you feel young, 'cause I made you feel alive. You can lie to yourself all you want, you can pretend you hate me, but I know the truth. I know what I saw. You think I'm some stupid little shit hustler that doesn't know anything? I know a whole bunch of stuff. I know you. You just don't get it yet. You will.

Silence.

BART: I'll say hi to Dillan for ya.

Bart leaves. Lights fade on Randolph.

Lights up on Dillan, dressed in his robe, sweating it out in the steam room of the bathhouse. His wig has wilted and his make-up is melting off his face. He has successfully set up the wig forms, which jut up out of the ground at odd angles, perched on the end of their sticks like the skulls of butchered drag queens.

He has a rock of cocaine loaded up in a pipe. He sparks it, inhaling deeply, holding it in.

He exhales with a great cloud of smoke.

DILLAN: Okay. Regroup. Lost in...

Silence.

Fuck, that's good shit.

Okay. Lost in the bowels of a third-rate bathhouse in Taipei, the mysterious Curtsy meets her vainglorious comeuppance, her inevitable conclusion. She sits, and she waits, knowing the young ingénue, Barblow, is making his way through the urban jungle of steamy filth, searching her out. Hers is an impenetrable darkness, a twisted deformed piece of wasted flesh lying at the bottom of a precipice where the sun never shines, where joy does not penetrate, where love is the enemy. On her melting ivory face she wears an expression of sombre pride, of ruthless power, of craven terror, of an intense and hopeless despair. What did she see in that moment? Did she live her life again in every detail of desire, and temptation, and surrender herself during that supreme moment of complete knowledge, crying out in a whisper at some image, at some vision, crying out a cry that was no more than a breath—

"The horror. The horror!"

Dillan holds the moment, and feigns a swooning death.

Bart enters, naked except for a towel. He grips something tightly in his right hand.

BART: Wake up. I got some more shit.

Dillan pulls himself up.

DILLAN: What the fuck does it mean?

Bart preps himself a rock with shaky hands.

BART: What the fuck does what mean?

DILLAN: Why would his last moment / be the horror?

/ Bart has the pipe loaded up and is about to take a hit. Dillan takes / it from him.

BART: / Hey! You dropped the rock, ya fucker.

Bart gets on his knees, combing the ground for the missing rock. Dillan shrugs it off, and nicks himself off another piece from the rock Bart has left on the bench.

DILLAN: It's a trick. That's what it is. It's a fucking trick. An / illusion.

BART: / You don't have to be / so fuckin' greedy.

DILLAN: / It doesn't mean anything. It's designed as / an enigma,

BART: / I'm out there selling my ass / for the rock,

DILLAN: / to fuck up the reader, to trap / us into a puzzle

BART: / I should have got / the first hit.

DILLAN: / that we can't solve.

Bart has found the missing rock, and is sitting there, fidgeting, waiting for Dillan to have his toke, which he's melting down, prepping.

If fucking Conrad had wanted us to know what it meant, he would have / told us,

BART: / Hurry up, / will ya?

DILLAN: / he would have left some sort of / clue,

BART: / I got the / fuckin' jeebies.

DILLAN: / some way to penetrate the character, a metaphor or / a... I don't know... A clue, or something.

Dillan lights up, sucks back a toke.

BART: / That last guy was gross. Fat ugly fuck made me lick his dirty fuckin' asshole.

Dillan, still holding his toke, passes the pipe to Bart, who quickly loads up.

I'm not goin' out again. It's your turn. I gone out the last three times, it's no fuckin' fair. You go sell your messed-up shit next time.

Bart takes his hit, too anxious to prep it, while Dillan exhales a huge cloud of smoke.

Silence. Dillan calms noticeably, ecstatically, while Bart holds his toke. A blankness comes over Dillan's face. He slowly slumps over during the following.

Bart exhales.

Oh. Oh, fuck. Oh, fuuuuck, is that good.

Bart sits, and breathes deeply.

Oh, man. That was worth it.

Silence. Bart breathes, and Dillan slumps.

What are you talkin' about, the horror? Is that your movie? You still workin' on your movie? That's some fuckin' strange weird-ass shit. I don't get it, you know? The one guy, or the gal, I guess, the one that runs away to Toopee or Tapee or wherever the hell she ends up, like what's her problem? Who the fuck does she think she is? She had it all, she was some big drag queen duchess bitch of the whatever, she was the centre of the whole fuckin' shit thing back home, and she throws it all away and she's totally fuckin' herself up, she just keeps going straight for the centre of fuckin' fuckin' shitville nowhere land, and she's got that guy that Barblow guy chasin' after her like she's some big mysterious gotta-know-all-about-her thing, and it's kind of obvious, you know? She hates herself, and she doesn't have the guts to finish it on her own, like blow her head off or somethin', and maybe she gets it, how hopeless the whole fuckin' thing is and it's like… Horrible. So she says it. Twice.

Dillan doesn't respond. He has slumped entirely over onto his side, staring ahead blankly. Bart gives him a nudge.

Dillan?

Silence. Their light fades to black.

Sirens are heard, and the sound of helicopters. The soundscape builds to a cacophony, and then slowly fades out as lights come up on Randolph, sitting in a hospital waiting area.

A long silence. Randolph gets up, paces, sits again.

Bart enters, now slightly dreamy and on the nod. He sits beside Randolph. Randolph gives him a look, then ignores him.

Another long silence.

BART: You okay?

Randolph doesn't answer.

You should get some of whatever they gave me. It's good shit. I haven't felt this relaxed since…well, never. You want some? It's just a shot, it doesn't hurt or nothin'. Want me to get a nurse? Just tell her you're tense. I betcha' she'll give you a shot. Tell her you did some crack. You'll get one for sure. You want me to go find her?

RANDOLPH: I'm fine, thank you.

Silence.

BART: Did you call his mom?

RANDOLPH: What?

BART: His mom. Did you call her? In the movies, or on TV or whatever, that's the first thing anybody does, is call the mom. I always thought it was pretty fucked. I don't have any folks.

RANDOLPH: You must have some sort of family. A guardian or something.

BART: I've been livin' on my own since I was fourteen.

RANDOLPH: You can't have been living on your own since you were fourteen. There are rules. Laws. Somebody had to take care of you.

BART: I guess they just lost track of me and quit lookin'. I'm like the Lone Ranger, eh?

Bart smiles at him, Randolph ignores it.

Silence.

You got parents?

RANDOLPH: Of course I have parents.

BART: You ever talk to 'em?

RANDOLPH: Sometimes.

Silence.

BART: You don't get along with them, or what?

RANDOLPH: We get along all right. We just don't talk that often. They never liked Dillan. I see them at Christmas.

BART: I always hated Christmas. I like the idea of it, presents and stuff, but I don't got anybody to give presents to, so the whole thing ends up being kind of a downer, ya know? I like the decorations. They're cool. All the lights and stuff. Makes everything look special instead of grey and shitty.

Silence.

So why did you hook up with Dillan?

Silence.

Is it 'cause of his...you know...his equipment? His freaky shit? That do something for you?

RANDOLPH: Why are you here? You can take off. There's nothing keeping you here. Why don't you...why don't you go roam the corridors. Go room to room. I'm sure you could scare up some business. There's no end of lonely people in a hospital. It could be an entirely untapped market for you.

BART: Naw. I've tried it before. They're all too sick to fuck.

RANDOLPH: Right. Of course.

BART: So how come you hooked up with him? He doesn't seem like your type.

RANDOLPH: And what would you consider to be my "type"?

BART: I don't know. Like a professional or something. Maybe a doctor. Or a lawyer, maybe. Not some wacko drug addict boy-girl guy. It just doesn't fit, ya know?

RANDOLPH: *(ignoring the question)* So what's your "type"? You apparently have this all figured out, so tell me. Who's the guy for you?

BART: Danny Boy Kane. He's a biker. A Hell's Angel.

RANDOLPH: Sounds like a real catch. How do you know him?

BART: I don't. One of my boyfriends told me about him, and I did some research, looked him up on the Net and all. He sounds about right. Somebody tough, somebody who doesn't take no shit. I figure he'd be a good boyfriend. I'm gonna check him out, anyway. The cops say he's dead, eh? But I think he's just hidin' out. I'm gonna find him, get rid of his stupid shit boyfriend, Simard, and I figure I'll settle in and that's that. I'm set.

Randolph is staring at him.

What?

RANDOLPH: So your "type" is a dead member of the Hell's Angels who already has a boyfriend.

BART: Yeah. He's got a wife and kids too.

RANDOLPH: Right.

BART: What?

RANDOLPH: It doesn't quite work that way, Bart. You can't just pick a guy out of the phone book and go after him. Especially a dead one, who also happens to already have a boyfriend and a wife and kids.

BART: Why?

RANDOLPH: It's a fantasy. It's not real.

BART: So why did you fall in love with Dillan?

Silence.

RANDOLPH: I don't know.

BART: It had to be somethin'. No offence or nothin', but he's a pretty out there kind of guy, or girl or whatever, he ain't exactly the catch of the day. So why did you two hook up?

A long silence.

I was in love once, maybe. I had a girlfriend when I was sixteen. That's who I started doing the crack with. I think maybe I loved her, or something about her, or maybe something about the two of us. And then she got pregnant. Pulled out of the whole drug thing, had her baby. A little boy. She's going to university now, eh? She's a fuckin' smart gal. She'll do okay. The kid'll be three in a couple of months.

RANDOLPH: Do you ever see him?

BART: She wouldn't let me, even if I wanted to. And I don't want to. I don't want him to know me, I don't want him to know what his dad is. I kind of hope she made somethin' up, like I died in the war or somethin', instead of "oh yeah, your dad's a crack ho. Hope you're proud of him."

Silence.

I'll get myself straightened out. Do good by him. Show up with his college money or somethin'.

Silence.

RANDOLPH: Thanks.

BART: For what?

RANDOLPH: For getting Dillan here, and calling me. I appreciate it.

BART: No biggie.

RANDOLPH: Yes, it is. It is a "biggie." Thank you.

Silence.

BART: He'll be okay.

RANDOLPH: I shouldn't have kicked him out. It was a stupid thing to do. I should have known better.

BART: Nothin' you can do about it now.

RANDOLPH: All I was trying to do was wake him up. Make him see what he's doing to himself, and he goes straight over the fucking edge, like it's a dare or something, he does everything in his power to make sure it's my fault, to make sure I fucked up, because if he actually cleaned himself up, if he actually did something good for himself, then I would have been right, and above all else, he will do anything in his power to make sure I'm not right. Even if it means killing himself.

Silence.

BART: Do you still love him?

Silence.

Bart moves over to Randolph, puts his arm around him.

It's okay to be scared. I'm scared all the time. You get used to it after a while.

Randolph leans into Bart, letting himself be comforted.

Their light fades to black.

The sounds of spring are heard.

Lights up on Dillan, sitting on a bench. It's a lovely day, sunny and warm. Dillan looks drawn and tired, but on the mend. He's feeding pigeons from a bag of bread crumbs.

Randolph approaches. He watches Dillan for a moment. Silence.

Dillan looks at him, and goes back to feeding the pigeons. Randolph makes his way over to the bench and sits beside him.

Another long silence. The pigeons coo.

RANDOLPH: You look good.

DILLAN: I look like shit.

RANDOLPH: The last time I saw you, you were trussed up in a hospital bed stuck full of tubes and as white as a sheet. Trust me, you look good.

DILLAN: Oh, that's right. Now I remember. I haven't seen you in...what is it? Two weeks, two days and fourteen hours, if I'm not mistaken. Not that I'm keeping track. I've just found it curious, that's all, that my partner of eight years should kick me out of the house, and then abandon me in rehab, leave me to heal myself with the generous support of fourteen of the most deplorable, desperate and, may I add, ugly people one could ever hope to spend time with. I speak of my "group." Four toothless, aging prostitutes, a gaggle of unemployed thugs, two professionals, a housewife, and little ol' me. Quite the collection. There's a story in there, somewhere, I'm sure. My next masterpiece. We have a lottery going, actually. Me and my "group." On this little tête-à-tête right here. We bet on whether you'd show up. I bet against you, by the way. You just cost me twenty bucks.

RANDOLPH: I can leave if you'd like. You can tell them I never came.

DILLAN: Too late.

Dillan turns and waves towards the building behind him.

Give them a wave, sweetheart. In the window there. Second floor. They're dying to have a good look at you.

Randolph remains motionless.

That's all right. I've made it abundantly clear what an asshole you are. A friendly gesture on your part could severely jeopardize my credibility. So, how are you? What's new?

RANDOLPH: I'm fine. How are you?

DILLAN: Oh, couldn't be better, really. Pounding headaches, and I've never felt so tired in my entire life. Listless, I believe, is the appropriate word. Overdosing on crack cocaine will do that to you, I suppose. They told me I had a minor heart attack. Imagine that. Thirty-four and my first heart attack. I'm rather disappointed that it was only minor. You know me. Go big or go home. Still, it is a marker of sorts. A first. I can't wait for your first. I hope I'm there to see it.

Randolph gets up to leave.

DILLAN: Oh, for heaven's sake. I'm kidding. Sit down. It's just a bit of good-natured ribbing. I don't care if I'm there for your first heart attack. As long as I'm there for your last. I hope it's a big one. Or better yet, a stroke. Something crippling and humiliating.

RANDOLPH: I didn't come here to fight with you.

DILLAN: I'm not fighting, dearest. I'm spewing. I've had over two weeks of empty, abandoned time to fill myself with no end of anger and bile, and I am now taking advantage of your presence to do some healthy spewing, that's all. All I'm asking is that you be a man and sit there and take it. It's the least you could do.

RANDOLPH: I'm sorry I haven't been to see you. I thought it would be better if I stayed away. I did what I could. I didn't leave the hospital until I was sure you were going to be all right, and then I got you in here. That's what I could do for you, and that's what I did.

DILLAN: Oh, I see. It was for me. You stuck me in here and then abandoned me for my own sake. How kind of you. How thoughtful. What a beautiful, heartfelt gesture. And what a pile of absolute bullshit. Really, Randolph. You're an intelligent man. You can come up with something a little more convincing / than that.

RANDOLPH: / What do you want from me? What am I supposed to say? What am I supposed to do? I don't have anything left to give you, Dillan.

DILLAN: Is that what you've based our relationship on? What you could give me? Is that what's been keeping us together all this time? What you thought you were giving me? Well, guess what, sweet cheeks. You have never given me anything. And I have never asked you for anything. So you can officially take that out of the equation.

RANDOLPH: You aren't going to get better until you have to, until you have no other choice, and as long as I'm there, you have a choice. You can just lean on me, and continue to abuse yourself, continue to kill yourself, and continue to punish me for it. I'm not going to do it anymore. When you are better, I will be there. I promise you that. I will wait for you, Dillan. But you have to get better first.

DILLAN: It's interesting, that you should know me so well. I don't know you at all. I do not know this thing that I see / before me.

RANDOLPH: / Dillan .../

DILLAN: / What? What! What is it you want from me? My blessing? Thank you, Randolph, for abandoning me? Thank you, Randolph, for being so generous and thinking of my well-being and fucking leaving me? Is that what you want? Well, fuck you! You're not going to get it. Fuck you all to hell, you weak, cowardly, pathetic little man! Fuck! You!

Dillan throws the rest of his bread crumbs at Randolph.

Silence.

So very sorry. My Thunderhoof is showing. I suppose you're right. I can be an adult and admit that. That you're right. For all the wrong reasons, of course, but you are right. I won't get better with you. I can no longer function as your damsel in distress. I like the role too much. I play it too well. I abuse it. Bart, I suspect, is much better suited to the part—a femme fatale who actually wants to be saved.

RANDOLPH: I don't love Bart.

DILLAN: You could pretend you do. That would be enough, certainly enough for him, and it would satisfy your own addiction. You must know, my sweet, that you are addicted to this thing called love. It's the only thing that drowns out the static in your otherwise empty soul. It brings you peace, and unfortunately there is no rehab for that, no methadone powerful enough. But unlike myself, you have the opportunity to use your addiction for good instead of evil. You could pretend to love him, and he will respond, and he will get better, and he will make you happy, and in the great and potent cycle of Pavlovian conditioning, your love for him will become real. You can save him, Randolph, and someone needs to be saved here.

RANDOLPH: I'm not going to leave you for Bart. That's not an option, Dillan.

DILLAN: I'm not giving you a choice. I don't want you anymore. I choose me, and in choosing me, I will save us all. It's grand and noble and befitting the exotic creature that I am. I can carry on with my head held high, knowing that I've done the right thing, relishing in the sting of self-pity, playing martyr and victim all at once. It's perfect, really.

RANDOLPH: No. No, it's not perfect. You're pushing me away so you can blame me, so you can escape unscathed. You're pushing me away because you're afraid I might not want to be with you. It's the coward's way out, and I won't let you do it. I will not let you blame me, and I will not let you give up on us. I will not let you do that. You are going to get better, and you will come home to me, and you will…

Silence. Randolph struggles.

You will fall in love with me all over again, and we will spend the rest of our lives together. That is what is going to happen, Dillan. That is the way that this will play out.

Randolph is crying, quietly. Dillan sighs, and gently rubs his back.

DILLAN: Do you know why you fell in love with me? Because I was someone that no one else wanted. I was safe. I was yours. And then I got fucked up on the drugs, and you couldn't compete with the drugs, could you? That's all it is. Imagine if it had been another man, or a woman. It would have killed you.

We both need to be with stronger people, Randolph. We both need a partner who can take care of themselves. I don't need someone to help me get better. I can do that on my own. But I will need someone, eventually, as will you, and that someone will need to be able to take care of themselves. We can't. We're both too weak.

RANDOLPH: So what have we been doing for the last eight years? Haven't we been taking care of each other? Isn't that what we've been doing?

DILLAN: No, sweetheart. We've been keeping each other company while we hide from the rest of the world. That's we've been doing, I think. Hiding.

Silence. Dillan removes his hand from Randolph's back.

You can go now. I'm done with you.

Dillan gathers up some of the bread crumbs, and returns to feeding the pigeons.

Randolph remains seated, silent for a long moment, while Dillan clucks and coos at the pigeons, throwing them bread crumbs.

RANDOLPH: I reread *Heart of Darkness.* I thought maybe I could offer some advice. Something.

DILLAN: You finished it?

RANDOLPH: ...Yeah.

DILLAN: How does it end?

RANDOLPH: What do you mean?

DILLAN: The ending. How does it end?

Randolph looks at Dillan, taken aback.

RANDOLPH: You don't know?

DILLAN: Oh, please. It was so wretchedly depressing. All those dark jungles and testosterone-fueled philosophical waxing. It was so fucking boring. I made it to Kurtz's death and simply couldn't go on. Much like Kurtz himself, I suppose.

Randolph is still staring at Dillan.

Okay, fine. Inform me, Professor. What do you think it means? The horror. What is that? Please. Share. Dazzle me with your learned insight.

RANDOLPH: I think he got to the end of his life, in search of the true heart of mankind, and he found himself. That's all there was. No big secrets. No big mystery revealed. Just himself. The great reckoning. We are all alone. Oh, the horror, the horror.

DILLAN: That is so. Fucking. Depressing. Why do you think I want to hear that? I'm stuck in rehab, I've just dumped you, I have nobody left, why do think I want to hear that?

RANDOLPH: You should have finished it. The ending is the best part of the story.

DILLAN: So what happens? Fuck, it's like pulling teeth.

RANDOLPH: Marlow does his thing, he futzes about contemplating Kurtz's last words, offering his opinion endlessly on what they may have meant, and then he goes back home and who should come calling but Kurtz's spurned lover, his intended, who he left behind when he went trundling off into the jungle. So she shows up and she's all distraught and seeking comfort, and Marlow's not being terribly gracious with her, I think he thought she was a silly little thing, although pretty, he does say she was pretty, but he didn't seem terribly fond of her. And then she asks what Kurtz's last words were, before he died. And Marlow looks at her, and he says, "The last word he pronounced was your name."

Silence.

I really liked that. That he should be able to muster some gesture of human kindness, just to make her feel better. In the end it was just another love story. A simple gal who needed to be reassured that the guy she loved loved her back.

A long silence.

DILLAN: Professor Randolph Evan Gitz.

RANDOLPH: Dillan Ramsey Delaney Azumu Thunderhoof LeFray Cocksworth Smith.

Silence.

Dillan gives him some bread crumbs. Their light stays up through the following, with both of them feeding the pigeons.

Lights up on Bart, at the bathhouse. He's wrapped in a towel, doing crack. He inhales a huge toke, holds it, exhales. The lights intensify, mocking a bright and sunny and beautiful Caribbean day. He addresses the audience while he reloads his pipe.

BART: You ever been to the Caribbean? Bet you it fuckin' rocks, man. Beaches for days, and sun, and hot guys all over the place. I bet I could find him, Danny Boy, the Angel's guy, I betcha' I could find him. It's not that big, the Caribbean. It's like an island or somethin', isn't it?

He sparks his pipe, takes another big toke, exhales.

I put myself into rehab, eh? I got Randy to find me a place, and he drove me down there and checked me in, and I wasn't too fuckin' happy about it at first, let me tell ya, but I stuck it out. I figured it was a place to sleep, and they fed me. And the meetings were okay, I guess. So I was in there for a couple of weeks, and I'm all clean and feelin' good, and I come out of the building, I'm going to catch a bus to wherever, I don't know, I had no idea where the fuck I was goin'. And there he was. Standing on the curb, all dressed up and looking pretty hot. And I started to bawl. I started to cry like a fuckin' baby. My whole inside just kind of fell apart, it just kind of melted when I saw him, like there was no one else in the whole world I would have rather seen there, waitin' for me, but I never hoped he'd be there, or maybe I did, but I never admitted it to myself 'cause if I did, it woulda killed me if he didn't show up. Hope, man. It can kill ya. But he did, I didn't ask him to, he just showed up, and he took me to this restaurant, and we had this big ol' dinner with wine and candles and everything. No one had ever done nothin' like that for me before. I get what that "in love" thing is. It's fuckin' hokey is what it is, but it's real. I get it.

Bart reloads his pipe throughout the following.

BART: He doesn't want to see me no more. He told me that, after we had our dinner and stuff. I wasn't really surprised or nothin'. I don't blame him. I get it. I guess…I don't know… I guess I'm too young for him or somethin'. That's okay. I'm okay. I'm into the shit again, but nothing like before. A little party now and again just keeps the edge off. I'm going to clean it up, get it together, go see my son, maybe. Or maybe I'll go find Danny Boy, see if that works out. It's going to be okay.

Bart takes a haul on his pipe, holds it, exhales. A long silence.

It's going to be okay.

Light fades to black on Bart in the bathhouse, and Dillan and Randolph sitting on the bench, feeding the pigeons.

The End

IN THE YICHUD ROOM

JOEL FISHBANE

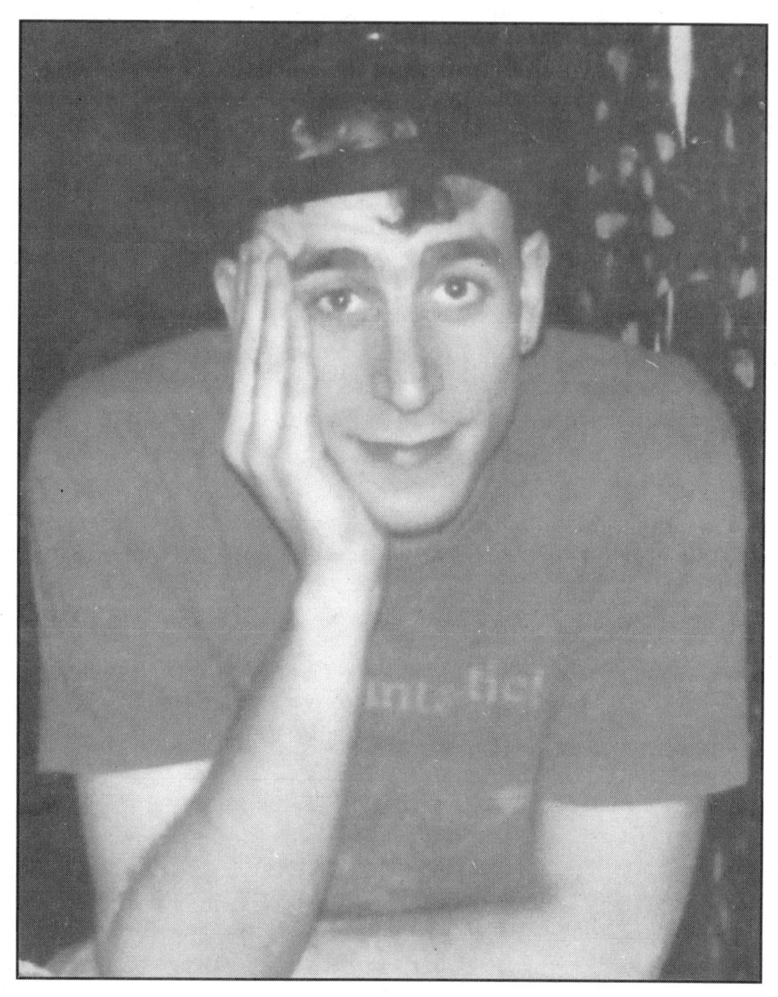

JOEL FISHBANE

ABOUT THE PLAYWRIGHT

Joel Fishbane is the artistic director of Pumpkin Theatre. He sometimes plays the clarinet.

PRODUCTION HISTORY

In the Yichud Room was written as part of the Toronto Fringe Festival's 24-Hour Playwriting Contest, 2000. It won second prize. *In the Yichud Room* was originally presented from March 10 - 13, 2004 at the Alumnae Theatre in Toronto, Ontario as part of the New Ideas Festival. It was directed by Andrew Lamb. The stage manager was Rachel McKinley, with Karie Richards as Amy, Ben Hunter as Sutler and George Bertwell as Chesterton.

For production rights, contact Signature Editions or Pumpkin Theatre: mrpumpkin@pumpkintheatre.ca, www.pumpkintheatre.ca

CHARACTERS

Amy Lauderer — The bride.

Sutler Brody — The groom.

William Chesterton — The former girlfriend's father.

SETTING

The play takes place in the Yichud, or bridal room, of a synagogue, but few specific set pieces are needed. At rise, we see the bride, Amy, in a gorgeous wedding gown and veil, and the groom, Sutler. They stand in isolated spotlights on either end of the stage. Whenever they speak to the audience they do so as if the audience members are close, personal friends. They may smoke or drink beer, if desired.

Yichud: The Jewish ceremony in which, immediately after the wedding rites, the couple are secluded in a room together for a single hour. In ancient times, this was in order that they could consummate the marriage.

Author's Note: Lines which end in a dash and then have a dash at the start of the next line are meant to indicate continuous flow of dialogue between speakers, so there is no break or breath.

PROLOGUE

Sutler and Amy, speaking to the audience.

AMY: Marriage.

SUTLER: Marriage.

AMY: The world's oldest profession.

SUTLER: The ultimate tradition.

AMY: Centuries old.

BOTH: Marriage.

AMY: This is how he did it.

SUTLER: This is how I did it.

AMY: We'd been dating for a while.

SUTLER: It'd been almost a year—

AMY: —I think I just assumed—

SUTLER: —I set it all up—

AMY: —we'd move in—

SUTLER: —took *forever*—

AMY: —or something—

SUTLER: —there's this thing they just put up—

AMY: —there's this huge gaudy sign—

SUTLER: —I don't know where—

AMY: —Dundas and Yonge—

SUTLER: —it's a billboard for one of those search engines, for the Internet—

AMY: —WebSearch Dot Something or Other—

SUTLER: —there's this monitor which tells you what questions are being asked right now—

AMY: —I've been against the Internet from Day One—

SUTLER: —Where's Madagascar? Where Can I Find This Book?

AMY: —it was invented as an excuse for lonely people to get cheap porn.

SUTLER: Where Can I Get Cheap Porn?

AMY: That's why it's there, everything else is a bonus—

SUTLER: —you won't believe what I had to go through to set it up—

AMY: —he takes me to the street corner—

SUTLER: —I got a friend to do it—

AMY: —won't tell me why—

SUTLER: —I told him to type it in at exactly 2:45—

AMY: —already I'm in a bad mood, I *hate* surprises—

SUTLER: —I'm looking at my watch, it's 2:50 and nothing—

AMY: —anyway, we're standing there and Sutler keeps looking at his watch—

SUTLER: —and then suddenly there it is—

AMY: —and then suddenly there it is—

SUTLER: —in big bold letters:

AMY: —in these huge red, digitized letters—

BOTH: "Amy, will you marry me? Love Sutler."

SUTLER: I wasn't nervous.

AMY: I remember thinking, how strange.

SUTLER: It was very peaceful.

AMY: "There's another Amy and Sutler in this city."

SUTLER: The question was there, there was nothing I could do.

AMY: Which is odd, because Sutler's not a very common name.

SUTLER: And all you can do is hold your breath and wait for it to end.

AMY: And then...

SUTLER: And then...

AMY: It hits me.

SUTLER: She looks at me—

AMY: —I was going to cry—

SUTLER: —she said yes.

AMY: I said yes.

SUTLER: The invitations read:

They both take out a wedding invitation and read from it.

AMY: *(reading)* You are cordially invited—

SUTLER: —to attend the union—

AMY: —of Sutler Willis Brody—

SUTLER: —and Amy Rachael Lauderer—

AMY: —at the Beth Israel Synagogue—

SUTLER: —Black Tie Optional—

AMY: —Dinner—

SUTLER: —Dancing—

AMY: —and Consummation to follow.

SCENE 1

Lights up on the centre of the stage: the Yichud Room. Sutler and Amy run into the centre, whooping with delight, happy and exhausted. They have just been married.

AMY: That was unbelievable.

SUTLER: I am so glad that's over.

AMY: It was too much.

SUTLER: I never want to marry you again.

AMY: Let's hope you never have to.

SUTLER: Wait, go back.

AMY: What?

SUTLER: Go back, I didn't carry you over the threshold.

AMY: That's for the hotel room.

SUTLER: It's for wherever I say it's for. Saddle up.

AMY: Uh-uh. Jews don't carry each other over the threshold. We prefer to dance over it. *(tries to dance with him)*

SUTLER: *(to audience)* I don't dance. *(to Amy)* It went well.

AMY: You think?

SUTLER: Don't you?

AMY: Absolutely. It was the perfect wedding.

SUTLER: Mmm.

AMY: You looked so scared walking down the aisle.

SUTLER: Did I?

AMY: It was a good turnout.

SUTLER: And why not? We're both very popular.

AMY: There was one thing.

SUTLER: Hmm?

AMY: This old dirty man.

SUTLER: My Uncle Rob. Never bathes.

AMY: No, no. This man was standing at the back.

SUTLER: Must be from your side of the family.

AMY: I've never seen him before in my life.

SUTLER: *(to audience)* This is where I lie to her. They say it's important to lie to your wife as soon as possible. It lets you know how much you can get away with. *(to Amy)* It was probably nothing. Some nut who likes to cry at weddings. Speaking of which, did you see my mother? Nearly drowned everyone in the pew, she was crying so much.

AMY: Her little boy's all grown up.

Pause. They enjoy one another.

SUTLER: So, hey, how long do we have to stay in here again?

AMY: An hour.

SUTLER: And this is tradition?

AMY: It's called the *Yichud.* The bride and groom are left alone for an hour following the ceremony.

SUTLER: To do what?

AMY: Consummate the marriage.

SUTLER: *(lasciviously)* Oh, really?

AMY: We're not married in the eyes of God until we do.

SUTLER: In that case, I think we got married a long time ago. *(he begins kissing her neck)*

AMY: *(enjoying it, but not too much)* Mmm. What are you doing?

SUTLER: Sorry, ma'am, it's tradition, just hold still and pretend you're enjoying it.

AMY: *(she pulls away)* Sutler, we're not actually going to do it.

SUTLER: We're not.

AMY: It took me two hours to get into this dress.

SUTLER: And it'll take thirty seconds to get you out of it.

AMY: Down, boy, down.

SUTLER: Wait a second. We're really not doing this.

AMY: With my family on the other side of that door? Can you think of anything more disgusting?

SUTLER: Yeah, your family on *this* side of the door. *(he kisses her again)*

AMY: Sutler, stop.

SUTLER: If we're not going to do it, then why are we in here?

AMY: I don't know. *(to audience)* This is where he starts acting unreasonable.

SUTLER: *(to audience)* I was not acting unreasonable. I simply told her I wasn't going to sit in there for an hour and do nothing.

AMY: We were not doing nothing. We were obeying tradition.

SUTLER: No we weren't. If we had been obeying tradition, we would have had sex.

AMY: He never understands anything.

SUTLER: What's not to understand? The tradition states you're supposed to have sex. I'd say that is one of God's clearer commandments. (*moving back into the scene*) Look, let's just go out there. We'll tell them I finished quickly. I'm tough, my ego can take it.

AMY: Sutler.

SUTLER: All right.

AMY: I appreciate this. I know it doesn't mean anything to you, but it's important to me. I'm sure you have your traditions.

SUTLER: Absolutely. Every Wednesday at 4 PM, my secretary gives me a blow job. You can't get angry, it's tradition.

AMY: I can't believe we're married.

SUTLER: I know. It's pretty wild.

AMY: It's exciting. I love you.

SUTLER: I guess I married the right girl then. Now come here, Mrs. Brody, and give your old husband a kiss.

AMY: Mrs. Brody?

SUTLER: You're going to have to get used to it. When this Yichud thing is over, we're going to go out there and everyone's going to call you Mrs. Brody.

AMY: But—

SUTLER: —you know they'll do that. They're going to do it for months.

AMY: No, they won't.

SUTLER: Yes, they will, they'll call you Mrs. Brody and think they're the first person to do it.

AMY: But I'm not taking your name. *(to audience)* You hear that? That's the bomb dropping on Hiroshima. *(to Sutler)* We discussed this, I'm sure we did—

SUTLER: —must have been your other fiancé, because I would have objected. Strenuously.

AMY: Sutler, I can't take your name. I'm the last Lauderer. If I change my name, it dies out.

SUTLER: It's going to die out anyway once the kids come along.

AMY: *(to audience)* And now for Nagasaki.

SUTLER: Amy? Amy, my son is *going* to have my name.

AMY: And my daughter is going to have mine.

SUTLER: *(pause)* When were you going to tell me this?

AMY: I'm sure I told you.

SUTLER: When?

AMY: Our first date. You said it was fine with you.

SUTLER: You can't trust anything I said back then, I was only trying to sleep with you.

AMY: Sutler, it's a new millennium. No one takes the other person's name anymore.

SUTLER: I do. You want my tradition? There it is.

AMY: No.

SUTLER: No?

AMY: No.

SUTLER: I see. So I have to sit here in your, your—

AMY: —Yichud—

SUTLER: —your *Yichud*, but I ask one little thing of you—

AMY: The *Yichud* lasts an hour. You want me to take your name for an hour, I will.

SUTLER: I'm going outside now.

AMY: Sutler—

SUTLER: —I am going outside because this is my *wedding*—

AMY: —we have to stay in here—

SUTLER: —to do what? To do *what*? I'm not fighting with you on our wedding day.

He exits.

AMY: *(to audience)* I refused to go. Tradition was tradition. I was prepared to sit here alone for an entire hour if I had to.

There is a knock on the door

But I didn't have to.

Amy, thinking it's Sutler, goes to answer it; it is Chesterton, old and dirty.

CHESTERTON: Excuse me, I'm sorry to bother you, but I'm looking for Sutler Brody.

SCENE 2

The lights change back to the spotlights at the start of the show. Sutler and Amy step into them; Chesterton freezes.

AMY: I was stunned.

SUTLER: Of course I had seen him at the wedding.

AMY: I thought he was homeless.

SUTLER: It was impossible *not* to see him.

AMY: I thought, have these people no respect?

SUTLER: I never made eye contact, though.

AMY: How did Sutler not see him?

SUTLER: That's why I wobbled when I went down the aisle.

AMY: Not *smell* him?

SUTLER: I was panicked.

BOTH: I was so scared he was going to—

SUTLER: —say something—

AMY: —ruin something—

SUTLER: And I'd have to explain. I hadn't seen him forever.

AMY: The ceremony started.

SUTLER: Do you take this woman—

AMY: —do you take this man—

SUTLER: —till death—

AMY: —unreligious, to keep Sutler happy—

SUTLER: —performed by a rabbi to keep Amy happy—

AMY: —marriage is about compromise, after all—

SUTLER: —can anyone show just cause why these two—

AMY: —should not be lawfully joined?

SUTLER: I held my breath.

AMY: Would someone speak up?

SUTLER: There was the beat—

AMY: —the prerequisite beat—

SUTLER: —not a sound—

AMY: —only thing I could hear was his mother sobbing—

SUTLER: —just my mother crying—

AMY: —blowing her nose like an elephant—

SUTLER: —and *he* wasn't saying anything—

AMY: —I thought, *this* is my mother-in-law?

SUTLER: I thought for sure he was going to say *something*.

AMY: But no.

SUTLER: But no.

AMY: No one said anything.

SUTLER: My balls feel like they're made of lead.

AMY: No one ever says anything, except on TV.

SUTLER: And I knew.

AMY: It all went smoothly.

SUTLER: If he was here, it had something to do with Sandra.

SCENE 3

Sutler leaves. Amy returns to the scene with Chesterton.

AMY: Sutler's out there. You can't miss him, he's probably the one getting drunk.

CHESTERTON: That can't be. The Sutler I'm looking for doesn't drink. He was always a dreadful bore at parties.

AMY: Well then, perhaps you've intruded on the wrong wedding.

CHESTERTON: No, it was him.

AMY: *(to audience)* I didn't want to be cruel. It's a bad omen to be cruel on your wedding day. But the *smell.*

CHESTERTON: It was a lovely ceremony, by the way.

AMY: Thank you.

CHESTERTON: I've never been to a Jewish wedding.

AMY: Yes, well, it's good to be cultured, Mister— ?

CHESTERTON: Chesterton. William H. Chesterton.

AMY: Well, Mr. Chesterton, I'm afraid, uh...look, you have to leave.

CHESTERTON: I really must speak with Sutler.

AMY: I don't think he is who you think he is.

CHESTERTON: I was going to say the same thing to you.

AMY: What was that?

CHESTERTON: Why is Sutler out there and you're in here, if I may ask?

AMY: *(awkwardly)* I'm not feeling well.

CHESTERTON: Ah. My wife was the same way at our wedding. Queasy stomach, my wife. Had something bad for breakfast. Her stomach gurgled through the entire ceremony like a river. "Do you"— *gurgle*— "take this man"— *gurgle*— she wasn't able to eat for days.

AMY: I'm sure I'll be all right.

CHESTERTON: Sutler will be back, though? To check up on you?

AMY: I suppose he will. If he thinks of it.

CHESTERTON: He will. He's a considerate man, Sutler. I remember—but no, I can't tell you *that* story. I'll wait instead.

AMY: You really can't.

CHESTERTON: Would you rather I go out there, look for him, call him by name? In front of all his new in-laws?

AMY: I'd rather you left altogether. It's…inappropriate for you to be here.

CHESTERTON: You will tell me, please, how you and Sutler came to meet.

AMY: I will do no such thing. Look, what do you want? I didn't bring my wallet with me. If you want, I can talk to the caterer about getting you some leftovers—

CHESTERTON: Is that all you think I would want? Money and food?

AMY: It's all you people ever want.

CHESTERTON: We people. What sort of people am I?

AMY: Homeless.

CHESTERTON: You think I'm homeless. How wonderful.

AMY: You're not homeless?

CHESTERTON: Just impoverished.

AMY: What do you want with Sutler?

CHESTERTON: I can't tell you that either.

AMY: I'm going to go get my father now. He's very big and very strong. He was a boxer.

CHESTERTON: So was I.

AMY: He went to Harvard.

CHESTERTON: So did I. Maybe I know him.

AMY: You went to Harvard?

CHESTERTON: Even the destitute deserve an education.

AMY: You boxed for Harvard?

CHESTERTON: I won too. But I'll let your father win, if it'll please you. Anything for Mrs. Sutler Brody.

AMY: It's Lauderer.

CHESTERTON: Sutler can't be pleased about that.

AMY: What makes you say that?

CHESTERTON: If I know Sutler—

AMY: I don't think you do.

CHESTERTON: Well I haven't seen him in many years. I dressed a lot better last time I saw him. I even wore socks. I traded my last pair of socks with a real homeless man, actually. It was for a book by Christopher Isherwood. *Goodbye to Berlin* it was called. It was that book, actually, that made me think of Sutler. It was he who got me interested in Isherwood. Practically swims in that man's work, doesn't he?

AMY: *(awkwardly)* I've never seen him read any of it.

CHESTERTON: Oh? Well, I suppose tastes change. And it has been a while since I've seen him, in any case. I didn't even know you two were engaged, until last night. I was using the announcement page of the newspaper to wrap my sandwich and there he was: Sutler Willis Brody and Amy Rachael Lauderer. You have a beautiful name.

AMY: Thank you. I don't really like it.

CHESTERTON: Then why are you keeping it?

AMY: I'm the last one.

CHESTERTON: The last one what?

AMY: The last Lauderer.

CHESTERTON: A Lauderer by any other name would still smell as sweet, I'd imagine.

AMY: I just...my grandmother asked me to keep it. She said she always wished she had kept hers. Esther Lillian. Now that was a beautiful name.

CHESTERTON: Is she here?

AMY: No. She died a long time ago. But she always told me, "Amy, keep your name. When you're born and when you die, it's all that you have. Everything else you own gets lost in between."

CHESTERTON: *(he checks his watch)* My, he's still not here to check up on you? Not a very good husband. Just out of the gate and already he's losing the race.

AMY: He's not losing any sort of race.

CHESTERTON: My wife would have castrated me. She tried to once, in fact. With a hot tea kettle. Not very bright, my wife. Thank God she only gave my daughter her looks and nothing else.

AMY: You have a daughter? I'm sorry, I just—

CHESTERTON: —you don't expect the poor and downtrodden to have families?

AMY: No. I...I guess I always thought you were people who had no people. Just each other.

CHESTERTON: Well, you're right. We're sort of like the Jews, wandering about the desert, looking for Canaan and trading our socks for a good piece of manna. I mentioned I traded my socks, did I?

AMY: *(amused)* Is that what you want from my husband? His socks?

CHESTERTON: It'll do for a start. But you're trying to get me off topic. I was speaking of my daughter. Her name is Sandra. She's beautiful, really. More than you, I'd say. She adores me. Here, let me show you something. *(he begins to lift up his shirt)*

AMY: You lift that shirt any more and I will call my father.

CHESTERTON: It's a scar. It's from the war. I won't tell you which one, that would reveal my age. But it's a shrapnel scar. Sandra loved it. She was fascinated by it, which is sort of morbid, I suppose, but a father takes what he can get.

AMY: Where is she now? Sandra?

CHESTERTON: I am so glad you asked that. Really, I am. Shall I tell you?

AMY: I asked, didn't I?

Lights change; Sutler appears in his spotlight. Chesterton speaks to Amy, Sutler to the audience.

SCENE 4

CHESTERTON: There's this tradition in my family.

SUTLER: Sandra's family had this absurd custom.

CHESTERTON: All the woman would go to Paris.

SUTLER: They'd go to Paris and live there for a year.

CHESTERTON: There's this beautiful old apartment.

SUTLER: There's some ancient, bohemian shithole.

CHESTERTON: It's the family heirloom.

SUTLER: It's the family curse.

CHESTERTON: It's inherited by each woman when she turns eighteen.

SUTLER: And she's supposed to go to Paris and live there for a year.

CHESTERTON: And they stay for a year and can do whatever they like.

SUTLER: At the end of a year, they had to go to the Eiffel Tower.

CHESTERTON: Now this started the year the Eiffel Tower was being built.

SUTLER: And walk— no elevator— *walk* to the top.

CHESTERTON: The woman has to stand at the top.

BOTH: And once there.

SUTLER: They take something of value—

CHESTERTON: —they take something, say a book, or a ring—

SUTLER: —and throw it—

CHESTERTON: —and throw it over the side.

SUTLER: The thing is, no one knows why.

CHESTERTON: Like all good traditions, no one knows why.

SUTLER: They just do it.

CHESTERTON: And everyone's done it.

SUTLER: Sandra's great-grandmother.

CHESTERTON: Sandra's grandmother.

SUTLER: Sandra's mother.

CHESTERTON: Sandra's mother. Except—

SUTLER: —only—

CHESTERTON: —the only thing of value—

SUTLER: —the only thing Sandra's mother had—

CHESTERTON: —the one thing she had that she thought was worth anything—

SUTLER: —was herself—

CHESTERTON: —and off she goes.

Pause

SUTLER: Almost nineteen.

CHESTERTON: Already married.

SUTLER: Had a daughter.

CHESTERTON: And the one thing she thought—

SUTLER: —the only thing she thought that mattered—

CHESTERTON: —was herself.

SUTLER: It came time for it to be Sandra's turn to go.

CHESTERTON: She was obsessed with going.

SUTLER: Sandra didn't want to go.

CHESTERTON: She loved the idea—

SUTLER: —she thought it was the most ridiculous thing she'd ever heard—

CHESTERTON: —it was what her mother would have wanted—

BOTH: I made her feel tremendously guilty.

SUTLER: I thought it was terribly romantic.

CHESTERTON: It's what tradition demanded.

SUTLER: She was so beautiful the day she left.

CHESTERTON: Her fiancé was there the day she left.

SUTLER: Her father was there.

CHESTERTON: Charming fellow.

SUTLER: Couldn't say goodbye in front of her father.

CHESTERTON: She kissed us both.

SUTLER: Couldn't say what I wanted to.

CHESTERTON: Got on that plane—

SUTLER: —she got on that plane—

CHESTERTON: —and off she went—

SUTLER: —barely eighteen—

CHESTERTON: —so beautiful—

SUTLER: —and we never heard from her again.

Pause.

CHESTERTON: She never arrived in Paris.

SUTLER: She was supposed to switch planes in London.

CHESTERTON: She got to London.

SUTLER: She never switched planes.

CHESTERTON: I had it investigated.

SUTLER: They couldn't find her.

CHESTERTON: They decided she was dead.

SUTLER: I assumed she met someone.

CHESTERTON: I didn't agree.

SUTLER: I went to see her father.

CHESTERTON: Her fiancé came to see me.

SUTLER: I was furious.

CHESTERTON: Mostly said things I already knew.

SUTLER: I needed to blame somebody. I said, "You and your traditions."

CHESTERTON: I was so goddamn sorry.

SUTLER: She didn't even want to do it.

CHESTERTON: I gave up on everything.

SUTLER: What the hell's the point of keeping a tradition you don't want to keep?

CHESTERTON: I didn't want anything.

SUTLER: I was so righteous.

CHESTERTON: I didn't think I was entitled to it.

SUTLER: But it was as much my fault as it was his.

CHESTERTON: And I never saw him again.

SUTLER: There was a time and for a long while—

CHESTERTON: —and every once in a while—

SUTLER: —I think I see her—

CHESTERTON: —I see her—

SUTLER: There was no good reason I should see her—

CHESTERTON: I'm a strong believer in chaos theory. Order in chaos.

SUTLER: This is a city of thousands of people—

CHESTERTON: —so many people and we run into ones we know all the time.

SUTLER: At the store.

CHESTERTON: Standing at a corner.

SUTLER: In bars.

CHESTERTON: Is that her?

SUTLER: The one standing in the checkout line.

CHESTERTON: Is that her?

SUTLER: The person in front of you at the movies.

CHESTERTON: Is that her?

SUTLER: The one who just stole your parking spot—

CHESTERTON: Is that her?

SUTLER: No.

CHESTERTON: No.

SUTLER: It's never her.

CHESTERTON: She's never there.

SUTLER: But I look for her all the time.

He leaves.

AMY: Mr. Chesterton, why did you want to see Sutler?

SUTLER: Sutler, yes, he'll be back soon, won't he?

AMY: Why did you come here?

CHESTERTON: Because last week I received some remarkable news.

AMY: News?

CHESTERTON: Yes. As luck, fate, and chaos theory would have it, *Ms.* Lauderer, my daughter is still very much alive.

SCENE 5

Sutler returns. He stops when he sees Chesterton.

AMY: *(to audience)* Sutler came in a moment later. You should have seen his face. I have never seen anything collapse like that. He suddenly looked very small and he staggered a bit, and dropped the beer in his hand and spilt it all over the carpet. I remember thinking, "They're going to charge me for the cleaning." Such absurdities. I kept staring at the beer as it seeped into the carpet, I barely heard the explanation, something about her sending a letter, I was hardly listening because I kept looking at the beer and thinking that this would be the last time I would ever see Sutler spill beer.

She stays there as the scene continues.

SUTLER: She's alive?

CHESTERTON: And ready to cakewalk all along the Champs Élysées. She's here. We just have to get her to Paris.

SUTLER: We?

CHESTERTON: Yes. Both of us. She wants to go, it's tradition, you know. You'll have to pay, of course. I don't have much, I'm on welfare.

SUTLER: She sent you a letter.

CHESTERTON: That's right. Such wonderful grammar, too, and she spelt everything properly, I taught her myself, did she ever tell you that?

SUTLER: All the time. She said you used those magnets you stick on refrigerators.

CHESTERTON: *(laughing, delighted)* Yes! Yes! Exactly!

AMY: *(to audience)* It was so strange, it was as if I wasn't even in the room and I was catching a glimpse of the old Sutler, the one who Mr. Chesterton had described, the Sutler I never knew or met.

SUTLER: *(smiling to himself)* Sandra.

AMY: How badly he loved her, I thought.

SUTLER: Sandra.

AMY: I could see it when he spoke her name. I marveled at it. Here was a Sutler I had never seen before and would probably never see again. The one who didn't drink and stayed up all night reading Christopher Isherwood.

SUTLER: How did she ever find you?

CHESTERTON: Oh, she's smart, our Sandra, you know she is. She found a way.

SUTLER: How?

CHESTERTON: Tracked me down, somehow, you shouldn't ask so many questions, boy. Sandra is alive, who cares about the details? Sandra's alive and she's ready to cakewalk. Remember that night you two did the cakewalk in our living room?

SUTLER: That was many years ago.

CHESTERTON: Funny, I think of it every day. Every day, and it makes me laugh, you and Sandra, and now you'll be together all over again.

AMY: *(to audience)* I was in shock. Sutler doing a cakewalk, you saw him, he wouldn't even dance with me. And what's that glint in his eye, do you see it? It's never there. This fucking jealousy rose up inside me.

CHESTERTON: We can be there tomorrow. Tomorrow, Sutler, do you know the first thing, the first thing she said, was that I should find you.

SUTLER: She said that?

CHESTERTON: First thing.

AMY: *(to audience)* First thing. I tried to picture this girl, this Sandra, roaming around, thinking of Sutler, thinking of my husband and I felt absurdly betrayed, as if he had been cheating on me.

SUTLER: God, I loved her.

AMY: *(to audience)* He was going to go. Why shouldn't he? I felt so horrid, how we had spent our only minutes of marriage arguing with each other. Probably the only time I'll ever be married and look at how I wasted it. We didn't even consummate it. In the eyes of God we weren't even married. In the eyes of God we were nothing.

SUTLER: Can I see the letter?

CHESTERTON: *(faltering; slightly)* What?

SUTLER: Can I see the letter?

CHESTERTON: I, uh, don't seem to have it on me.

SUTLER: Where would you have left it?

CHESTERTON: Probably in my other pants. Which I had to sell to get train fare up here, so you see, I don't have the letter—

SUTLER: William. There was a letter, wasn't there?

CHESTERTON: Of course. Of course there was. We have to leave, right away. Right away, Sutler.

SUTLER: Where is she now? We have to get to Paris, right? So where is she?

CHESTERTON: She's here, she's here.

SUTLER: In the city?

CHESTERTON: *(faltering)* We need to get her to Paris. It's tradition.

SUTLER: William.

CHESTERTON: I got a letter.

SUTLER: No. You didn't.

CHESTERTON: Sutler, please—

SUTLER: —I'm married, now. I'm going on my honeymoon.

CHESTERTON: Honeymoon! With who? With, this, this *thing?*

SUTLER: I'm sorry, William.

CHESTERTON: Yes, here it is, I did get a letter. *(produces one)*

SUTLER: Let me see it.

CHESTERTON: Why can't you just trust me?

SUTLER: *William. (he takes the letter)*

CHESTERTON: It came to me last week.

AMY: Dear Mr. Chesterton, it said.

CHESTERTON: It was in the dead-letter office. And that's what it was—

AMY: —we regret to inform you—

CHESTERTON: —a *dead* letter—

AMY: — a body was recently found—

CHESTERTON: —some nut decided to deliver all the dead letters—

AMY: —it has been positively identitifed—

CHESTERTON: —fucking do-gooders.

SUTLER: *(to audience)* It didn't come as much of a shock. Like if God came down, you'd think, "Well, there, you see, I was right." I could have done without the details, mind you. *(to Chesterton)* I'm so sorry, William.

CHESTERTON: Don't say that. I hate it. Every day, people looking at me with sad looks and saying how sorry they are. "Oh look, let me help you," they say. "Oh look, I found a *letter.*" Why couldn't you just believe me? We could have been in...look, we have the flat, we'll stay there, it's just for a year, you can come back and marry this girl all over again.

SUTLER: I'm sorry, William. I promised her I'd only marry her once.

CHESTERTON: Then to hell with you. She deserves better than you, deserves better than to just be forgotton. What am I supposed to do? I have to go get her.

SUTLER: I don't understand.

AMY: Sandra's body had been waiting. In the letter it said you had 60 days to claim it, but the letter was almost five years old. They had buried the body in a public cemetery.

CHESTERTON: They just threw her in the ground.

AMY: Pauper's funeral.

CHESTERTON: Like she meant nothing.

AMY: He wanted her cremated.

CHESTERTON: She deserves to be in Paris.

AMY: He wanted her ashes thrown from the Eiffel Tower.

CHESTERTON: And here you are getting married.

AMY: I didn't know what to do. There were two men, mine and Sandra's. The one who didn't drink and the one who does; the one who reads Christopher Isherwood and the one who doesn't; the one who was married to me...and the one who loved Sandra Chesterton. I thought, this can only end badly. But it didn't. *(entering the scene)* What if we took her to Paris?

SUTLER: You mean...

AMY: What if we brought her to Paris?

CHESTERTON: Why would you do that?

AMY: Because my husband loved her. And because it's tradition.

SUTLER: It's not mine. It's his.

AMY: *(to audience)* Sutler was right. It was Mr. Chesterton's tradition. So we offered to take him along.

CHESTERTON: You would take me to Paris.

AMY: You'd have to clean yourself up.

CHESTERTON: But it's your honeymoon.

AMY: Well, we won't keep you around for the whole time.

Amy leads Chesterton out.

SUTLER: *(to audience)* Once we were alone, I didn't know what to say. I kept thinking, what if Sandra had been alive? What if she wanted me back? What would I have done? I have no idea what I would have done. She was such a long time ago. We were so young.

Amy returns

I should have said something.

AMY: What would you have said?

SUTLER: I could have told you.

AMY: Told me what? That you were in love once? We've all been in love once. Why do we try to pretend that we haven't been hurt?

SUTLER: I don't like you knowing that I loved someone else.

AMY: You loved her that much?

SUTLER: Yes.

AMY: And you still fell in love with me?

SUTLER: Yes.

AMY: I think that's the most romantic thing I've ever heard.

SUTLER: I'll tell you everything, if you want to hear it.

AMY: I do. But not now. We only have twenty minutes.

SUTLER: What do you want to do?

AMY: Well it's the Yichud Room, isn't it? Help me out of this dress.

They kiss.

EPILOGUE

Amy and Sutler separate and go into their respective spotlights.

AMY: Marriage.

SUTLER: Marriage.

AMY: The world's oldest profession.

SUTLER: The ultimate tradition.

AMY: Centuries old.

BOTH: Marriage.

AMY: We waited until the hour was up.

SUTLER: Once it was finished, we went out.

AMY: People called me Mrs. Brody.

SUTLER: They called her Mrs. Brody.

AMY: I didn't correct them.

SUTLER: I did.

AMY: Marriage is about compromise, you know.

The end

SUICIDE NOTES

KENNETH T. WILLIAMS

Photo: Stefen Winchester

KENNETH T. WILLIAMS

ABOUT THE PLAYWRIGHT

Kenneth T. Williams is a Cree playwright and journalist. His plays *Thunderstick*, *Suicide Notes* and *AWOL* have been produced across Canada. His newest play, *Three Little Birds* (former title: *A Box for Bones*), was workshopped and read at the 2007 SpringFest in Saskatoon. He worked for over six years as videojournalist for the Aboriginal Peoples Television Network's national news program. He now edits a TV series in Saskatchewan called "Art InCLINEd." He has two feature-length screenplays in development, *Café Daughter* and *The Red Majesty*. He resides in Saskatoon, Saskatchewan.

PRODUCTION HISTORY

Suicide Notes was produced in 2004 by Fu'Sha Theatre for the Summerworks Theatre Festival in Toronto. Vinetta Strombergs directed, with Brenda Kamino as Ange, Michelle St. John as Cat and Ryan Cunningham as Pete.

For production rights, contact Signature Editions, production rights agent Charles Northcote—Charlie@coregroupta.com, 416-955-0819, or the author at kennethwilliams@shaw.ca.

CHARACTERS

Ange — A homeless woman who writes suicide notes.

Cat — A forty-something novelist who hasn't written in fifteen years.

Pete — A poet, and Cat's twenty-something boyfriend.

SETTING

Ottawa, today.

SCENE 1

Spotlight on Ange.

ANGE: The darkness is a mother's warm embrace
She comforts
Hides me from the snarling icy jaws of sadness
The metal shrill crippling anger
She knows I'm tired of fighting the bright glaring lie of joy
I paint on my smile
They can smell weakness and they will tear you apart
Taunts from the wild dogs feed on you
I lean deeper into the darkness and she covers my ears with her soft hands.
Shhhhhhhhhhhh she whispers
Shhhhhhhhhhhhh, they won't get you here.
You are safe with me.
She doesn't try to stop my tears
And hums me to sleep with a lullaby of emptiness.
Goodbye.

Spotlight on Pete.

PETE: Don't drink and jah, young urban Indian male.
Weed makes your dick droop.
Your back stoop and kills the warrior within.
Spliffifying your need to kill.
Killin' your need to speed on the warpath four-oh-one.
Grill-smashed-in-BMW-jump on the Don Valley.
Parkway.
No way home.
But young urban Indian male, which way is home?
Rhythms call, call from the heartbeat of the nation, call from SystemSoundbar-Docks-Phoenix-Government-Boa-boom-boom-boom-boom-boom-boom of a million mini-warriors mate-dancing fancy.
Is this home Toronto Tonto?
Visions flood in L-S-D-driven rain dances, dances on fire, fire-burned retinal shapes, spiraling voices, voices of the walking dead, spare-change elders and tricksters accost angels in blonde Gucci wings.
Invisible walking.

Unseen 'cause no one will look you in the eyes.
In this new land, the warrior hunting beer, proudly bearing a beer-claw broken necklace.
When are you coming home, young urban Indian male?

SCENE 2

Lights up on Cat in her kitchen. Marley's "No Woman No Cry" plays in the background.

CAT: The Minister of Intergovernmental Affairs is pleased to announce...pleased? No, not "puhleeeezed." Her people will just edit that out anyway. The Minister of Intergovernmental Affairs announces the conclusion... Announces the conclusion? The minister of I.A...what? Goddamn it, I don't even have the What and I still have Who, Where, When and Why to go! All right all right all right. I'm stressing over a press release...a press release about the Infosync initiative that'll align the information systems between the feds and all the provinces and who the fuck cares that I spent all day on this crap that's only going to end up in some stupid reporter's recycle box. It's not that this promises anything new or exciting or lifesaving. Promises. Promises. Broken promises.

Pete enters. He sings along.

PETE: "And then we'd sit and drink oatmeal porridge."

CAT: Fuck you! It's cornmeal porridge!

PETE: 'Kay. Whatever.

CAT: I'm going to be calm I'm going to be calm I'm going to be calm. He comes in here, and the first thing I do is attack, shouldn't do that, because I'm going to be calm, even though he's been gone for five fucking days!

PETE: You're talking to yourself again.

CAT: Five days, Pete! Where the hell have you been!

PETE: This has got to wait, baby. I got a reading tonight. At Club Babylon. You know the one. On Bank.

CAT: Oh great! Another reading! Are you going to blab to them about me as well?

PETE: Blab?

CAT: Five days without calling or leaving a note.

PETE: I was at a reading...

CAT: How could you! It's the only thing I've ever asked you not to do.

PETE: In the moment, you know, when you just let the mind flow and the words unfurl and the rhythm of the—

CAT: You were high.

PETE: Probably, but...you know...

CAT: Some professor of Native Lit at the University of Ottawa knows I'm here. She wants me to give a reading to her class.

PETE: Hey, that's cool. Maybe we could team up.

CAT: No, it's not cool!

PETE: I'm sorry, Cat. I—

CAT: After all these years of trying to stay out of the spotlight, you just threw me back in there! I'm not ready for it. And for five days I've had to sit here and wonder who else you've told.

PETE: Fine. Sorry. I don't understand the freak-out value.

CAT: You made a promise and you broke it.

PETE: It's just a Native Lit class, Cat. How many people do you think will be there?

Silence. No response from Cat.

I've been learning how to play guitar. Wanna hear? I'm getting pretty good. Been practicing on my own.

CAT: Don't you know what they're going to do? They're going to ask where I've been all this time. Why haven't I had anything published since *Dreaming Child*? They'll want to know if I've got anything new and I'll show them this.

She throws her notebook at Pete.

PETE: "I'm going to kill that motherfucker when he gets home. Why I put up with this, I don't know. He's dead. Dead. And I can be free." Well… It's emotionally raw, revealing truth. At least it's not a press release.

CAT: You really suck at this comforting thing.

PETE: You're making a big deal out of nothing. So what if some people know you live in Ottawa now?

CAT: I just want them to forget me.

PETE: Babe. Even after fifteen years, people aren't forgetting you. They're more curious. You should hear some of the things I hear about you. Weird conspiracy theories. You were abducted and murdered by police. You died in a sweat lodge. You're living alone in a cabin, deep in the bush, armed with a shotgun to chase away trespassers.

CAT: Yeah, just be thankful I don't have a shotgun.

Pause.

PETE: Are you coming to the reading?

CAT: I'm still pissed at you.

PETE: Understood. Can I borrow the guitar?

SCENE 3

Pete is now onstage doing a reading. Light on Pete. Cat is seated, watching him.

PETE: Okay, all. I got a new one for you. It's called "raving is my sun dance." No, not raven. Not the bird. You know, raving. Ray-vingggga. But it's kinda cool that, you know, the words sound alike. Okay, here goes.

The e takes
Tae-tae-tae-tae-tae
TAAAAAKES hold
Spinning
Beat beat beat

Of a hundred thousand hearts
All one
All none
All gone
All done
Staring at the lights
Lost souls
Dead
Not knowing we were alive
Wanting
Seeking
Speaking
In visions
In-duced
Juiced
By ecstasy
The new warriors of light
Can
Kiss
MY
Fucking
Ass
We scream at light
We run in darkness
Driven by
Powered by
The reverend of revolutions
The 33 and a third
aaaR Peee emmmmmMs spinning disks of visions visions visuals laser burned into my eyelids
raving is my sun dance

Thanks. Thanks. Got another one for you…

Pete continues in the background. Cat outside, getting some air, fuming. Ange approaches.

ANGE: Suicide note?

CAT: Sorry?

ANGE: Suicide note?

CAT: I'm sorry. I don't understand.

ANGE: You need a suicide note. You look depressed.

CAT: Not really your business—

ANGE: Usually a sign. That look. You know it. I know it. I see it all the time.

CAT: See what?

ANGE: No one seems to see it anymore. It's like they don't care. If you need a suicide note you should leave a suicide note. Here you go.

CAT: I'm not taking that.

ANGE: Leave it someplace obvious. You don't want them looking for it. Don't want them thinking that you didn't care to write one. Can I have a smoke?

CAT: Sorry. I don't smoke.

ANGE: You should…helps you relax.

CAT: Look, do you want something?

ANGE: Her memory stolen from me
The smell of her hair ripped
From my dreams
My hands cuddled her
Stroked her cheeks
Dressed her in the casket.

Pause.

Did you see the sunrise? God, it was beautiful. You look terrible.

Ange starts to leave.

Bobbie Snow didn't leave a note.

CAT: What!

ANGE: Just remember to say goodbye.

Ange puts a note on the ground and exits. Cat picks it up. Light on Cat. She reads.

CAT: I am from nowhere.
I don't belong here.
I cannot feel your arms
your smile
your love.
I hold you
I tell you I love you
but I don't understand your smile
or the look in your eyes
It's too much for me
to keep pretending
or that I should stay…
here.
Please forgive me.
I am from nowhere
and I don't belong with you…
or anyone.
Goodbye.

Lights on Pete.

PETE: Okay. One more. Then I'm done for the night. Just got back from Detroit from a reading down there. Gone for five days. It's a weird story how I got there. But I'll save that one for later. But Detroit, man. That's fucking cool. Lots of cool Nishes down there. What's a Nish? Glad you asked. This one's called Nish-Now-Be.

Anishnawbe you can call me
Nothin's free
Especially Anishnawbe
Used to be free Anishnawbe
Where can you see
It's time to flee
Nish now be
Stand free
I am what Nish now be
Long hair
Gone
Canoes
Gone

But I'm still here
I'm a Nish now ME

Applause. Pete joins Cat at table.

PETE: Well?

CAT: Detroit, eh?

PETE: I didn't tell you?

CAT: No.

PETE: It was when I…uhhh…went to that rave in Hull. It's kind of a funny story, really. I ran into some cool—

CAT: Save it. I'll just chalk it up to the Peter Matthews experience.

PETE: Okay. What do you think of the guitar? I think it works.

CAT: You're a little rough.

PETE: Nothing a little practice won't hurt.

CAT: You know some of the street people around here, right?

PETE: Yeah, why?

CAT: I just met someone. A woman. She offered me a suicide note.

PETE: That's Ange. She's been around a couple of years. She hands them out to people. Like a public service or something.

CAT: She knew my book.

PETE: Don't look at me. I didn't tell anyone you'd be here.

CAT: Calm down. I'm not blaming you. She tries to bum a smoke. Then gives me a suicide note. And says something like "Bobbie Snow should've left a note."

PETE: She didn't leave a note?

CAT: No!

PETE: Come on! It's been years since I read your book. I can't remember every tiny dee— I mean, yeah, she didn't. Of course. That moment really must've resonated with Ange.

CAT: Go on. Keep digging that hole.

PETE: Okay, okay, what about Ange and her note?

CAT: I didn't know what to say. I wanted to talk to her but she just disappeared.

PETE: No explaining some fans. What you think of the guitar?

CAT: You remind me of the Sex Pistols. All proud you don't really know how to play. Make it part of your act. You think she's a fan?

PETE: She's knows your book. She knows you. She can now tell all her friends in the crazy house she met the elusive Catherine Walker. And what do you mean, "my act?"

CAT: Yeah. Your shtick. You know, the wild modern young Indian. But it was how she said it. "Bobbie Snow didn't leave a note." Most fans want an autograph, they tell me their favourite parts of the book, and then ask, "When's your next one?"

PETE: She's crazy. Don't worry about her. And it's not an act. It's the truth.

CAT: Your "act" is just you making observations, which isn't the same as telling the truth. And how do you know she's crazy? At least she didn't ask for an "authentic" Ojibway blessing.

PETE: I hear you can make good money doing those.

CAT: See! There it is again.

PETE: What?

CAT: You're being glib. You're being cynical. But there's no meaning to it. You blend a lot of images—like your poetry. But I don't know what's underneath. It's so…disconnected. I wonder what she's disconnected from?

PETE: Reality. Me, though, my generation is disconnected from the past. I'm just not moaning about it. I celebrate the disconnection. Gives me a chance to create myself on my own terms.

CAT: But you're just combining bad guitar playing with drug-addled rantings. It's just noise, after a while. If you want to express disconnection, I've got to know what it is you're disconnected from. But all I hear you do is make fun of our culture.

PETE: I'm not making fun of it. I've just never experienced any of what I've read about. Not in a real touch-it-or-taste-it sense. I won't make shit up about tricksters, grandmother spirits or white buffalo if I don't really know it.

CAT: But you can know it. There are still elders and teachers out there. Who knows, maybe Ange is some kind of grandmother spirit? No! No, forget I even said that.

PETE: And what elders should I see? The one who takes credit cards for his sweat-lodge-of-the-month club? I don't know who's genuine or not. Hell, one "elder" was taking passages out of *Dreaming Child* and calling them the ancient teachings of his people. The guy wasn't even Ojibway! He was a—

PETE & CAT: Brown-skin New Ager and born-again Indian.

PETE: Exactly. Because of them, your book is next to Carlos Castenada and Lynn Andrews, instead of in the lit section where it belongs. We're surrounded by these people, Cat. If I can't trust what they know, then I can only trust what I know. That's why I do what I do. Like the time I lived on the streets. I wanted the experience. To see what it was like. To taste it, know it, stuff you can't understand by simply reading about it.

CAT: But it's still not real. You're middle class, from an affluent suburb. It was no different than a summer camp…only with the homeless.

PETE: Well, I learned one thing…growing up in the suburbs don't give you much decent to write about.

CAT: That's who you are, Pete. That's real. You could be the first angst-ridden suburban Native author.

PETE: Angst-ridden? That's so grunge. Blah blah blah hate-my-parents blah blah blah hate-my-life. Been done. I want to carve my own path. Make a new mark.

CAT: By comparing a rave to a sun dance?

PETE: Tell me what the difference is! I dance. I sweat. I stare at the lights. I have a vision.

CAT: Is that all a sun dance is about?

PETE: Well…uhhh…it's kinda the same.

CAT: Uh huh. How can you say that, when you've never touched it or tasted it, as you like to say?

PETE: All right, all right, you win.

CAT: Not about winning, Pete. It's about being as truthful an artist as you can be. Imagine yourself as a lake. Your poems are like stones skipping on the water. You need to dive. You need to reach deep inside yourself. Deeper than your fears. Strip away the layers of ignorance, doubt and, finally, your own brutish ego. Until you're laid bare. Exposed. Vulnerable. Only then can you experience truth.

PETE: Laid bare…exposed and vulnerable.

CAT: Stop it…you're making fun again.

PETE: You're the one talking dirty. Is that how I should be? Exposed…vulnerable…laid bare.

Pete stretches over the table, arching his back, facing the ceiling.

CAT: Get off the table.

PETE: Your eyes are a lake…I'm drowning in your gaze. Your body is the soft, sandy bottom…holding me as I die in your embrace…vulnerable…exposed…laid…bare.

Pause.

CAT: You do have a way with words.

PETE: That's just the first stanza.

CAT: There's more?

PETE: Lots more.

He moves in to kiss her.

But it's more of a performance piece.

CAT: It better be a hell of a performance. You have to make up for five days.

PETE: Then you'd better call a cab. I need to save my energy.

He kisses her. Lights out.

SCENE 4

Cat at her favourite spot in the park. She's working on some papers. Ange approaches from behind.

ANGE: Paper!

CAT: What?

ANGE: Paper! I need paper!

Ange reaches for the pile on Cat's table. Cat pulls them away.

CAT: Hang on a second.

ANGE: Please! I need paper.

CAT: I want to talk to you.

Ange walks away. Cat rips out some notepaper and runs after Ange.

Here here here. Here's some paper.

Ange takes the paper, pulls out a stubby little pencil and writes feverishly.

I saw you a couple of nights ago. Do you remember me?

Ange waves her off.

ANGE: Must not forget must not forget!

CAT: Forget what?

Ange finishes her note. Sighs.

ANGE: Demand is high. I can hardly keep up.

CAT: Will you sit down for a second?

ANGE: Best place to leave it is in your pocket. They always look there. Of course, you can also leave it somewhere else. It's up to you.

CAT: I'll buy you a coffee.

ANGE: A double-mochaccino latte would be nice.

CAT: Latte. Okay.

ANGE: Not too much cinnamon.

CAT: Anything else?

ANGE: Dreams would be good too.

CAT: Well…we have something in common.

Ange starts rummaging through Cat's notes.

Hey! What are you doing!

ANGE: It could be here!

CAT: Do you need more paper?

Cat rips out some pages from her notebook and hands them to Ange. Ange looks over them, like reading some invisible note, then tosses them aside.

ANGE: Not here. Not here. Not here. *(to Cat)* Staring is rude.

CAT: Sorry. Do you know me?

ANGE: My name is Ange.

CAT: That's pretty. Is it short for Angela?

ANGE: Could be. I never asked. Your name?

CAT: Cat.

ANGE: Cat.

CAT: Yes. Cat. That's my name.

ANGE: Cat?

CAT: It's short for Catherine.

ANGE: That's not entirely true. Not true at all. You wrote the book. You wrote…a long time ago…a long, long time ago…the book.

CAT: Yes. Shhh.

ANGE: She looked like she was dreaming. A dreaming child.

CAT: Yes. That's me. Just keep it down.

ANGE: You are… I found you… I found you…you are…you are!

Ange grabs Cat's hand; she stares deep into Cat's eyes.

You are Catherine Walker. I found you.

Cat pulls her hand away. She walks away.

ANGE: Bobbie Snow didn't say goodbye!

Cat stops.

Page 112. No goodbye. Tell me where it is.

CAT: Where what is?

ANGE: Was it in her pockets? They didn't look in her pockets. Or was it on the dresser? They looked there but they may have missed it. Please tell me where it is!

CAT: What is it you want to know, Ange?

ANGE: The sun is beautiful and warm. But you look awful. Was it something like this?

Ange hands Cat a note.

Or this.

Another note.

Or this one or this one or this one.

More notes. Cat takes the notes and reads them quickly.

CAT: Can I have these?

ANGE: They're suicide notes.

CAT: I know.

ANGE: You gotta say goodbye. Because people forget. They have everything else prepared but they forget that. The most important thing.

CAT: Do you have more notes?

ANGE: I gotta go now.

CAT: Ange. Please.

ANGE: Thanks for the paper.

CAT: Can I see more of your notes?

ANGE: You only need one.

CAT: I know a lot of people. Who need to say goodbye.

ANGE: Are you some sort of misery magnet?

CAT: Let's get your latte.

SCENE 5

Cat's apartment. She enters first and looks around. She's clutching Ange's notes.

CAT: Pete? You up yet?

Pete enters. He's awake...well, almost.

PETE: Hey, baby. Where you been?

CAT: Getting coffee.

PETE: You bring me one?

CAT: Sorry, baby. Forgot.

PETE: No worries. I can make my own. Whatcha got there?

CAT: Some of Ange's suicide notes.

PETE: Really? She gave them to you?

CAT: No. She kind of let me borrow them. In a manner of speaking. She insisted on meeting the people I said needed to see the notes.

PETE: What people?

Cat points to Ange.

ANGE: Hi.

Pause.

PETE: Hi.

ANGE: Suicide note?

PETE: Can we talk?

CAT: Sure.

PETE: Alone.

ANGE: Is this about me?

PETE: Yes.

ANGE: You want me to leave?

CAT: No.

PETE: Yes.

CAT: Not the apartment. We... Pete and I need to talk about...

ANGE: Me.

PETE: Yes.

CAT: It's okay, Ange. I think Pete's just a little surprised.

ANGE: I've seen you around.

PETE: I hang out. Sometimes.

ANGE: You have a nice place here.

PETE: It's not mine. It's Cat's place.

ANGE: But you live here.

PETE: Well, yeah, but—

ANGE: Nice place.

CAT: Thank you, Ange.

ANGE: I thought you were a social worker.

PETE: Who? Cat?

ANGE: No. You.

PETE: Me?

ANGE: Always hanging out. Always talking to people. Made me think you were a cop too. Too friendly, you. Buying us coffee and stuff. But always asking questions. Too many questions. Made me nervous. I'll get out of your way. You want to talk. Bathroom?

CAT: Down the hall. To the left, Ange.

Ange leaves.

Okay. Before you start. If you watch her close enough, you notice that the crazy thing comes and goes. She's been pretty lucid for the past hour and drinking one latte after another. Maybe the caffeine helps, I don't know.

PETE: But—

CAT: She's walked into my life. Just like you did. There's a reason for this. I don't know what the reason is, exactly. And I know nothing happens without a reason.

PETE: Okay, but—

CAT: But that's not all. Her notes. They're beautiful. They're like poetry.

PETE: Hang on a second! Poetry?

CAT: They're heartbreaking...testaments about life and sorrow. I cry every time I read them. They should be published.

PETE: Published? She writes them for people she thinks are about to cap themselves. Who's going to publish that?

CAT: They're more than that, Pete. Just listen for a second. I have an idea. A proposal. I think I could take this to my agent and publisher. A collection of poetry called "suicide notes." As discovered by Catherine Walker.

PETE: What!

Pause.

CAT: Say something.

PETE: That's...that's... That's the fucking craziest thing I've heard.

CAT: Just listen to me. I don't claim to write them.

PETE: No one's going to believe that. Your readers have been waiting fifteen years for a new book. They'll think you made her up as a literary device and wrote these notes yourself. It'd be a fucking brilliant stunt if the truth wasn't so despicable.

CAT: Nothing despicable in finding a gifted writer, Pete! I had to convince you to write down your "stream of consciousness rantings" that "were too pure for the page." And you haven't been giving me shit about that. What is it now, four books? She deserves to be printed as much as you did.

PETE: All right. Fair enough. Have you thought for a second that maybe only you think they're poetry?

CAT: I know they're poetry.

PETE: Then what's with this discovered-by-Catherine-Walker stuff? You didn't do that with me.

CAT: Because you could do the readings.

PETE: You'll do the readings?

CAT: She can't...obviously.

PETE: You're taking advantage of her.

CAT: I am not. I'm being practical.

PETE: So at each reading and interview you can talk about this mysterious homeless woman who gave you these suicide notes. But everyone will just think you've created a trickster-grandmother figure. Just like before.

CAT: Look. The only way they could get published is if someone's name was attached to them. And in no way do I imply that I wrote them. I'll make sure it will all be perfectly legal.

PETE: It's all perfectly fucked!

CAT: She'll get all the royalties. Her name will be on the contract as the author.

PETE: You're messing with somebody's life and you think this is about money?

CAT: She writes poetry and doesn't know it. She just does it. I haven't written anything worth publishing in fifteen years. Not one short story, poem, hell, not even a review. And these magical notes pour out of her...like breathing...like when I met you. You made me feel alive again. The way you stand there, at the mic, so confident, so sure of yourself, speaking to the world, knowing it wants to listen...needs to hear you. And your words just spill out. A torrent...raw...uninhibited. It's so easy for you...and impossible... At least I can say I discover talent. That's what's left for me.

PETE: Oh please, Cat. You're a writer, not a fucking martyr.

CAT: Listen to me, Pete! You think it's easy for me to finally see that I can't fucking do it anymore! Maybe *Dreaming Child* was the only book I had in me. Now that's gone and I can't even dream anymore.

PETE: I'm not going to play along with your pity fantasy. Yes, I know I suck at the comforting thing! But I'm telling you the truth because I love you.

CAT: You could sugar-coat it a little. Bastard.

Ange enters.

ANGE: Any coffee?

CAT: Sorry, Ange. We're not done.

ANGE: You're done talking about me, right?

PETE: Were you listening to us?

ANGE: Yes. Coffee? One cream, one sugar, if you got any.

PETE: That was private.

ANGE: Then you should keep your voices down.

SCENE 6

Cat alone in the park, writing in her notebook.

CAT: The sky is…blue…what other colour would it be…the sky is…sky blue…why is it so easy for him why is it so easy for him why do I keep repeating the same line over and over…trap…fell into it again…always writing about not writing and this one will be—

Cat rips out the page.

Again. It just pours out of them…like water from a…tap…stream…waterfall… FUCKFUCKFUCK…

Cat rips out the page.

My coffee is brown. The grass is…brown… My hair is brown. My day sucks. I have nothing to put in my diary…diary…this is not a diary but it's turning into one…my dreams were…dull…I stopped remembering them years ago…who's going to want to read this? Dear world…goodbye…it's so simple for Ange…great…just great…more about someone else again…more and more and more… Where do I start? Dear whoever finds this diary…

SCENE 7

Pete and Ange in separate spotlights.

ANGE: you're repeating yourself, he said. certainly am, i said. need to. need to remind myself.

PETE: acid night in the crazy house
the sugar cubes were a different colour that night
the meds worked like magic
no one screamed
not once
in the insane asylum.

ANGE: people talk to themselves a lot these days, i said. for whatever reason, i see more and more of them. not all are crazy. shit. most of them just seem lonely.

PETE: insane asylum
no longer has any meaning
the insane have no asylum.

ANGE: lonely, eh? he asked. well, if they're talking to themselves, then they ain't talking to me. is that important? i asked. i hate being disturbed, he said, especially by disturbed people.

PETE: the inmates were let loose
left to their own devices
to find their own asylums
didn't leave much choice
we'd gather
speak our tongue
create a new homeland on the streets and alleys
within the cracks left wide open for us
hidden beneath the feet of the passersby
lost in the dark corners of their eyes

ANGE: like you? i said. like me, he said. i'm certifiably disturbed. been so for as long as i can remember. what do you remember? i asked. not much. it's the pills. these fucking blue ones. make me forgetful. constipated too.

PETE: no one wants to see us
ruins the day
punctures their reality balloon

pop
blast
a bloody shower
the death of illusions
never pretty

ANGE: they're supposed to make you constipated? no, he said. i'm not really sure what they're for. but they make me sweat. and give me the shakes. if i take those blue bastards i sweat and shake like a sonofabitch.

PETE: especially on lsd
i hoped it was only lsd
acid and meds
the ride is gonna be good
a rollercoaster with no seatbelts
the earth breathing like a million tibetan monks chanting
the eternal ohhhhhmmmmmmm
what are those monks seeking?
what kind of asylum do they need?

ANGE: and you can't take a shit. nope, he said. they cram me up good. need them yellow and red ones 'cause of those blue ones. they help me shit. well, do you have any idea what the blue pills are for? he thought about this for a second. can't recall, he said.

PETE: and we sit alone
we know the invisible predators stalk us in the daylight
will kill us in the night
but we are protected in towers of pills

ANGE: you just take them? i'm supposed to, he said. they give them to me and i take them. ever ask them what they're for? well, he said, i'm sure they know what's best for me. that's why i'm here. they put me here. in this home. it's a cardboard box, i said. but it's mine, he replied.

PETE: the insane asylum

ANGE: he showed the pills from his pocket. see, he said. they're here when i need them. he swallowed them before i could tell him they were tiny stones and pieces of broken glass. see you later, i said. see you later. he smiled. blood on his mouth.

PETE: i can see the stones and glass in the old man's stomach
the pills
the glass will help him shit
blood
it cuts up his guts
lacerating the muscles pushing them through his intestines to his asshole
and he'll die screaming locked in a spastic fetal vise grip shitting bloody clots of colon
stabbed to death from within.
but no one will know the agony of his final hours.

ANGE: the old man will need a note. he needs to say goodbye.

Pete joins Ange at the kitchen table.

PETE: So?

ANGE: Yeah?

PETE: What you think of that one?

ANGE: Okay. I guess. Kind of long. Got a smoke?

PETE: I don't smoke. What part was long?

ANGE: All of it. Yeah. I need a smoke.

PETE: No one here smokes, Ange. The whole poem was too long. All of it.

ANGE: No smokes?

PETE: Oh, Jesus. Can you stay focused for a second?

ANGE: Well...it was really boring. I zoned out, you know. Your shirt's nice, though. I like red. Is there any coffee?

PETE: In the cupboard.

Pause.

You want me to get it for you?

ANGE: Two creams, please.

PETE: Do it yourself.

ANGE: Okay.

Pause. She sits there, staring at him.

ANGE: I'd really like a smoke.

PETE: It's about that old man you told me about.

ANGE: I know.

PETE: Only I'm changing the perspective. Coming at it from a different angle. Like that of a young street prophet on LSD.

ANGE: Got that.

PETE: Okay. But I wanted to show how I would relate to him. How we're really the same.

ANGE: You're not the same. He's crazy. You're not.

Pete storms out. Pause.

People need to relax. *(louder)* Smoking helps me relax.

Cat enters.

CAT: Hi, Ange.

ANGE: I think Pete is mad at me. He read me his new poem. I told him it was boring. Are you making coffee?

CAT: You said what? Boring?

ANGE: Two sugars, please.

Cat puts on the kettle.

CAT: I can tell you, he's never been told that about his work.

ANGE: He wouldn't make me coffee.

CAT: He's not used to harsh criticism.

ANGE: He said it was about a friend of mine. He didn't leave a note. What were those fucking doctors thinking? Why would they do that to him?

CAT: What friend?

ANGE: Notes are good. Doctors give us notes all the time. Notes for pills. Notes for shots. Maybe Bobbie saw a doctor. He could've given her a note. Did Bobbie see a doctor?

CAT: Ange… It's just a book.

ANGE: But you saw it first! That's why you wrote it, right? You saw it and wrote it and knew her, so you should know. Did she see a doctor? She needs a note.

CAT: It's not like that…

ANGE: Stop! Stop it and just tell me!

CAT: There's nothing to—

ANGE: You said you'd help me.

CAT: I am— Pete!

ANGE: No you're not! Are you too tired to help me? To help Bobbie?

CAT: Bobbie's not real!

ANGE: Over and over she kills herself. Page 112. She doesn't say goodbye! She had to say goodbye. Just that. That's all I need. That's all I need. I need her to say goodbye! Just tell me where she put the fucking note and I won't bother you again!

CAT: Ange, please—

Pete enters.

PETE: What's going on?

CAT: Ange. I'm sorry. I'm sorry.

ANGE: Just write her a note. Put it in the book. Someplace where I can find it!

CAT: I can't!

PETE: Ange. She can't do that!

ANGE: Why not? She just has to go to page 112 and put in a note. Tell me why she dies. Please please please tell me why she did it! Tell me why she did it! I need to know why!

PETE: Because she was alone.

ANGE: But she wasn't alone. She had me. She had a family. She had everything and then she was gone. And I don't know why! I need to know why! Why is she gone? Why is she gone? Why is she gone!

The kettle whistles. Pause.

ANGE: Got coffee?

CAT: Sure.

ANGE: Black.

SCENE 8

Pete on stage. Cat in a park on her cell phone. Ange watching television in Cat's apartment.

CAT: Okay, okay, okay, don't give me the "I told you so" speech. I butt in. I know. But even you couldn't have predicted this kind of mess. What was I supposed to do? Just leave her there? Out on the street! I was taught to be generous. But I wasn't taught what to do when...when... Pete?

PETE: Two and two is four is the best answer I can give
It's solid
It's real
It's without question, correct and right
So it must be morally true
Numbers are soldiers
Well trained and reliable
You always know what they'll do

ANGE: I like war movies, eh...see, they're limping around in mud...just going forward because that's the way they were pointed and who cares what's in front...don't think about it...just keep limping...just keep moving.

CAT: I'm just tired. That's all. I thought I could handle this. I don't know what to do now. I'm way out of my league here. But, goddammit, give me some credit. I didn't just write her off as some crazy woman. I saw something more. Something special. And she came into my life because I could see what she truly was.

PETE: One plus one plus one is three
It's the only answer that I know
I'm happy with these facts
Because facts are truth and truth is good

But what is this
Someone's messed with my equation
One A plus One B plus One C equals...
What?

CAT: This is something you understand more than I do. You know the streets. We can't just open the door and chuck her out. It was only one freak-out.

ANGE: Oh, I like this show better...it's about a boat that flips in the ocean...that's why I don't go on boats...don't want to flip in the ocean and scream and run around like that...people dying...mostly of embarrassment...should've known that the ocean would do that...does it every time I see this show.

CAT: Maybe I need to take a break. Get away for a while. And everything will be all right when I get back. Right? Pete? Everything will be all right?

PETE: Before I can figure what this all means, here comes a Seven D, Nine E, Fourteen F, Three-hundred-and-sixty-six X and Eighty-eight-to-the-power-of-eleven-squared Zed!

How am I supposed to figure anything out if you keep fucking with my answers!

ANGE: What I like about these boat-flipping shows is that someone always freaks out...screaming and screaming...they mostly annoy the others, but they're always stuck with her...and when she dies, because she always dies, they all look sad...only deep down, you gotta know they're relieved they never have to hear that sound again.

SCENE 9

Pete enters. He sees Ange. She stares at him. He sits in front of her. Pause.

PETE: She's gone.

ANGE: She didn't say goodbye.

PETE: She'll come back. I just don't know when.

Ange starts rocking.

ANGE: Who's going to make me coffee and get me paper?

Pause.

PETE: Ange. Do you have a place to stay?

ANGE: One sugar.

PETE: We can't stay here, Ange.

ANGE: Is she going to see Bobbie?

PETE: I can take you somewhere.

ANGE: If you like.

PETE: Where?

ANGE: The basement.

PETE: Sorry?

ANGE: They found her in the basement. They said she'd probably been there for hours. Nothing could be done, they said. She and you have the same colour eyes. She never said goodbye. I think she was angry at me. Why are you so angry, Peter?

PETE: Who was angry at you, Ange?

She reaches into her pocket and pulls out a small bottle of pills.

ANGE: They're always here when I need them. But they take my dreams away. My memories of her.

PETE: Let me see those.

He reads the bottle.

ANGE: I need to go home.

She hands him a note.

Goodbye, Pete.

SCENE 10

Lights up on Cat, onstage reading.

CAT: "The darkness is a mother's warm embrace
She comforts
Hides me from the snarling icy jaws of sadness

The metal shrill crippling anger
She knows I'm tired of fighting the bright glaring lie of joy
I paint on my smile
They can smell weakness and they will tear you apart
Taunts from the wild dogs feed on you
I lean deeper into the darkness and she covers my ears with her soft hands.
Shhhhhhhhhhhh, she whispers
Shhhhhhhhhhhhh, they won't get you here.
You are safe with me.
She doesn't try to stop my tears
And hums me to sleep with a lullaby of emptiness.
Goodbye."

Applause.

Thanks, thanks. Wow. I haven't done this in a while. I'm still a little rusty, but I feel so good to be back. I know some of you have some questions. The one everyone has asked so far and I'll tell you right now is, yes, Ange is a real person. I didn't make her up. And she has inspired me. I'm writing again.

We now see Pete standing in the park with the guitar case. He slams on the guitar in an unholy union of rage against the machine mated to a fancy dance song.

PETE: Creeeeeatoooooor
Gave me this land
Creeaaatoooor
Took it away
Creeeeeatoooooor
Gave me this land
Creeaaatoooor
Took it away
I'm supposed to pray
I'm supposed to say
I'm very thankful
To see this day
But with every sunrise
I see more skins die
Paved under grey skies
Their souls are sucked dry

Hey-ya-hay-ya-ha
Hey-ya-hay-ha-ha
Hey-ya-hay-ya-ha
Hey-ya-hay-ha-ha

Pete stops. Weak scattered applause.

Thanks, you're too kind.

Ange enters.

Ange!

ANGE: Peter? Your name is Peter.

PETE: Yes, it is.

ANGE: I think I remember you.

PETE: You stayed with me and Cat for a little while.

ANGE: You have a cat? What kind of cat?

PETE: No, no, Cat's my girlfriend. Was my girlfriend. She brought you home and you just stayed. For a couple days. I took you back to your sister's. Remember?

ANGE: My sister takes care of me.

Pause.

PETE: Are you all right, Ange? Can I get you a coffee?

ANGE: No. I can't stand the stuff.

PETE: Neither can I. I'm through with stimulants. I'm trying to see life through unfiltered eyes. Life on drugs is—

ANGE: There's too much missing! I'm supposed to remember... something. Do you know what it is? I didn't tell you, did I? Your name is Peter. Peter. I like your shirt.

PETE: Thanks. Ange...

ANGE: Yes?

PETE: Do you know your way home?

ANGE: I know the way to my sister's. She takes care of me. Something's missing.

PETE: Let me walk you home, okay?

ANGE: Did you see the sunrise this morning?

PETE: I did. It was beautiful.

ANGE: It's been so long I hardly know her face when she visits me in my dreams.
I only know her by the anger shooting out her eyes like glass dust blown in the wind.
But even in my bloodied pain I still long to embrace her.
To hold her one last time.
To smell her hair.
Feel her neck against my breast.
Leaning in.
But she runs from me and won't look back.
Baby, what did I…?
It's been so long…I'm forgetting her.
And there will be nothing.

(to Pete) That's all…something's missing. Will you help me, Peter? Help me find it?

PETE: Sure. Come on. Let's go home.

He holds out his hand. She takes it and they exit. Back to Cat.

CAT: And I have a little announcement to make. Well…a big announcement really. My new novel will be coming out next month. Thank you, thanks. I know, sixteen years. But I had to make sure that it was really good. I'd like to read something from it. It's called *The Diary of Bobbie Snow.*

(she reads) "Dear whoever finds this note. Where do I start? From the beginning? From the time they told me I was adopted. That my "real parents" abandoned me? I sometimes think I see them in my dreams. All I know is I'm seventeen years old. My life sucks. Maybe you know me. My name is Bobbie Snow.

Pause. Blackout. The end.

CANADA HOUSE

J. KAROL KORCZYNSKI

Photo: Dave Stevens

J. KAROL KORCZYNSKI

ABOUT THE PLAYWRIGHT

For many years Karol Korczynski drifted as an itinerant general labourer from Inuvik to Istanbul as well as plenty of places in between. He has been a guest in some of the finest flophouses, hiring halls and county jails of our time. Over the years he has participated in a number of bitter workers' struggles, including as a union steward in London, England and the Yorkshire coalfields, as a farm worker in Alentejo, Portugal and as a political organizer and journalist in Canada and the United States. *Canada House* is his first completed play. It was written over the winter of 2002 in a well-known, recently closed Toronto beverage room. He has followed up *Canada House* with a thematic sequel, *Canada Steel,* which will be staged in February 2008 at the Tarragon Theatre in Toronto. Karol has also written *Hoozgow,* a one-act play concerning an eventful weekend in a West Virginia jailhouse. He is now completing a novella, *Tales From The Business Cycle,* based on a rather unfortunate residency on Vancouver's notorious Skid Row some years ago. Ironically, Korczynski now works for a bank.

PRODUCTION HISTORY

Canada House premiered at the Theatre Passe Muraille Backspace in Toronto on November 12, 2004 and closed in early December after a successful three-week run. The production was critically acclaimed in local, national and international newspapers and webzines. *Canada House* was produced by the Canada House Artistic Cooperative. It was directed by Graham Cozzubbo and starred two-time Gemini nominee Daniel Kash as Louis, Shaw Festival stalwart Wendy Thatcher as Sally, and Brian Marler as Ray. Rob Thomson designed the lighting, Nicholas Longstaff composed the soundscape and Lee Wildgen designed the set.

For production rights, contact Signature Editions, or the author at bixdjango@yahoo.ca.

CHARACTERS

Sally — Female; fifties; a down-at-the-heels phone sex worker; a barfly.

Ray — Male; mid-twenties, sharply dressed; a “boiler room” telemarketer.

Louis — Male; forties; a shoplifter; a displaced Québécois, also a barfly.

ACT ONE

SCENE 1

A young man listening on a cell phone reclines on a La-Z-Boy chair. There is a large, rusting sign resting against one wall. It reads "DOMINION." The man is wearing a bathrobe and breathing heavily, gasping, moaning throughout; one hand roams underneath his robe; he has a plastic bag over his head; he reaches for a syringe and violently jams it into his leg. Over his gasps, we hear an emotional female voice…

SALLY: …all the kids moved out of the sandbox when they saw her comin'. This tiny, little—I don't know—old-man girl standin' there with her bucket and spade lookin' like the breeze was gonna snap her clean in two…

Lights slowly come up on other side of stage, revealing the source of the voice; a telephonist.

…Had a big head like a light bulb. You probably seen a kid like that on the TV. Six years old goin' on a hundred. One kid kept yellin', "It's ET. Look out. It's ET," but the girl didn't take no notice. Too busy bakin' cakes outta sand. Stickin' crab apples in them like they was cherries or somethin'. Then she looks over. Wants to know if I wanna buy a cake. She's tryin' to lift the bucket to serve me up a slice but the damn thing's too heavy for her. Just then one of them monarch butterflies comes floatin' in between us. The kid looks up at me all smiley with this big, toothless grin… Do you like butterflies, she says? Pretty soon I'm gonna be a butterfly.

RAY: *(ripping off plastic bag, frustrated, gasping for air)* Jesus. Fuck. Nothin!… *(still gasping)* That's sad?… *(still catching breath)* That's fucking sad to you?

SALLY: Damn right it's fucking sad.

RAY: Butterflies? Are you kidding me? What the fuck is that?

SALLY: Just about the saddest thing I ever saw. That's what you want, right?

RAY: *(getting up to pace the room)* Saddest thing *you* ever saw? Hey, it's my fucking dime, bitch. Remember?

SALLY: Hey! Take a Valium, fer Christ's sake. I'm doin' my best. Okay?

RAY: Jesus. Twenty bucks a minute for this shit? Butter fucking flies? I'm tellin' ya. That ain't sad! It's... I don't know what the fuck it is.

SALLY: It's a little kid, man. That's dyin'.

RAY: Yeah. Well, save it for the funeral.

SALLY: Jesus, will ya cut me some fuckin' slack? We only been at it a few weeks, fer Christ's sake. Maybe...maybe if I knew ya better.

RAY: C'mon, Brandy. Get with the program. It's phone fucking sex.

SALLY: *(sad, bitter)* Yeah, don't *I* know it.

RAY: *(gets a shiver)* Jesus. Now the crank's kickin' in. Girl, you are messin' me up.

SALLY: Yeah? Then maybe ya oughta try the ManLine.

RAY: Okay. Okay. Chill. It's just I'm cranked. All right? It's just...you and me. Somethin's cookin'. I know it.

SALLY: You're a hard man ta figure, Frederick. That's for fucking sure.

RAY: Listen. You workin' Tuesday?

SALLY: Yeah. I'm workin'.

RAY: You know, I think the needle's helpin'. Gettin' them juices flowin'.

SALLY: Well. We're gonna need all the help we can get on that one, huh?

RAY: Okay. So, Tuesday right? Just don't give me any more of them dyin' kid sob stories. Okay, Brandy? And no cancer mom or lost dog ones either. You're better than that.

SALLY: *(sadly)* Yeah. That's what I keep tellin' myself.

We hear a fearsome woman's voice yell down to Ray... "Ray. Get up here."

RAY: *(to himself)* Ah, Jesus... *(then, getting up, walks towards DOMINION sign)* Listen. Gotta go. Big week ahead of me. Business. Up, down and fucking sideways.

SALLY: Yeah. Well, let's you and me work on the "up."

We hear the same woman's voice again; sharply... "Ray!"...

RAY: Listen. Tuesday. We'll talk... *(hangs up, calls pleasantly to wife)* Be up in a minute, Georgia... *(audibly shivers, running hands through hair)* Jesus. All jagged up, nowhere to go... *(begins to polish DOMINION sign; light out on Ray)*

SALLY: *(hangs up, shaking head)* Fuuuck, man... *(checking pockets)* Jesus. Where's my fuckin' Percodans...? *(phone starts to ring, she finds pills, swallows them with a slug from a bottle, looks at phone, then answers)* Carol's Kinky Cunts. Brandy speakin'... *(takes a drink while she listens, then)* All right, Wormboy. On yer fuckin' knees...

SCENE 2

The next night. The stage is dark. There are sounds of conversations, glasses tinkling. Music. A big-screen TV comes on. It is broadcasting war news, scenes of bombing, social unrest. A karaoke song ("Georgia On My Mind") is being sung. The stage is slowly illuminated to reveal a dingy Canadian beverage room. On the wall, we see a large official portrait of Prime Minister Paul Martin that acts as a dart board. A poster reads "Buy War Bonds." A neon sign exhorts "New! Try a Molson's Labatt's." We see a well-dressed young man (Ray) singing karaoke. Sally, an extremely drunken woman, heckles. As the karaoke continues, Louis, a French Canadian, enters from the washroom, talking loudly over the song.

LOUIS: How da hell do I know it was one of dem two-way mirror?... *(Louis laughs heartily) Cinquante*, Andy! ...And don't forget da tomata juice! I'm gonna need da vitamin!"

RAY: *(dressed in smart black leather jacket, nice slacks)*

Georgia, Oh Georgia.
No peace, no peace I find.
Just this old sweet song
Keeps Georgia on my mind
I said just an old sweet song
Keeps Georgia on my mind.

To sporadic applause, some heckling from drunken woman, an announcer's voice: "Big round of applause for Ray Bidwell, ladies and gentlemen. Ray Bidwell. Ray's practicin' for his fifth anniversary shindig, folks. Gonna surprise the little lady. And don't forget. It's Poutine Night at the Canada House. For a plateload of lip-smackin' frits just place your order with my man Andy, as always, over at the bar. This is Karaoke Ken and I'm takin' a pause for the cause, a brew for the crew." As Ray moves towards Louis' table, Sally continues heckling.

SALLY: *(barely conscious)* ...piece of shit...

LOUIS: *(wearing a tatty nylon Toronto Maple Leafs jacket) Tabernac*! Dat was what you call *magnifique*, Ray. *Très* fuckin' *magnifique*.

RAY: *(sitting down, glaring)* Yeah? You were talkin' through the whole goddamn—

SALLY: *(opening a pill bottle; calling to waiter)* —Channel Eleven.

LOUIS: Oh, no. I was listenin', Ray. Me. I was listenin' real goddamn good.

SALLY: *(taking a last pill)* ...S'hockey... Fuckin' war... S'all bullshit...

A hockey game replaces scenes of war on the TV.

RAY: War's over, grandma.

SALLY: *(to Ray)*...Ya gotta match?

RAY: Yeah. Your face and my ass.

SALLY: ...Too good fer me, eh?

RAY: Yeah, me and the rest of the fuckin' planet.

SALLY: ...Gimme a light...

RAY: Jesus, Louis. Who the fuck is this?

LOUIS: Now, boss. You listen. Dat Sally. You don't want to know her.

SALLY: *(touching Ray's shoulder)* I didn't take nothin'.

RAY: *(agitated, raising hand)* Get outta fuckin' here. Goddamn meatslap.

SALLY: *(retreating)* Big Shot—

LOUIS: Hey, Sally… Sally!

SALLY: …Huh…

LOUIS: Ain't dat yer friend over dere?

SALLY: …Huh…

LOUIS: Yeah. See. Da Big Pollack.

SALLY: *(gazing off, shouts)* Gene… *(gets up)* Ya commie bastard… *(stumbles away)*

LOUIS: Dat one crazy broad… *(then to waiter, who is always offstage)* Andy! *Cinquante*!

SALLY: *(moving offstage to Gene, who is, like Andy, always offstage)* Ya gotta light?…

LOUIS: Fucking women, eh, boss? Dey always trouble.

RAY: Don't I know it. Always wantin' somethin'. Squeezin'…and fuckin' with ya.

LOUIS: Dat's dem, Ray, for sure.

RAY: *(mimicking wife)* Ray, we need a new fridge. Ray, we need a new house. Ray, junior's got a cough. Ray, come to fuckin' bed.

LOUIS: Dey never be 'appy. Dat fer sure.

RAY: Yeah. Twelve hours a day telemarketin' ain't good enough for her. Cold callin' on straight commish. Everglades timeshares. Mexican miracle cures. Elvis DNA. It ain't no fuckin' cakewalk, dude.

LOUIS: Thank god we do da work on da side dere, eh, boss?

RAY: Free enterprise, Louis. A man's gotta make his own way.

LOUIS: *Certainement.* And he get da pay for doin' it, eh?

RAY: *(smiling, pulling envelope from pocket, waving it)* Greedy bastard. You never miss a payday, do ya?

LOUIS: Louis. Dis guy. He don't miss much.

RAY: *(tosses envelope to Louis)* Come the big prize night, that's gonna look like chicken feed.

LOUIS: You really tink you gonna win da big prize, boss?

RAY: *(confidently leaning back, putting hands behind head)* C'mon. Is it gonna rain frogs on Judgement Day? *(dreamily)* The Social Market Foundation, Louis. The Time and Motion Man of the Year Award? When I win that big boy, I write my own goddamn ticket. A whole new snack bracket. The sky's the fuckin' limit!

LOUIS: You be walking down da easy street, dat for sure.

RAY: Big dog's gotta eat! Ain't been a winner yet hasn't ended up with a fat contract from the Foundation. I'm talkin' wallet share, Louis. Big time!

LOUIS: I tink you gonna buy da big boat. Da new car. Maybe a present for dis guy too, eh?

RAY: *(annoyed)* No. No. Ya see, that's loser thinkin', Louis. Ya save yer wad. Ya don't go blowin' it. Fuckin' dipstick. Me? I'll be looking to one kick-ass investment. That's fer sure.

LOUIS: What dat, boss?

RAY: No, dude. That's fuckin' personal... Somethin' I promised the old man...before he... *(snaps out of daydream)* Ah. Anyway, ain't won the fucker yet.

LOUIS: I tink you be lucky dis year.

RAY: Luck ain't got nothin' to do with it. Read the Foundation manifest. "To wipe out any and all barriers to the free accumulation of personal wealth." Hell, we even got guys workin' on turnin' the law of the jungle into nothin' but a fuckin' guideline. Like it says on the trophy. Cheaper, Faster, Lesser. Hell, Louis, I'm a goddamn shoo-in!

LOUIS: Well, dat's the way I seen it too. Back to dem dere basic...da old-fashioned way.

RAY: And that's why I'll win, man. Tradition! 'Cause I'm producin' a good honest product. Something folks can use. At a good honest price. Washtub Methamphetamine, Louis. Twenty-five cents a unit. Five hundred per cent mark-up... *(then defensively)* Hey, it's the war... *(continues)* At a thousand units a day. *(waving hand smugly)* Well, you figure it out.

LOUIS: *(admiringly)* Figure it out? Hey, da number make my head swimming.

RAY: Hell, I'm talkin' some of the best numbers this side of fuckin' Cleveland! But that ain't the beauty of it, dude. It's the way I got the time and motion cracked. Why, when them judges get a load of that broad from Pango Pango all chained up tight and cookin' meth 24/7… Well, shine up the trophy, baby! 'Cause I'm takin' it home.

LOUIS: So dem judges. When dey coming over to da shed?

RAY: The twelfth… *(chuckling)* Figured it was a nice touch workin' them boys on a Sunday… *(self-satisfied, drinks, looks at watch)* Jesus, will ya look at the fuckin' time.

LOUIS: Hey, it early.

RAY: *(drinking up)* Nah. Gotta go, man. My two little guys will be gettin' outta skatin'.

LOUIS: Ah. Dem boy. Dey gonna play fer da Leaf one day, for sure, eh?

RAY: Leafs?

LOUIS: Hey, maybe *Les Canadiens,* eh?

RAY: Hockey? It's figure skatin', Louis. She's got 'em in fuckin' figure skatin'. The way they pedal their little asses around that rink. They look like a coupla fuckin' Ottawa pussies… *(gets up to leave)*

LOUIS: Hang on dere a minute. I'll walk ya as far as da *pissoir* dere… *(walking offstage)* So, ah, Ray. Ya win dis here trophy, what d'ya tink of gettin' dis guy Louis Lemaire inta dat big shot Foundation, eh?

RAY: *(putting arm around Louis' shoulder)* Well. It's like I been tellin' ya. A dude's gotta be able to see the big picture, Louis. First off. Ya gotta love yerself. Totally. Abso-fucking-lutely. You a family man, Louis?

LOUIS: Me? *Non… (proudly)* Louis got no one.

RAY: That's gonna help. Lookin' after Number One. That's the tough part. You do that. Maybe we got a spot for ya.

LOUIS: Hey, for da Foundation, I would do anyting.

RAY: Well, maybe I'll just take you up on that. Ya know, Old Pango Pango can take a kick better than most. Ya can't deny it. Still, broad ain't made of iron either.

LOUIS: What you need, boss?

RAY: Well, I don't wanna jinx the project, but maybe you should keep your eye out for another cook. You know. A backup.

LOUIS: Like dem goalie. Johnny Bower and dat Terry Sawchuk. Or da Gumper wit...uh...dat...dat other guy.

RAY: Business continuity, Louis. It's the latest fuckin' thing... *(walking)* Now tell me, you been sellin' them names like I told ya to?

SCENE 3

The next day.

SALLY: *(speaking to Andy, the bartender)* The perfect crime, Andy. Murder. That's what I was goin' for. Live, onstage in a strip joint bar. With everybody watchin'. Tall fuckin' order. I can tell you. 'Specially with a shaved pussy hangin' out. But that's what kept me dancin'. The fuckin' challenge. To see if I could waste one of them droolin' stageside jack-offs and get away with it. Trick was to pick a fat one. Give him a good show. Plenty of pink. Full body alphabet. V's and A's. Legsplit Y's. Hell, I'd even give 'em some of them Chinese letters. Get him thinkin' about that piece of liver waitin' back home in the fridge. When the fat fuck was breathin' real hard, I'd ask him up for a dance. Fool him, though. No dry bonin' slow stuff like he was expectin'. I'd play Meatloaf or the Stones. Get that slob movin' real good. Sweatin' under the lights. Fuckin' heart attack just awaitin' ta happen...

Louis enters, sits down at a nearby table.

...Never got one, though. House rules. No customers on stage. Bouncers would break it up every fuckin' time. Go figure. Turns out the personal touch is bad for the face sittin' business. People can be so much fucking shit.

LOUIS: *(wearing a booster coat—large shoplifter's coat with many pockets)* Andy. *Cinquante!*

SALLY: Case in fuckin' point... Hey, Walnut Dick! Hey, Andy! The hell with the *cinquante.* You should be servin' up smallboys for ol' Louis Bob Lemaire. Yeah, with a short to chase it.

LOUIS: Eh, Andy. She jerk off tinking of dis guy plenty of time. Don't you worry about dat ting.

SALLY: Hey, Andy. I need ya to tell me why a man with a dick the size and shape of a Loblaws walnut— and I ain't talkin' about the whole nut, mind you, just the wrinkly bit inside—why a man with a dick like that is gonna wanna let her hang on the busiest night of the goddamn month.

LOUIS: Ah! You don't know one fucking nothing.

SALLY: Wanderin' from table to table. Just layin' the thing out for everybody's gander. The whole thing goes against everything I ever knowed to be true about a man, queer, straight or indifferent.

LOUIS: Sandpaper Sally Carew...fuck-ing idi-otte.

SALLY: Well, that's just what I been tryin' to tell ya, Louis. I *gotta* be a moron. I mean, a man with a dick as sorry lookin' as yours is naturally gonna wanna keep quiet about it. But there you are, runnin' it up the flagpole just to see who salutes.

LOUIS: *Plotte*! You talk bullshit.

SALLY: Yeah? Remember goin' off with that patchy-haired broad—what's her name? The one that knows all the capitals of South America... Yeah. Jackie Squat.

LOUIS: *(taking out bottle of olives from his coat pocket)* Dat junkie?

SALLY: Kept askin' her about backups...or up the back, if I fuckin' know you.

LOUIS: Yeah? Your big nose. It everywhere, huh?

SALLY: *(laughing)* Man, I hope ya used Saran Wrap!

LOUIS: Dere ain't no way. Andy, dat broad. She got a hole in her goddamn leg...*(grimaces)* All poison... No. No. No. Dat. I would have remember.

SALLY: Pleadin' blackout, are ya?... *(mimicking Louis)* "*Tabernac*, Sally. One minute I'm drinking at da Canada House and da next, well it's mornin' and I'm drivin' a T Bird in Rosedale with a goddamn fish sticking outta my sock and a wad of jism dripping off of the dash..." *(loses accent)* Nah. You ain't gettin' off that easy.

LOUIS: I tink you are out of dem Percodans. Dat your problem... Fucking *guidoune... (cell phone rings; to the tune of MacDonald's "You deserve a break today...")*

SALLY: Don't you call me no—

LOUIS: *(short tempered)* Hey, I got business...Lemaire...Hey! Black Jack Shellac. How is my favorite undertaker? ...*Pas de problème...* Just a minute... *(as he shuffles around in coat pocket, bringing out a hammer first, eventually bringing out a little notebook, we hear Sally grousing)*

SALLY: *(mimicking Louis)* Business... Yeah, right...*Pas de problème...*

LOUIS: *(still searching, to Sally)* Fuck off!

SALLY: Ahh!... *(turns attention elsewhere)* Hey, Gene. You write that in the pisser? ...Better to die on yer feet than to live on yer knees—

LOUIS: —Blackie? Okay. I got dem name. *Bon.* Dere is Irma Rosentag in da St. Mike Hospital...*Non.* Car crash... *(flipping through notepad)* Dere is Maria Costello... Greg Jackson at da City General. Both with da cancer. Dat right. All in da phone book... Yeah... Yeah—

SALLY: —Plenty of ways to live on yer knees. There's carpet layin'. Religious work. Blow jobs...

LOUIS: *(continuing phone conversation) Pas de problème.* Ray, da boss man. He guarantee dem guy. Yeah. Yeah. Yeah. Dey gonna need to buy a funeral... *(laughs)* Hey. Dat snack bracket. It gonna get bump, for sure, eh? ...*Bon.* Later, gator... *(all smiles, puts phone away, proudly)* Hey. What can I say? Dat my broker... *Cinquante*, Andy! And back it wit dat Jack Daniel. A *big* one!... *(laughing)* For da *big* dog. He got to eat something too, eh?

SALLY: *(pauses, staring at Louis, shaking head, disgusted)* Jesus H. Christ, you still sellin' sick folks' names to them funeral parlours?

LOUIS: *(aggressively)* Yeah. Dat right. Two word. Tele-fucking-marketing.

SALLY: Louis. You are one scum-suckin' pig.

LOUIS: Supply and demand, *ma petite fleur*! Free enterprise! What da matter? Ain't ya read da program?

SALLY: I got a room right over this here bar, pal. Just like you. I *live* the fuckin' program.

LOUIS: Den maybe you don't hear?... *(with emphasis)* Dat what da booze is for!

SALLY: *(takes drink, long pause)* Hey, Android. Ya know that poem we been talkin' about fer behind the bar? Yeah. I'm thinkin' of makin' a couple of changes. How's this grab ya? "This beverage room is dedicated to those merry souls who make drinkin' a pleasure. Who obtain contentment long before capacity. And who, whatever they may drink, prove able to carry it, enjoy it..." *(turns to Louis)* "...and keep their fuckin' dick in their pants."

SCENE 4

The next day.

LOUIS: *(wearing his "booster coat"; unloading comically large amounts of loot from inside pockets throughout his monologue —CDs, cuts of meat, shirts still in their packages, etc; talking to Andy)* So, dem two Labrador, dey jump over da side and dey start swimming around dat canoe. Da day, it hot, and dem dog, dey just cooling demself like dey always do, when dese two Yankee, dey pull up dere alongside. In deir boat dey got dis here wet bar and one of dem Bob Izumi Sonar Fish Finder dat ya see on da TV show. But dem poor bastard ain't caught a goddamn fish in the whole fucking morning. "Any luck?", dey say and *mon ami* old Blackie Shellac, he hold up dis string of fish dat would choke one of dem bear. "Jesus. What you boys usin'?" say one of dem Yank. Well, Blackie, he just wink at me and he look at dem two dog paddling around dat lake. "Pickerel Retriever," he say... *(big laugh)* Pickerel Retriever! *Crisse*, dem Yank, dey don't know whedder to shit or buy a dog... *(Sally enters, takes off coat, sits down at her own table, Louis still laughing)* Pickerel Retriever... *(then, to Sally)* Hey. Dis guy. Got good T-bone...

SALLY: *(pointing to her ass)* Yeah, T-bone fuckin' this... Two more days till karaoke, Andy. Jesus, I can hardly fucking wait.

LOUIS: *(holding up steaks)* Maybe you and me, eh? I cook dem for you.

SALLY: *(ignoring Louis, looks around, calls out)* Hey, Bernie! Workin' hard or hardly workin'? *(laughs; aside)* Fuckin' Bernie... *(then)* Hey, Berner, how's the twins?

LOUIS: I got da Jack Daniel. Be just like de old day.

SALLY: The old days, eh?

LOUIS: At Dominion.

SALLY: I got news for ya, Louis. Fuck the old days.

LOUIS: In my room. I got smokes, too. You know me. Da Bargain Mart. One-stop shopping.

SALLY: Shoppin'? Boostin's more like it.

LOUIS: *(holding up bottle of pills)* I got you some painkiller.

SALLY: *(grabs bottle)* Jesus, Louis. Now yer cookin' with gas... *(takes two pills, then, suspiciously)* Whatddya want for it?

LOUIS: Hey. Don't worry. Dis guy. He been working... Don't know at what. But da job, it pay fifteen buck by de hour.

SALLY: Mystery job, eh? That's a new one. What about the... *(gets distracted)* Hey. Watch this... *(calls out)* Hey, buddy. Go home... *(laughs heartily)* Yeah, you heard me. Go home. Ya been in here long enough... *(still laughing, to Louis)* Always cracks him up...

LOUIS: Hey, dat Big Gene Vitkowski. You watch dat guy. I trust him as far as I can spit da ditch water.

SALLY: Homeless Gene? Getta outta here. Only guy don't treat me like a fuckin' whore.

LOUIS: *Socialiste*! Goddamn Equalizer. Dat what he is. Why, dose guy, dey want to equalize the whole fucking world.

SALLY: Ah, get off his back. He reads books.

LOUIS: Me too.

SALLY: Skin books.

LOUIS: Comrade Gene J. Vitkowski. The "J," it probably stand for genius, huh?

SALLY: Hey, watch this… Hey, Gene! What d'ya call a commie without a girlfriend? …Homeless… *(laughing)* No. You go home! …No. You go home! …No. You go home!… *(sits)* Aaah, ya laugh or ya fuckin' cry… *(refocuses)* So. Nimrod. Lemme get this straight. Ya been workin' a job but ya don't know what it is you're doin'. Some kinda government work?

LOUIS: Well, dat da long story.

SALLY: Yeah? Cost ya a Homo.

LOUIS: Maybe I tell you up in my room, huh?

SALLY: Look, Louis. It's early, okay? Just gimme my fuckin' drink.

LOUIS: Yeah, you always like da Homo, huh? Andy! Jack on top of a tallboy, eh?

SALLY: *(leaning back in chair)* That's better. Well, c'mon. The mystery job.

LOUIS: *Ecoutez.* A few week ago, I am waiting on da corner hoping somebody swing by. Maybe hire some tank wipe or a guy to strip some asbestos.

SALLY: So what? Skid Row Labour Exchange. Been there. Done that. Got the bruises. Course I always found the money better after sundown.

LOUIS: Well, Louis. He ain't so pretty like you.

SALLY: No shit.

LOUIS: So, dis one morning, a pickup, she pull up and dis big neck, how you say, ramrod, he jump out and yell, "Da job, it pay fifteen buck by de hour. Cash in da hand!" Fifteen buck by de hour! I tell you, he don't have to say it three time… About twenty minute later, we all jumping out in one of dem forest ravine and getting handed dese axes.

SALLY: You're lumberjackin'! In goddamn fuckin' Trawna... *(laughs)*

LOUIS: Only dere is dis one problem. Dem axes. Dey don't got no axe head... *(incredulously)* ...We standin' dere but all we got are da freaking axe handle! Da sharp part. We don't got. Da guy next to me, well, he say something smart and old Bull, he just belt him one right in da mouth. Fire his ass right dere on da spot. Dat ramrod, he say dere's more of da same for any man wit another question.

SALLY: *(rubbing jaw)* Sounds like that wrestler you used ta like. The Mad Dog Vachon.

LOUIS: Dat for sure. So, we let da Bull space us out. All ten of us. Standing in front of dem tree wit a goddamn axe handle and a stupid look, like dat guy Bush. Well, dat ramrod, he say he want eighteen stroke by da minute and dere's hell to pay for anyone dat don't keep up. And dat's what I been doing for da last eight week. Hitting a goddamn tree wit one of dem fucking axe handle... It a damn ting. I tell you. A damn fucking ting.

SALLY: So lemme get this straight. You been whackin' away for over eight weeks with nothin' but a cut fuckin' stick and pickin' up over a hunnerd dollars a day for yer trouble! Jesus. Sounds like cakeboy work if you wasn't so ugly... *(thinking hard)* Cut a log yet?

LOUIS: Only way a tree ever gonna fall if one die from getting pissed on three time every day. Wished one got cut, though. You know, whacking away without no hope. Well, it take a toll on dem men. Fifteen buck an hour or not, ain't seen no guy last more than three or four shift since da job start...Well, nobody excepting Louis Bob Lemaire. Dat for sure.

SALLY: What the fuck do they expect? Most people wanna feel like they're doin' somethin' for their money. Hell, even Sidewalk Stanley gives ya a fuckin' pencil for your chump change.

LOUIS: *(still proud)* Well, Louis. He ain't most people. Non! As far as dis guy see, long as ol' Bull keep up wit da payroll, who da fuck is dis guy to go looking for da suggestion box?

SALLY: So what's your fuckin' problem?

LOUIS: Well, Louis. He is off the fucking payroll. Dat what. Friday quitting time. Bull, he tell me don't show up no more. Say for me to sit tight right here in da Canada House. Say ta expect somebody about two o'clock today.

SALLY: Two o'clock? Almost that now.

LOUIS: Probably gonna get my walking paper. Dat da thank I get. Only man dat stay and he pull me off the fucking job. Just look at dese blister. I am telling you, Sally. Dat what wrong with dis here country. Getting so one guy, he can't do no honest day's work no more.

SALLY: Somethin's up, all right. But it ain't no firin'… *(chuckles)* Maybe it's one of them Candid Camera shows. Like "Stupid As A Monkey"…Yeah. They probably got you on a split screen hackin' away alongside some chimp, smearin' Deep Heatin' VapoRub on his balls or somethin'. But you outlast him. Louis Bob Lemaire! Stubborn as a mule. Stupid as a monkey. TV guys comin' here with the prize. That's what! Why, you're goin' to fuckin' Disneyland!… *(laughing, finishing drink)* Thanks for the drink, big boy… *(exiting)* …Hey, Gene! What the fuck's this war about, anyway?

LOUIS: *(calls after her)* Yeah. You a funny broad, huh? …So, Andy. You gonna buy some merchandise? Maybe dis here shirt. Da lady, dey gonna like dat on you, eh?

RAY: *(approaches Louis' table, sits down)* My man, Louis. Shop till ya drop, huh?

LOUIS: Da Big Guy. Hey, look at dis. You take something, eh?

RAY: *(examining merchandise)* Bargain Mart? Ya know, you really should be doin' the uptown stroll.

LOUIS: Hey, dat some good stuff dere.

RAY: Nothin' I'm lookin' for.

LOUIS: Hey. What you want? I get you anyting, man.

RAY: *(getting comfortable)* Yeah? How about axe heads, dude? Whaddya say? Ya think ya can locate me some nice, shiny axe heads?

LOUIS: *Tabernac.* What you say?

RAY: *(grinning, putting feet up on table)* If it ain't Paul Fuckin' Bunyan. Up close and personal.

LOUIS: *(incredulous, like a man surprised by Candid Camera) Non... Non... Crisse, d'epais! Non.* You are kidding, me. *Non.*

RAY: What is it? Eight weeks now? The Zen Buddhist of the Don Fucking Valley.

LOUIS: *Calisse! Trou d'cul!* Dat? Dat was your business? ...You are a bastard, my friend. A goddamn bastard.

RAY: Hey. Gimme a break, dude. We had to be sure. Foundation don't take any Tom, Dick and Froggie.

LOUIS: And dat guy, Bull. Da ball breaker... Hey. What? What you mean? Da Foundation.

RAY: That's how we separate the men from the boys. A dude's gotta lumberjack them trees for eight weeks runnin'. He slows down or starts askin' questions... Well, you met Bull.

LOUIS: Shit! I will be dat uncle's monkey. So. Dis was da test, eh? For Louis Bob Lemaire. Bastard.

RAY: Was the only way, Louis. Foundation ain't no social club. We got fish ta fry. And you're gonna be one of the cooks.

LOUIS: *(very excited)* No shit? Me? Dat guy? I am in da Foundation?

RAY: If ya want it.

LOUIS: Want it? *Tabernac!* For two whole year, it just my dream!

RAY: Now you'll be on probation, mind ya. We'll start ya out with an easy job. See how ya handle it.

LOUIS: Hey. You don't worry about nothing. Louis. He will make you da money... Ah, *Crisse...* Look at dis. You make me cry.

RAY: Andy. A coupla Jacks... And one for my partner here. We got business!

LOUIS: Hey, you don't wait around. What you got?...ah...partner.

RAY: Pango Pango. My cook. That's what I got. Fuckin' broad's dead.

LOUIS: What?

RAY: You heard me. The bitch is fuckin' dead. Three days until the judgin' and "Miss I Can't Stand the Pain" decides to OD on fuckin' meth.

LOUIS: Dead? *Crisse.* What you gonna do?

RAY: What the fuck am *I* gonna do? No. Wrong question, dude. What the fuck are *you* gonna do?

LOUIS: Me?

RAY: It's Game Seven, Louis. Johnny fuckin' Bower time.

LOUIS: Ah… Yeah…da backup… Yeah, sure…I…I know plenty people we could hire.

RAY: Hire? Jesus, Louis. Where's your fuckin' respect? This is the goddamn Foundation Award.

LOUIS: Well, I—

RAY: Duderator. Lookit. You're gonna need somebody without a family. Okay? Who nobody's gonna miss. Somebody that's used to livin' like shit. Okay? Who won't go to pieces considerin' the circumstance. Reason I keep doin' business down here. 'Cause of the skill sets.

LOUIS: Ah. I don't know, boss. Kidnapping. Slavery. Dat never was my line of work dere. Louis Bob Lemaire. He more like da back office guy.

RAY: Listen, you goddamn wannabe. You're in the Foundation, now. Not the fuckin' Boy Scouts. You wanna stay in, you line me up a cook. Understand?

LOUIS: But Ray, I—

RAY: You understand!

LOUIS: Okay, Ray… *Je comprends.*

RAY: Yeah. Okay. *Je comprende.* Now you're talkin' my lingo… So, listen. I'll swing by Friday to pick up the package… *(getting up)* Gimme a chance to try the new knockout drops. Maybe catch a little karaoke… *(turns to leave)* I'm countin' on ya, Louis. Don't mess this fuckin' up.

SCENE 5

Later that week. We hear phones ringing and women's voices answering. "Carol's Kinky Cunts," "Carol's Kinky Cunts"… Lights up on Sally, who is on phone in a cubicle.

SALLY: Charles and Camilla dinnerware? Jesus, honey. Do *you* have a wrong number… *(disconnects)* Jesus… *(phone rings again, lights up on Ray, preparing his arm for an injection, DOMINION sign still omnipresent)* Carol's Kinky—

RAY: It's me. Frederick.

SALLY: Frederick! How ya doin', man?

RAY: I'm talkin' to some bimbo on a 1-900 Line. How d'ya think I'm doin?

SALLY: Same old Frederick.

RAY: All right. I'm on the clock here. Gimme some sad. Kick-ass style.

SALLY: I've been doin' some thinkin'.

RAY: Lemme have it, baby.

SALLY: About my first haircut…

RAY: Hey, this ain't another little kid story?

SALLY: Well. I was just a kid. Six or seven years old. But this ain't about me, man.

RAY: *(injecting, puts bag on)* All right then… Turn it loose.

SALLY: Well, it was probably back around '62. I remember 'cause the ol' man was on strike down at the foundry. Hard times all around. So, they set up this canvas tent out in the scrubs where ya could go and get a hot meal, play a little horseshoes, get yer family a free haircut. I musta been pretty scruffy-lookin' 'cause my dad takes me down one day to get my ears lowered. Musta been about a hundred folks come before me though 'cause I had to wade ankle deep in hair just to get to the cuttin' chair. Well, the ol' man, he goes over and starts kiddin' around with the other dads. But there was this one fella wasn't joinin' in. Little, funny lookin' guy. He just kept starin' at that pile of hair.

And then he just started cryin'. Not bawlin' or nothin'. Least not yet. But tears were runnin'down his cheeks and soakin' his beard. Then he started to take off his clothes. First his shirt. He had a real scrawny chest and some kinda numbers tattooed on his arm. Then he just strips off naked and falls down on the ground. He was really bawlin' now and screamin' out people's names, all the while scooping up these great, big handfuls of hair and smearin' it over his body and into his face. I remember lookin' in his eyes and seein' somethin' I ain't ever seen before or since. It was like he was empty and full to explodin' all at the same time. Ya ever seen anybody like that, Frederick? You ever seen somethin' like that? Dirty fuckin' Krauts was all my ol' man would say when he took me outta the chair. Dirty fuckin' Krauts...

RAY: *(has taken his bag off halfway through the story and is laughing intermittently)* Fuckin' dirty Krauts, huh?... *(laughs)* You're kidding me, right?

SALLY: Jesus.

RAY: Girl. That is just wrong in so many ways.

SALLY: *(rolling eyes)* Here we go...

RAY: First off. What are ya doin' askin' me questions right in the middle of the damn thing? If I'm workin' up a lather—which I wasn't there—but if I am, a question's liable to break my stroke, now isn't it? Second. The story's too long. Gotta be quick and clean. Like a smart bomb on a...on a Cairo hospital.

SALLY: What? You timing me now?

RAY: Damn it, Brandy. I got a plastic bag over my head fer Christ's fuckin' sake. Now, correct me if I'm wrong. But you ain't gonna make a hell of a lot off a dead man, now are ya?

SALLY: So, now you're my pimp too, huh?

RAY: Bottom line's a bottom line. Take my word for it. I know about these things.

SALLY: *(confrontational)* What about the man in the tent, Frederick? What about him?

RAY: Yeah, I was comin' to that. You ever study history, babe?

SALLY: Enough to know what that fella was screamin' about.

RAY: Great man once said history is bunk, girl. But you mighta misheard it. Figured maybe he was sayin' history is spunk. Figured maybe that's the way to ol' Frederick's heart, huh? Well, in future, just leave the fuckin' Germans out of it. Okay? Got enough of a bum rap, already.

SALLY: *(can't bite her tongue anymore)* Ya ever watch nature shows, Frederick? Like the one they had on the other night? All about this African stink worm. Looks like them big, white grubs ya see from time to time. Got a stink on it you wouldn't believe. Skin chemical. Lets 'em live in them termite hills, slurpin' up bugs without ever gettin' bit. Problem is, once and a while, well, don't one of 'em just get too fucking fat. Chemical just turns itself off. Well, pretty soon them little termites are swarmin' all over the damn thing...eatin' stink worm... *(Ray is starting to feel an erotic reaction)* He can't swat 'em away. He's a goddamn worm for god fucking sakes. He's just gotta lie there and take what's comin'... Ain't nature wonderful?

RAY: *(tearing up, looking sad but excited)* Oooooaaaaah. Yeah. I'm feelin' it, babe. Oooah. I'm feelin' it!

SALLY: Jesus fucking Christ. What the hell am I doin' here?... *(hangs up in disgust, takes a pill)*

RAY: *(still carrying on)* Ooooooh, Brandy... *(tearful)* Big guy's helpless...he can't even swat 'em away...

We hear Georgia's voice yell down from upstairs: "Ray. Where's the fuckin' gin?"

SCENE 6

The next day.

SALLY: *(with a Walkman headset, high, in a joyful, excited, girlish groove, talking to someone —offstage— in the bar)* And the violins are goin' Dada dah dada dah. Dada dah. Dadadadada dadada. And it's soundin' just like a choir's singin'...and then the horns come in... Ba. Ba. Ba. Ba. Bah. Bah... And the strings keep goin' dada dadada dah daah. dada. da... Like they're all jacked and just singin' away...only they're not... It's just instruments, man... *(incredulously)* there's no fuckin' singin'...*(falls back in chair exhausted, joyful, grinning)* That's entertainment...Right, Gene...*(no answer)* Hey! ...Gene! ...Skid Bro! You were right, man. Wolfgang fuckin' Mozart, eh?

LOUIS: *(on cell phone, stressed)* No. No. Dat Jackie Squat no good. Too wasted... *Crisse...*You sure ya got nobody? ...I need da backup... Fuck. Fuck... You know, Blackie. In dis Foundation, da new guy, he get all da shit job, huh...*(shocked; unbelieving) Quoi?* ...*Non. Non.* We split from Ray? No. No. No. I am loyal... *Non... Non...* Shut up...*(hangs up)* Independent? *Tabernac!*

SALLY: *(overhearing)* What fuckin' now?

LOUIS: *(still to himself)* Dat Blackie. He ask too much.

SALLY: Boyfriend trouble, eh?

LOUIS: Dere ya go all da time. Busting my ball. *Crisse.* I got my own problem.

SALLY: Yeah. Like where ta spend yer first million, eh?

LOUIS: *Plotte!* You are jealous of me. *C'est ca.* It kill you dat I always been a businessman.

SALLY: Well, that ain't entirely true, now is it Louis? You maybe fergettin' Dominion?

LOUIS: *(flustered)* What you go bringing dat up for? ...It been ten year. A guy, he learn from dat mistake.

SALLY: Yeah? Well, maybe that was the only time you had it right.

LOUIS: *(indignant)* Right? Right? ...Dominion Fibreglass. You forget what we call dat place? Huh? Da Hell Hole!

SALLY: I was there, Louis. Remember?

LOUIS: Yeah, you was dere, all right. In shipping. I was in da fibre wool. Remember?

SALLY: Yeah, I remember.

LOUIS: *(getting more emotional)* Standing at dat heat press for eight hour, dat pink shit in your mouth like bad cotton candy...acid wiping dat wool chopper six fucking hundred time all day. And god help you if dat acid get in your eye...

No. No. No. I don't forget... Dat ramrod trying to figure a hundred and one way to let you know you are nothing but a piece of shit... And when dem fibre sliver get pack too tight inside your body... *Attention*, 'cause dem bastard. Dey coming out! Da Fibreglass poison. Fever. Everywhere swollen. Dat pus. Dripping out of my ball, my armpit, from da nose. When you start sweating out dat shit. *Crisse!* It like you got inside one thousand little razor blade. *Crisse.* Da drug pusher in dat plant. Don't worry. Dey do some business.

SALLY: Yeah. Well, that's what the fight was all about.

LOUIS: *(angrily) Non*! If dat was all, maybe I could stand it. *Crisse*, dat was da easy part. But den you have to go home. *Ah, oui.* Maybe you snort something in da car. But sooner or later you are sitting in da kitchen and the wife, she lifting da baby to see where she left da booze... Or maybe she just stare nowhere, waiting for you to save her and yelling 'cause you can't. And da boys. Da fucking boys. Bouncing dat hardball on da bedroom wall. All da goddamn night... *(punching fist into hand and maybe his kids, too)* Bam! Bam! Bam! ...Dere. Dat da hard part... When you finally realize dat between da job and da wife and da kid and the whole goddamn world...nobody own demself... Somebody else own you. You don't even know who. Well, fuck dat! I got out! To hell wit you!

SALLY: Yeah. You got out all right. With the fuckin' strike fund. That was our money. And you took it like a thief in the fuckin' night. Left us out there to fuckin' rot!

LOUIS: Kingston. I—do—my—time.

SALLY: You just don't fuckin' get it. We was tryin' to own ourselves too. But together. Do ya remember that part, Louis? Do ya?

LOUIS: Fuck off!

SALLY: You was our leader. We couldn't say nothin' to the ramrods. Hell, half the plant was just off the boat. But we knew you'd say somethin'. And whenever ya did…well…we all kinda felt like we was sayin' it too.

LOUIS: *(does not want to listen, shouting)* Andy!…Andy! Another drink here. Now!

SALLY: And I'll tell ya another thing, buddy boy. I worked the downtown stroll long enough to know a little somethin' about bein' owned… By the fuckin' hour. You ain't the first to feel that way and ya won't be the last. But what ya don't understand is what it takes ta stop that feelin'. And I ain't talkin' about the fuckin' booze either. It's stickin' together and fightin' it out. Feelin' like yer part of somethin' other than a fuckin' bowlin' team. That's what ya ran out on, Louis. Ten fuckin' years ago. The chance *not* to be a fuckin' slave.

LOUIS: *(calls across bar)* Hey, Gene. You brainwash another one, eh?

SALLY: Bullshit! This is between you and me, you little fuckin' weasel.

LOUIS: For Christ sake, Andy! Where da hell is my fucking drink?

SALLY: Hey, Andy! Pretty funny, eh? Big Louis here don't believe in nothin' but his self. Then there's me. Don't even got that… And here we are livin' over the same fuckin' shithole…in the same fuckin' world… *(stands, mock toast)* Well, here's to ya, pal! Louis Bob Lemaire. Businessman… My fuckin' hero!… *(snaps back drink)*

LOUIS: *(very angry, shouting) Oui!* I am a fucking businessman. A damn good one… I…I buy and sell people just…and dey just like you. You hear me! Just like fucking you!

SALLY: *(shaking sarcastically)* Ooooh. Ya got me shakin' in my boots… *(waving hand, leaving)* Ya big fuckin' zero.

LOUIS: *(apoplectic) Non!* You. You. You are da fucking zero. You cunt! I ain't no nothing. You will see… *(then to convince himself)* I ain't no nothing.

SCENE 7

Louis sitting at one table. Sally is at another. There is a jug of beer on Sally's table. We hear the closing refrain from Gene's karaoke tune... "And that's why you've never seen a unicorn to this very day... You've seen green alligators and long... (forgetting words) da da da da dada da and some monkeys too, some cats and rats and elephants and sure as you're born, are we ever gonna see another unicorn?"

SALLY: *(karaoke ends)* Irish Rovers. Jesus, Gene. You're a fuckin' unicorn... Okay. I'm up... I'm tellin' ya, Andy. I'm feelin' young tonight!

Walks over to karaoke area, picks up microphone. Lights go down, except on Sally, who has placed a drink, cigarette on a stool. She moves around area comfortably, like she's been on cheap nightclub stages before; tapping mike.

...How's that? Everybody hear me?... *(blows into mike a few times, then looks at it)* Reminds me of a guy I used to date...Jewish fella... *(takes a drag from cigarette, grimaces)* Fucking filter tips. Like suckin' on tit through a fisherman's sweater... *(pointing into audience, nodding, smiling)* Yeah, Ramona. You know what I'm talkin' about... Hey... Don't get me wrong here... This broad don't make no lesbian jokes... *(an aside)* Dykes might kick the shit outta me... I'm tellin' ya. Feel like a million bucks tonight... Yeah, Canadian... Name's Carew. Sandpaper Sally Carew to some of ya. Pimps gave me the name when I went independent— Men... Brings ta mind the difference between a cactus and a corvette... With a cactus, the prick's on the outside... Hey, Kenny Boy. Sure this mike is workin'? ...Fuckin' Ken. Only fella I know who keeps track of his family by watchin' "Crimestoppers"... *(blows kiss to Karaoke Ken)* I love ya, man. Cue it up, pal... Number 42... *(sings "Leaving on a Jet Plane").*

"My bags are packed, I'm ready to go. I'm standin' here outside your door. I hate to wake you up to say goodbye..."

As Sally is singing her song, lights go up on Louis' table. A bit later, Ray enters, passing Sally. Ray sits down with Louis...

Sally continues to sing... Ray gets comfortable. Listens. Then looks around, takes a small baggie filled with white powder out of his coat. Holds it up for Louis. Gives it to him... Sally still singing... Ray looks around again...takes a gun out of his pocket...slides it over to Louis... Louis looks surprised, pushes back gun. Ray pushes it back. Louis pushes it back again... Ray does a "why not" shrug, puts it back in jacket... Sally still singing... Ray says something to Louis... Louis points, maybe a bit reluctantly, to Sally... Ray checks out Sally, who is still singing...sits back in chair, nodding his approval... Sally getting to crescendo of song... Ray looks at Louis and nods a "go ahead" motion... Louis gets up...moves to Sally's table, takes out bottle of knockout drops...empties it into Sally's jug of beer...just as Sally hits final notes..."Leavin' on a jet plane. Leavin' on a jet plane" ...Lights down!

SCENE 8

Sally is drugged, sluggish, lying on meth lab floor, chained.

RAY: *(sitting at small desk, speaking on cell phone, exasperated, whinging)* I'm tellin' ya I did it, Georgia. Yeah. Outta the chequing account... Yeah. Patio furniture's covered... And the figure skatin'... Whaddya mean attitude? I love ya, hun. I ain't got no attitude... I know it's your money, babe... Yeah. I know... Okay!.. Ah. Listen, babe. I'll probably be workin' late tonight... I don't know. Just a function, honey. You know how it is...Yeah. That's right... At the club... Yeah. Yeah. Sure, babe. What d'ya need? ...A quart of gin. Mix. And them potata things... No... I did not eat... I did not... Georgia. Lookit. I did not eat all the Cheetohs. All right! ...Yeah. Okay. Bye... *(hangs up)* Fuckin' women. Can't live with 'em. Can't kill 'em either... *(to Sally, with a kick)*...Well, not usually. Eh, babe?

SALLY: *(sitting up, looking around, getting her bearings, examining washtub, then with wavering bravado)* This one of them bleedin' shops? 'Cause if it is. I ain't gonna be no good to ya. Hepatitis. Yup. Hep B. That's what I got. Scout's honour. S'why I'm always a bit yella. Kidneys, lungs, liver. All shot. Ain't nothin' I got ya can get a price for. Might as well just turn me loose. Won't say nothin', man. Just walk away. Won't say a fuckin' word.

RAY: *(laughing)* Bleedin' shop? Don't flatter yourself, grandma. You'd be dried up after a couple of milkin's.

SALLY: *(noticing chain, lifts it)* Wait a minute…You ain't some kinda fuckin' pervert…

RAY: Tell me. You done much cookin,' grandma?

SALLY: Yeah. Look at me. I'm a regular Martha Stewart.

RAY: First thing you're gonna do is learn… *(kicks, Sally grunts)* some fucking… *(kicks, Sally grunts)* manners… *(pointing finger)* I'm not fucking around here.

SALLY: *(hands shielding head, expels long, painful moan, says nothing)*

RAY: *(calming down)* That's better… *(adjusts clothing)* Now, like I was askin'…

SALLY: *(learning fast, holding ribs, grimacing)* Whaddya want, mister?

RAY: *(pleased)* Ya see there? Was that so hard?… *(kicks again)* Crank, baby. You're cookin' crank. Methamphetamine. Crystal Flake. Vancouver Turnaround. Ten pounds a day or I poke yer eyes out.

SALLY: New York… *(pulling up to a sitting position)* or Mexican?

RAY: *(pleasantly surprised, nodding)* That's it…Mexican style. The Hot Tamale. Ephedrine. Pinch of acid. Bucket of that red phosphate… Just take care you don't spill any on yerself. Shit burns right through ta breakfast.

SALLY: If it don't blow me up first.

RAY: *(grabbing her hair)* Hey, look at that. Bitch knows her way around a kitchen.

SALLY: Pays for a broad to know women's work.

RAY: Well, I got news for ya, grandma. Job pays squat! Exceptin' of course for the room and board… *(handing over piece of paper)* Here's the recipe. Follow it close… *(exiting, turns back)* Oh, yeah. Got some fellas stoppin' by later to check on the operation. You do good, well maybe we can find some room in here for a stereo or somethin'... *(looking at watch, goes back to desk, places phone call)* Yeah, put me through to Carol... Did I say I wanted to speak to you, Holly? You think maybe I'm just dyin' to talk to the first stretch-pant bimbo that answers the phone? I bet you think yer somethin' special, huh, Holly? Thinkin' no one can tell that yer really a three-hundred-pound piece of goo... *(Sally begins to take notice of conversation)* So, let me say it one more time, lard ass. Put me fuckin' through to Carol... *(while he's waiting, Ray notices Sally listening. He gets up, goes over and kicks her one)* What the fuck you lookin' at?... *(regaining some control as Carol comes on the line)* Yeah. Carol. I called earlier. Frederick... *(Sally taking notice again)* Listen, she come in yet? I been tryin' to reach her all fucking day... No. I don't want to talk to anyone else... *(losing it again but trying to retain his cool)* Listen. I'm lookin' for Brandy. No. Nobody else. Lookit. Just tell her to call me, all right? Yeah. Anytime. Just give her the number. Okay? Just give her the fucking number... *(hangs up. Smashes phone against wall repeatedly)* Fuck! Fuck! Fuck! Fuck! Fuck! Fuck! Fuck!

Still looking up from her chains, Sally reacts.

(recovering composure) Nobody's gonna miss ya, babe... *(one last kick)* Get to fucking work...

Lights down on lab.

SCENE 9

Lights come up on Louis, extremely drunk back at the Canada House.

LOUIS: *(now wearing a tatty nylon Montreal Canadiens jacket; violently reciting poetry, extremely rapidly in staccato as if he is afraid he might forget it otherwise, pointing, drunk, out of control)* "We are da dead. And now we lie. In Flander Field. To you wit broken hands we throw dat torch; for you to hold it high..." Andy! Put dat behind da bar, asshole...Flander Field. Good enough for da dressing room of da fucking Montreal Canadien! Sally. Her shit don't stink, eh? *Guidoune!...* *(takes drink)* Beliveau. Richard. J.C. Tremblay. Dat guy Rejean Houle. Guy LaFleur...Johnny Bower... Fucking English!... *(spits, dials cell phone)* ...Hey, Blackie. Maybe you are right, eh? Why dis guy Ray take all da profit? Maybe we run a few ting on our own, eh? ...Sell some name. Run some dope... *(laughs) Oui. Independent.* Like in da song... *(chorus of Separatist folk anthem "Gens Du Pays") "Gens du pays c'est votre tour. De vous laisser parler d'amour"... (trailing off) Oui. Je me souviens... (then loudly, to entire bar) Je me souviens!*

> *Lights fade on Louis. We hear glasses tinkling. A hubbub of voices, drum roll... An announcer's voice: "May I have the envelope, please! ...And now, without further ado... on behalf of the Board of Directors of the Social Market Foundation, it is my pleasure to announce this year's Winner of the Time and Motion Man of the Year Award... And the winner is... Washtub Methamphetamine. Ray Fucking Bidwell..." Loud applause, lights come up on podium, Ray holds a large trophy over his head, ecstatic, puts trophy down, acknowledging people in the crowd.*

RAY: Don't ever give up on your dreams. Not ever!... *(more applause)* Ya gotta own it, man. Ya gotta own it... *(calming down)* Whew. This is unbelievable... Okay...I would like to thank Mr. Frank Barzini, without whom this project woulda never had the seed money to take off and fly. I'd like to thank Detective Superintendent Spear... *(shading eyes, squinting, nods to Spear in audience)* Thanks, bud. You and the boys have always been there... Hardware Depot for supplying...what can I say, just the absolute top of the line. Canada Customs Niagara Falls for a damn fine job on the distribution... The First National Bank of Curaçao... I know I'm gonna forget somebody here... My Lord and personal saviour, Jesus Christ... My wife, Georgia. Love ya, hun... Who else? ...Um. Black Jack Shellac. Louis Lemaire. And Pablo and Jawon and...what the hell, Sandpaper Sally Carew for cookin' up one hell of a storm... *(reaches out to touch trophy, contemplates a moment, looks skyward, mouths words "Thanks, Dad," very emotional)* And I wanna thank my dad... *(looks skyward again)* Dad. I know you're watchin'... *(fighting the tears)* I want to thank my dad for teaching me all about... *ownership*. About hard work and priorities and keepin' what ya have, no matter what. Well, I did it, Dad. Maybe you always had your doubts. Maybe it's a little late comin'. But it's me holdin' the trophy tonight... And there ain't nobody can take that away. Ya hear me? Nobody... *(holding trophy over his head triumphantly, applause building, shouting)* Wait till next year! ...You ain't seen nothin yet! ...You ain't seen nothin' yet!...

Lights fade on Ray. Come up on Sally. Working in the lab.

SALLY: *(her face horribly beaten, cuts, black eyes, tuning a radio, talking/ psyching herself up)* Bastard leaves me nothin' but a AM radio. Stereo, he says. My fuckin' ass... Okay. Get yer shit together, girl. You been in tougher jams than this one... Hah. Like hell you have! Well, buck up, girlfriend, 'cause if you don't go through with this, *you're* gonna be the saddest story ever told. *(Sally finds a station she likes...we hear Freddy Mercury singing "I've Got To Break Free")* ...Hah! Freddy... All right. Percs. Percs... Ah. Okay... *(has reached in pocket, pulled out bottle, takes everything)*

Sally goes about preparing mixture. She takes a sample and drips it on her manacled wrist, winces, hops around in terrible pain. Goes back to mixing. Lights still up.

Music continues; lights now also go up on Louis. Totally hammered. Sitting in Canada House. Mumbling, gesticulating, shadow-boxing. Agitated. Pulling at his crotch. Pulls open fly. Lumbers off through bar... Sally continuing to labour in her lab... Lights down on Louis.

Lights go up on third part of stage... Ray is sitting in his La-Z-Boy recliner, trophy by his side, he has his plastic bag, his cell phone, but Brandy isn't there. He paces angrily and throws his phone against the wall... Sally continuing to labour. Lights go down on Ray.

Music building to crescendo... Sally lifts manacled arm...with gritty determination she plunges it into acid/red phosphate washtub in order to dissolve flesh and free herself from manacles...her face contorts in indescribable pain. She faints as the curtain falls on Act One.

ACT TWO

SCENE 1

One year later. It's near sunset. There are street sounds, traffic noises. There is a lighted telephone booth in the background. We see a flashing red light and hear a voice on a megaphone: "This is the Police. In the interest of public order, nightly curfew has been extended until further notice. Please proceed to your place of residence ... This is the police. In the interest of..."

Lights up on Sally. Her arm is inserted inside a shoebox through a hole punched in its end. She is at the front of the stage, as if addressing passersby...

SALLY: *(addresses audience)* Wanna see what's in the shoebox?

RAY: *(lights up on Ray, wearing a business suit, around the corner, happily dialing his cell phone)* I'm gonna get the plant. Ya hear that, Dad? They're sellin'. I'm gonna get back the fucking plant!... *(cross-fade to stage front)*

SALLY: *(to unseen street passersby)* Only five bucks to see what's in the box. C'mon, folks. Get on over here. Sally's back in town.

RAY: —Jesus, Georgia. This is my *dream* I'm talkin' about. Ten years I been waitin' for this. Ten fucking years since those bastards drove Dad under and now—

SALLY: —C'mon, pal. Slow down. Curfew ain't fer another hour... *(shaking head)* ...Curfew. Fuuuck... Hey, c'mon over here. I wanna show ya somethin'...Yeah, in yer dreams, asshole!—

RAY: No. No. That's what I'm tryin' to tell ya... Lookit. I got it all figured out. Them work riots are makin' a lotta folks jumpy... Food riots, war riots, whatever. Point is, the owner wants to bail. We move now, we pick up the plant for a piss in the driveway—

SALLY: —C'mon, people. Slow down. My mortgage payment's comin' due... Step right up. See the seventh wonder of the fuckin' world—

RAY: —No. Listen to me, Georgia. Will ya just fuckin' listen? ...Okay. We remortgage the house, cash in the bonds, then marry it all up with the prize money from the next Foundation Award—

SALLY: —Oh yeah, pal? You try holdin' down a job with an infection!

RAY: —Yeah. I'm pitchin' it tomorrow, girl... Whaddya mean, if? ...I'm tellin' ya right now, Georgie. It's a fucking shoo-in—

SALLY: —Don't worry. Gotta ambulance on standby. Yeah. In case of fuckin' heart attack. C'mon. See what's in the shoebox. Five bucks and ya get to tell your grandkids—

RAY: *(now wincing, agitated)* —Jesus Christ, Georgia. We need the cash now... Look. The hell with the Montessori... Yeah? Well, who the fuck needs Mozart anyway?—

SALLY: —Hey, you. Yeah. With the hat. Can ya help a girl out here? I just wanna show ya somethi— *(frustrated)* Jesus fucking Christ. Lookit. I need some money. Will ya just get over here?

RAY: —Oh, baby. I can see it now. Just like the old days. Dominion Fibreglass. Got the sign as good as new... Don't worry. This is gonna work. I promise ya... Listen, I gotta go... Yeah... Yeah. Gin and some mix... Lookit... No. No. I am not gonna forge your signature... No. Now, that was different... No. *You* don't understand... Hello. Hello... *(flips phone shut)* Fucking cunt—

SALLY: *(addressing passersby again)* —All right, folks... Gimme a break, will ya? Only cost ya five dollars... C'mon, people. The GO Train can fucking wait... Step right up, now... See what's in the shoebox... Seventh wonder of the... *(she sees Ray, tries to hide her face)* Jesus—

Ray walking across the stage, on phone again. He stops near Sally; talking.

RAY: That's right, sir. 545-2123... No problem, sir. I got the cash. Hey, Mr. B. You can call me anytime... *(flips phone shut; ecstatic)* Yessss!... *(begins to walk, slows down, looks back)*

SALLY: Shit!

RAY: *(returning)* Well, if it isn't little Miss Martha Stewart. Long time no see.

SALLY: *(brandishing shoebox)* You keep away from me.

RAY: *(excited, admiringly)* Jesus. You fuckin' did it. Plunged that hand right in there. Only way out and you took it. Man, you just can't dee-fence somethin' like that.

SALLY: I got friends, ya know… Gene… Gene!

RAY: Hey. Take it easy. I got no hard feelin's… *(shrugging)* Sold the lab, anyway.

SALLY: No hard feelin's? Jesus fucking Christ.

RAY: *(mocking)* Aw. Martha's feelin' sorry fer herself.

SALLY: Look it. I just don't want no trouble. Okay? I kept the cops out of it, so fuck off!

RAY: Smart move. Captain had a piece of the operation. Man, was he pissed.

SALLY: You are some piece of fuckin' work.

RAY: Okay. Okay. My bad. There ya go. A Grade-A Ray apology and…what the hell, it's my lucky day…here's a twenty. So. What? Am I off the Indian List?

SALLY: Get the fuck outta here. What d'ya think I am?

RAY: Heeey. Ya wanna go there? Do ya? 'Cause I think we both know the answer to that one… We're just negotiatin' the price.

SALLY: Yeah. You like payin' for it. Don't ya?

RAY: Huh? What the fuck you mean by that?

SALLY: Oh, nothin'.

RAY: You don't know nothin' about me, bitch.

SALLY: That's right. Yer just a guy that likes beatin' on women.

RAY: Fuck you! That was business.

SALLY: Whips and chains and shit.

RAY: No. That ain't me.

SALLY: Yeah. Well, then just who the fuck are you?

RAY: Jesus, you got me goin' there. Didn't ya? Jesus. Will ya look at me. I'm havin' a conversation with a one-handed meatslap.

SALLY: Yeah. What's wrong with that?

RAY: Me and you? In a conversation? That's what's wrong with that.

SALLY: You ain't no better than me.

RAY: How about them Blue Jays. Nice weather we're havin'. Sorry about the hand. Yeah, right. Listen, babe. It's been a slice. Maybe I'll see ya at the circus sometime?... *(begins to walk away)*

SALLY: *(to herself)* Fuck it... *(calls out)* I'll let ya see what's in the shoebox.

RAY: *(stops in his tracks)* Yeah?

SALLY: Yeah. For...how do you call it...a little face time.

RAY: Face time, huh?

SALLY: It's mighty sorrowful.

RAY: Ah. Gotta be a fuckin' angle.

SALLY: Maybe there ain't. Maybe I just wanna see if you got the stomach to look at what ya done... Anyway, what do you care? I'm about to show you the Seventh Wonder of the fuckin' World.

RAY: *(thinking)* A business proposition, huh? I'll give ya three minutes.

SALLY: And no hittin'. No matter what I say.

RAY: *(rubbing hands together)* Start talkin', Martha.

SALLY: *(an outburst)* You cocksucker. You fuckin' bastard. Just who the fuck do you think you are? Kidnappin' me like that... And...and fuckin' beatin' me. You piece of shit. I never done nothin' to you. Nothin'!

RAY: Whoa. Looks like you plan on gettin' your money's worth.

SALLY: Yeah. The big funny man. Well, you don't fool me, buster. I seen guys like you all my life. Yer all the fucking same. Folks are nothin' but things to you. Things to squeeze and twist just ta see if ya can use whatever comes spurtin' out.

RAY: Oozes out, honey. Don't exaggerate. With you. It oozes out.

SALLY: *(pause, shaking head)* Ya know. I'm just tryin' to picture you as a kid. Catchin' grasshoppers or playin' road hockey… Can't fuckin' do it.

RAY: Yeah? Maybe cause I was workin' for a livin'. Yeah. Even back then. Work. Ya ever try it?

SALLY: Yeah, I tried it… Never cared for it.

RAY: *(proudly)* Yeah? Well I worked in my old man's factory. For a few years anyway. Till it went under. Pop was groomin' me. Started out in the warehouse. Was runnin' the shrink-wrapper before I was twelve years old. The Laminator. That's what they called me. Like Schwarzenegger. You wanted plasticizin'. You had to see *me*.

SALLY: Yeah, I used to do factory work… The Laminator, huh?… *(starts chuckling)*

RAY: What the fuck's a matter with you? You find that funny? A thing like that…that's funny to you?

SALLY: Ah. Lighten up. I was thinkin' of somethin' else.

RAY: Yeah. Well, what the fuck do you know? We happened to take pride in our work…at least until the big strike… Fuckin' Equalizers. Freeloaders. Just like you… Bastards drove Dad to the fuckin' wall, man. Broke him with all their squeezin'. And for what? Dominion Fibreglass—

SALLY: *(startled)* —Domin—

RAY: —Out of business. Turn out the lights. Everybody loses. But you'd probably find that funny too… The way he just sat at home afterwards. A failure. A fuckin' suicide. I had to change my fuckin' name! Another family chewed up by the likes of you…*(mimicking workers)* We want more. We want more… *(then)* Ta hell with initiative. Ta hell with private property… *(again as a worker)* Give us more. Just give us fucking more… *(then)* Whatdya mean? You never done nothin' to me… *(snarling)* You done every fuckin' thing!

SALLY: *(holding up stump)* Well, fuck you too.

RAY: No! Fuck you! 'Cause I'm gettin' back the fuckin' plant.

SALLY: What goes around comes around, eh?

RAY: Yeah. You got that right.

SALLY: Your dream come true.

RAY: *(dreamily)* Yeah… *(then, angered by his honesty)* You know, bitch. You talk too fuckin' much. Open up the fuckin' box. I got a function to get to.

SALLY: *(cynically)* Deal's a deal. Right?

RAY: Open it!

SALLY: Yeah. Yeah… *(lifting lid, looks away, sadly, with some distaste)* …feels like my first time strippin'.

RAY: *(immediately impressed)* Whoa!

SALLY: Yeah? You should see the other guy.

RAY: Man. You weren't kiddin'. That is one sight for sore eyes. Musta fuckin' hurt, eh?

SALLY: Percodans. Turns out, you burn your hand off, ya get 'em for free.

RAY: God. Looks like some kinda rake…with some leaves stuck in it… *(tries to touch it)*

SALLY: Hey! Back off. No touchin'.

RAY: …It moved. Did you see that! The fuckin' rake moved! What else can it do?

SALLY: It can poke yer fuckin' eye out.

RAY: Hey. Take it easy. I'm a fan. All right?

SALLY: Didn't ya say ya had a function to get to?

RAY: *(checking watch)* Damn… *(getting up reluctantly, takes last look)* Man! That is one helluva conversation piece… Tell me. Can ya… Can ya feel anything?

SALLY: *(looking away)* To tell ya the truth. I don't fuckin' know anymore.

RAY: Ah. Buck up, babe. Could be worse. Listen. There's this circus guy I know. Sideshow Sam… Ya see what I'm sayin? …The

Fuckin' Rake Lady... Think about it... *(laughing, arrogantly handing over a business card)* Yeah. Here's my card. Gimme a call. We'll do lunch... *(exits)*

SALLY: *(darkly, looks at card, slowly, to herself)* Sideshow, eh? Okay, Frederick. Let's just see who's the fuckin' freak... *(starts begging)* All right... C'mon, people. Curfew ain't till ten. Who can change a five spot here? Hey, buddy. Can ya break a fin? C'mon...I need some quarters... *(then, ominously)* Gotta make an important phone call...

SCENE 2

Tinkle of forks on plates, murmur of conversation. Lights up on Ray dining at a head table. Louis enters wearing an ill-fitting, powder-blue wedding suit, and takes a seat beside Ray.

RAY: *(eating)* Yer fuckin' late.

LOUIS: *(tipsy)* Yeah. Like da rabbit at da tea party.

RAY: Jesus. Pissed again.

LOUIS: Maybe. Or maybe I am just happy. I do my job. Don't you worry.

RAY: Yeah? You catch another fish today?

LOUIS: *(cocky)* Hey, *pas de problème.* Kid from Temiskaming. At da bus station.

RAY: *(impatiently)* Well... How'd it go?

LOUIS: Ah. It go. Pick him up. Drop him off. Same shit. But da day is different... *(Louis reaches for bottle of wine)*

RAY: *(fixing a stare)* You getting cocky? Don't get cocky on me, Louis. Just do your fuckin' job. All right? Got too much at stake here... *(grabbing bottle from Louis)* And go easy on the booze, will ya? You're at a Foundation function, fer Christ's sake.

LOUIS: *(reclaiming bottle, loudly)* Louis Bob Lemaire never shirk nothing.

RAY: *(embarrassed, looking around)* Okay, Louis. Okay. C'mon, dude. Chill. This is a big night for both of us. I'm just saying, keep it fucking together. Okay?

LOUIS: *Oui. Oui.* No problem. Everyting is in control.

RAY: You betcha. Consolidated Microbe, the new client, ain't never been happier. You got yourself a credit card. Foundation's makin' you a full member. Just ride the wave, dude... Here, try some of this here chicken. Got some kind of pepper cheese thing goin' on. Mama.

LOUIS: *Non. Merci.*

RAY: It's fuckin' sweet, man.

LOUIS: *Non. Non...* Okay. *C'est vrai.* Maybe I am a little bit nervous.

RAY: Ah. You just never gave a speech before. That's all. Listen. What say we get it outta the way. Then maybe ya can let your hair down.

LOUIS: Den we start the big party? Okay. Now you cook with some gas.

RAY: *(tapping on a water glass, then standing)* All right fellas. Settle down now. Cherry pie will be along in a minute. But first... Please... If I could have your... *(firmly)* Hey, Sammy! Can it! Will ya? ...All right. Now. Before we get started, how about a big hand for the girls in the kitchen. Wasn't that chicken something else? I'm tellin' ya. Father Dan there's thinkin' of runnin' off with the fuckin' cook... Now, I got a coupla quick announcements here before we get to the main event... *(reading from cards)* There's still room for a few more foursomes to the big Stockwell Day Memorial Golf Tournament. Just sign up over there with Sam... *(new card)* Big news. Presentations start tonight for the next Foundation Awards. Now, entry fee's gone up a grand... But, hey. I'm goin' for the ree-peat, so why throw your money away?... *(new card)* Willy, call the wife... *(laughs, makes whipping noise/motion. New card)* And last but not least, don't forget the deadline's Saturday for the Grand Marshall nominations to next month's Crack Pride Parade. And gentlemen. Please. This year, only one vote to a customer... And now to the business of business. We got here today the newest member of the organization. He's done his probation. Got a new suit along the way. And he's ready to do some steppin' out. Currently working on the Consolidated Microbe account, here he is—the man who put the sub into sub-contracting...*(solemnly)* Ladies and gentlemen... My protegé...Louis Bob Lemaire!... *(Ray applauds as he sits down. He stifles a laugh to someone in the audience)*

LOUIS: *(gets up, returns to drain wine glass, to podium, very nervous, referring laboriously to notes)* Okay. Maybe I come from da different neck in da wood than most of you, eh? But here goes something. Okay. I am suppose to talk to you tonight about dat guy Allan Smith wit dat hand dat is invisible.

Split stage. Lights back up on Sally who, with hand now wrapped in a plastic bag, gets up from street and moves slowly toward telephone booth.

RAY: Adam.

LOUIS: Huh...

RAY: *(like a school teacher) Adam* Smith and the Invisible Hand.

LOUIS: *(going back to his notes)* Oh..uh... *Certainement...* Dis guy Smith, he figure you can do anything you wanted cause dere was dis Invisible Hand thing dat nobody can see but it was taking care of everything so that everything, it work out no problem. Kinda like dat CIA.

Sally has now entered the phone booth and begun to dial.

—Ray, he gimme dis quotation dat maybe explain it better...*(shuffling paper, clears throat)* "It is not from da"...*(looks up)* okay, now dis is dat guy Smith talking..."it is not from da kindness of da butcher, da brewer or da baker dat we expect our dinner, but from deir regard to deir own interest. We address ourself not to deir humanitay but to dat dere self love—

RAY: *(his phone rings, he answers, oblivious to Louis' speech)* Make it fast. I'm at a function here—

LOUIS: *(flummoxed by interruption, tries to continue while Ray talks, grinning sheepishly)* ...*Excusez-moi*...where was I?...oh, yeah...at da self love—

SALLY: Hello, Frederick.

RAY: *(shocked, getting up to absent himself from podium)* Brandy? Jesus Christ. I don't believe it. It's fuckin' Brandy.

Louis, still flummoxed, grabs Ray's wine glass and drains it as lights go down on the podium.

SALLY: Hey, babe. Long…time…no…wank.

RAY: Girl, I been lookin' all… I mean, Carol… She said you stopped comin' in.

SALLY: Yeah. Well, maybe I just gone freelance. Lookin' up some of the old customers. What do ya say, Freddy? Still got yer plastic bag?

RAY: Jesus. I'm at a goddamn function for Christ's fuckin' sake!

SALLY: Take it easy, big boy. I'm off the clock. Can't a girl make a little conversation?

RAY: No, that's okay, babe. Sure ya can. It' just that I'm at a function, that's all.

SALLY: Ya miss me, Frederick? Ya never said ya missed me.

RAY: Are you kiddin' me? That last session? I still got a woody. We were getting close, babe. Real close… *(shivers, pained)* That termite stuff…all over that little grub…like a fuckin' mob… I don't know… *(almost embarrassed to admit it)* Big guy takin' shit. Just gets to me.

SALLY: Ah. You liked that, huh? You know, Frederick. It's like…I don't know… Like I'm really startin' to get ta know ya.

RAY: *(vulnerable)* I know… I tried some of the other girls after you left…but they was just goin' through the motions… You know. Boo hoo. I lost my boyfriend. That shit. Fuckin' airheads. You're not like that… You listen…like you really care.

SALLY: Got to. Like I always said. Yer a hard nut to crack.

RAY: Ahhh. You know. I got pressures.

SALLY: Tell me about it… Listen. Tell ya what I'm gonna do. Seein's how I'm startin' up my own jerk stand, what d'ya say I give ya one on the house. Off the clock. You know, the works.

RAY: *(excitedly)* Yeah… Yeah. Like a Customer Appreciation Day… I like it. Put me down for one motherfuckin' sad story, will ya?

Whatever's on yer mind... *(getting pen from pocket, upbeat)* What's yer new number, babe?

SALLY: *(looking at surroundings)* Ah...I'm kinda just settin' up my new place. What say I give *you* a call this time...say...what? ...tomorrow night?

RAY: Tuesday? Yeah. Yeah. That'll be fine... *(hits forehead)* No, wait a minute. Damn. Judgin' a karaoke Tuesday. Wednesday night too. Some kinda marathon. Keeps the poor folks happy.

SALLY: Aw. Frederick. Couldn't ya get out of it?

RAY: Geez, I don't know, Brandy. It's a network opportunity. What else ya got?

SALLY: How about the Thursday?

RAY: Thursday? ...Yeah. That'll work. Round about midnight. Man, it's gonna be just like old times, babe. Listen. I gotta get back. Breakin' in a new guy tonight. Real fuckin' loser... *(heartfelt)* Hey. Brandy. Thanks for phonin'.

SALLY: Don't mention it, Frederick. I reckon I owe ya one... *(hangs up, lights down on Sally)*

Ray hangs up, returns to head table. Lights up on Louis, still at the podium.

LOUIS: *(drunker, draining a wine bottle)* Dem dog, dey swimming around dat canoe like a coupla Florida shark. Well, dat Black Jack Shellac, he just look over at me... "Pickerel Retriever," he say. *Crisse.* Dem Yank, dey don't know whether to have a shit or buy dat dog...

RAY: *(stares incredulously at Louis, gets up, starts applauding, eases Louis from podium)* Louis Lemaire, ladies and gentlemen. Louis Bob Lemaire... *(Louis sits)* How about that Invisible Hand, huh?... *(shrugs)* Go figure... *(looking out)* Is that the pie comin'? Yeah? Okay. Cherry pie, folks... And remember. Cash bar proceeds go to the Kids for Christ program, so keep 'em comin'... *(sits, slaps Louis in the head)* What's the matter with you? You can't lay off the booze for ten minutes?

LOUIS: I tink it go pretty good, eh?

RAY: Well, I need to discuss the Microbe account...like, before you start showin' off yer dick.

LOUIS: Ah *crisse,* Ray. You don't listen. Dat gotta be some other guy.

RAY: *(beginning to eat again)* Yeah. Whatever. Bullshit walks. Right? Now listen up. I'm givin' you a new detail. Want ya to stop bringin' the runaways over to Consolidated's germ testin' unit. Got another guy workin' the supply side...sister's kid... *(shrugging)* Hey. What can I tell ya? It's family.

LOUIS: *(a bit hurt)* But I was signing two, three kid by da day. And what about dem twin I got yesterday? Eh? Nobody coulda done dat.

RAY: *(continuing to eat)* Yeah. Yeah. You did good. Got no complaints. But my sister... Lookit. I'm puttin' ya on the night shift, Louis...movin' ya over to disposals.

LOUIS: Disposal? What do you mean, disposal?

RAY: *(shrugging, obviously)* Disposals. Round about three in the mornin', ya back the truck in behind the...whatdya call it? ...the...the decontamination unit there. Pick up a box or two... Look at me, Louis... You don't look in 'em, ya hear me?

LOUIS: Yeah. Don't look in dem.

RAY: That's right. Then cart 'em over to Blackie at the incinerator... *(shrugs)* Disposals.

LOUIS: You mean I get to run da Chevy?

RAY: Pick up the keys from Sam over there. And get a curfew pass while you're at it... Big part of our Award Project, Louis. I don't mind sayin', we're on track for two in a row... *(still eating)* Which reminds me... Saw an old friend of ours today. Broad from the shed. Big mouth. Got a way of getting ya talkin' too much.

LOUIS: *(fumbles for a cigarette, surprised) Qui?* Sally?

RAY: Regular medical fuckin' marvel.

LOUIS: *(pleased)* Sally? Sally Carew? She live? *Tabernac!* Dat broad.

RAY: The old goat's sleepin' over a grate out back of the train station. Red Cap entrance. Got no hand... *(grimacing)* shoebox hangin' off her arm… Can't miss her… *(stops eating, salts food)* There's a can of gas in the back of the truck… *(takes out a big cigar, turns to Louis, pulls lighter from pocket, flicks lighter)* Want ya to kill her, Louis.

LOUIS: What?

RAY: You heard me. Nobody runs out on Ray Bidwell. No fuckin' body… *(lighting Louis' cigarette)* Oh, yeah… When ya strike the match…tell her The Laminator sent ya… *(Ray lights his cigar, Louis is stunned)*

SCENE 3

RAY: *(illuminated by a single light, supremely confident, smoking a cigarette, with a glass of scotch in his hand, pitching)* Okay, gentlemen. Just two words…Social Robotics… Remember them to your broker… Picture it. A process that can provide to you…at a price yer gonna like…a hand-picked supply of specialized labour power…for the…ah…more sensitive jobs. Now, I'm talking a pool of workers devoid of anything but the most basic of desires. A little food. A little booze. A little Don Cherry. And in return? Imagine, gentlemen. Workers who'll do what ya tell 'em…without question, without reflection… without… *(searching)* …compunction. Without a nightstick bustin' a bowel or a big payroll at the end of it. And isn't that really what the Foundation Award is all about? Now, more than ever. Motivation. Low overhead. Discipline. You wanna get it done? Well, I'm here to tell ya. Ray Bidwell's got the jam, gentlemen. For the second year running, I got the fucking jam. No cattle prods, no union backhanders, no annual performance reviews. Just ready-made guys, ready to go to work. No questions asked. Whatever the job. Think about it. It's simply a question of a viable selection process… And gentlemen, this I will guarantee to you today. Ray Bidwell knows how to pick 'em… So, if you'll now turn to the dossiers in front of you, I wanna show you my latest prototype…Louis Bob Lemaire! The New Workin' Man!… *(lights cross-fade)*

SCENE 4

It's dark, just before sunrise. In the dark we see a lighter being flicked on and off repeatedly, its holder rocking back and forth.

LOUIS: *(very conflicted; still wearing powder-blue outfit)* Dis beverage room, dedicate to dose merry soul… Me too. We was all dere, Sally. Happy. In da beverage room. *Moi, aussi. Oui. Tout le monde. Oui.* Me too. Me too. Me too…*Non! Non!* Dey never like you. *Tout le monde.* You and dem. Dey never like you. Merry soul. Dat bullshit. Dat bullshit—

As (day) lights slowly come up, we see Louis, drinking from a bottle. He is sitting on a stoop over top of Sally, who is snoozing in a sleeping bag. A shoebox lies near Sally. Her hand is wrapped in a white plastic bag. There is an overturned gas can near Louis. He's whimpering, looking at his feet, rocking, flicking lighter. Sally wakes up, startled.

SALLY: What the fuck?

LOUIS: *(startled, jumping up, last whine, then brandishing lighter)* …You don't move! Just stay dere. I…I ain't kidding.

SALLY: Jesus Fuck. Louis Bob Lemaire.

LOUIS: *(flicking lighter)* You just stay dere!

SALLY: Look at you. You look like Barry fuckin' Manilow.

LOUIS: Dis ain't no joke. I am telling you.

SALLY: It's the middle of the night. Yer damn right this ain't… *(sniffing air)* Hey, wait a minute. You smell somethin'…

LOUIS: Like maybe gas?

SALLY: *(checking sleeping bag, smelling sleeve)* Jesus Christ! Gas!… *(Sally tries to get out of sleeping bag)*

LOUIS: *(moves to hold her down, flicks lighter)* I will fucking do it!

SALLY: *(struggling)* You bastard!

LOUIS: *(now sitting on top of Sally)* I will burn you, Sally. So help me. I will do it.

SALLY: *(stops struggling, face to face with Louis, defiant)* Well. What are ya waitin' for?

LOUIS: You just can't shut your fucking trap, eh? Sandpaper Sally Carew and dat big flapping booze hole. You were smart-mouthing wit da boss, eh? And now, I got to do dis. Women! Can't keep yer fucking yap shut. Always push. Always dig. *Ah, oui.* Don't worry. You will get torched…When *I* am ready.

SALLY: Jesus Christ, Louis. What the fuck is goin' on here?

LOUIS: What da fuck it look like? Boss want you done. Like da fucking dinner… Oh, yeah… Compliment of da Laminator.

SALLY: Laminator? That cocky motherfucker.

LOUIS: You say yer prayers.

SALLY: Will ya just wait a minute! …Christ… Ain't I s'posed to get some last words or somethin'?

LOUIS: Dere. You see. Always wanna talk.

SALLY: Yeah. And why don't ya get off of me first. I ain't goin' nowhere.

LOUIS: *Ah, oui.* Just like in dat meth lab, eh Sally?

SALLY: He was gonna kill me.

LOUIS: Dat what you say.

SALLY: Hey. Lookit, Louis. You got gas all over yer suit there.

LOUIS: Huh? Ah, shit!

SALLY: Unless yer plannin' on a murder-suicide, I'd be gettin' offa me.

LOUIS: *(getting up, pulling at trouser inseam) Crisse.* It only new just yesterday.

SALLY: *(buying time over next few minutes, slowly extricating herself from sleeping bag)* Yeah? Bargain Mart?

LOUIS: *(indignant)* Da Wedding Store.

SALLY: Christ. Poor fuckin' broad.

LOUIS: No. It not like dat. Me. Today. I make a big speech. Louis Bob Lemaire.

SALLY: Ya boost it?

LOUIS: *(defensive) Non.* I pay for dese... *(takes out wallet, flips it open)* Credit card... Don't you worry. With Ray and then Black Jack on da side. I make plenty.

SALLY: What? Killin' folks?

LOUIS: No. No. Disposal.

SALLY: Disposals, huh?... *(shaking head)* Ha. That's a good one... How much ya gettin' for me? A coupla grand?

LOUIS: It not like dat. For you I get nothing.

SALLY: Nothin'? ...Jesus.

LOUIS: *Non.* I told you. It ain't like dat. *Non*!

SALLY: Yeah? Well then just how is it, Louis?

LOUIS: What? You don't know? Da whole goddamn world on fire! Dat how it is. One guy. He can do nothing. Me? I look out for Louis Bob Lemaire. Whatever work. Da rest...well, da rest...dey just take care of deir own damn self.

SALLY: *(holding up arm)* Yeah? Like this? This the rest?

LOUIS: *Oui.* Dat right. When you run. You just think about Number One. Like everybody. Just like you try to run now... *(flicks lighter)* Return into dat bag!

SALLY: You flick that thing one more time, Louis. I swear, I'm gonna latch onto you like it's our fuckin' weddin' night. Rubbie flambé. That's what yer gonna get. Yeah. The whole world's on fire, all right. And you and me too, if that's the way ya wanna go.

LOUIS: Don't go fooling, Sally. You...you return into dat bag. Eh!

SALLY: You had yer chance. And ya didn't take it.

LOUIS: Me? I could fry you. No problem.

SALLY: Well, not to-fuckin'-day, pal. Lookit. My man, Gene. Yeah. Remember him? Hey, Gene. Over here... *(smiling triumphantly at Louis)* Lookit. It's Walnut Dick Lemaire.

LOUIS: *Chienne... (flicks lighter)* You will see. I will fuck you up.

SALLY: Yeah. Over here. Gene.

LOUIS: You fucking bitch... *(flees)*

SALLY: Hey, Gene. I'm thinkin' of quittin' smokin'.

SCENE 5

Split stage. Lights on Ray.

RAY: *(at home; talking to his children; polishing white skates with dark polish)* C'mon, boys. Chill. I ain't afraid to tell her. Boys' skates are black, for Christ's sake. Hell, ya don't see Elvis Stojko goin' around in no girlie skates. Yeah. No frilly tights either. He's got that karate chop. Don't you worry. I'll tell her. I'll tell her tomorrow. Yeah. That's what I'm gonna do... *(puts down skate, touches up own shoes)* So, what d'ya think? The old man look like a karaoke judge or what?... *(calling out, plaintively)* C'mon, Georgie. I gotta go...Georgia?...*(to kids, as Ray walks to doorway)* Mommy and her little drinkypoos... *(then sings in hopes of placating wife)* Georgia. Oh. Georgia... *(doesn't succeed)* Okay... So, I signed the house over without ya. I was under the gun, honey. The old guy needed a little cash up front. You know. To hold the deal till the big prize comes through... Listen. Ya know that mink coat ya keep lookin' at? Well...after we get the plant tied up...it's yours. Hell, I'll even take you out to the Club for supper. You in yer mink coat and me in my...my shiny shoes. We're gonna turn some heads all right. Walkin' down Bay Street. Mr. and Mrs. Ray Bidwell. The Fibreglass King!... *(lights cross-fade)*

LOUIS: *(in Canada House, quite drunk; talking to Andy. The large Buy War Bonds poster is now splattered with red paint)* Ya, I fuck her. Before she start wit dat whoring. Back in da plant when I save her mother, eh? I never forget dat. All dem female inside... *(shudders audibly)* Look like dis big greasy balloon or something. Just came plopping out dere by da wool stacker. Dat Old Lady Annie Carew, she rolling, trying to push dat damn thing back up inside her body. Da wool, all jamming. Everybody screaming. Foreman. He running like some kind of blue ass fly. Got to keep dat line moving. Stack dat fucking wool. Keep working. Well, fuck dat I say. Annie need me. So I reach over and hit dat Stop Button. After dat. *Crisse.* It was like I was dat guy Leon fucking Lenin…I tell you…Having everybody depend on you… *(thoughtful pause)* Well. Dat a helluva fucking thing… *(lights cross-fade)*

SALLY: *(in alley, excited)* Jesus, Gene. I never knew ya could move so fast. One minute the cop's got me by the neck, the next. Outta nowhere. Bam. Right in the fuckin' balls. That'll teach the fucker. And them curfew goons by the stage… *(shadow boxing)* Pow! Bam! The whole crowd was on 'em. Lookit, one of 'em dropped his cell phone. Oh. You were right, man. We don't have to take this shit. Jesus, Gene. Never knew a political meetin' could be so damn excitin'! It's like…I don't know… Like…like fuckin' Mozart, man… Now. Tell me that part again about gettin' treated like human beings. You know. When folks take over the fuckin' world.

SCENE 6

Ray is sitting at a karaoke judging table. We hear the final strains of a karaoke … "God Bless America"…

RAY: Sweeeet, man. So sweet… *(choking up)* Fuckin' says it all… *(writing on paper, holding it up)* Aw, hell, folks. I'm givin' it a perfect ten… Ken, I'm tearin' up, here… Let's take five… *(takes a drink)* Louis! Get over here.

LOUIS: *(nervous, sitting down)* You want to see dis guy, Ray?

RAY: You do what I told ya?

LOUIS: *Certainement.* I did everything. Burn dat broad real good.

RAY: Yeah? Well how come it didn't register in the papers? Homeless body count last night was a big, fat zero.

LOUIS: I put her in one of dem germ boxes. You know. For da disposal. Dump her at Blackie's. With all dem others.

RAY: Others? You been lookin' in the boxes, Louis? I told ya not to go lookin' in the fuckin' boxes.

LOUIS: *Non. Non,* Ray. I close my eye. I remember. You say don't look.

RAY: Blackie. He only billed me fer four last night.

LOUIS: No. No. You got dat all wrong. Four, five, three. Who is counting? I just do what you order.

RAY: This better not be one of yer fuckin' schemes, boy.

LOUIS: I don't know what you say, boss. I don't got no scheme.

RAY: That ain't what Blackie says.

LOUIS: Blackie? Bastard!

RAY: You think I'm stupid, Louis? You think I'm a fuckin' idiot?

LOUIS: Okay. So, we do a few ting on da side. Big deal. I still work for you.

RAY: *(grabbing Louis' lapel)* Listen asshole. I got a lot riding on you. Don't fuck with me, boy. Ya understand?

LOUIS: *Oui. Je comprends.* I do your job. Don't worry. She dead. *Pas de problème.* Dat fucking broad. I tell you. She dead!

RAY: Dead, huh?

LOUIS: Like dat burning toast.

RAY: Well, if she ain't, she better be. Ya follow?

LOUIS: *(pauses, then falls for trap) Oui.* Don't worry. Me. Louis Bob Lemaire. I take care of it.

RAY: Take care of what?

LOUIS: You know. Dat ting.

RAY: Yeah. Well if she's dead, Louis, just what the fuck do you have to take care of?

LOUIS: I… I don't know about nothing! You are fucking me up! Andy! *Cinquante!*

RAY: You lyin' piece of shit. You didn't do the fuckin' job. Killin' one of yer own. That was gonna be the cherry on the cake. You backstabbin' son of a bitch. You don't think the Foundation judges are readin' the papers this mornin'? Lookin' at the homeless body count?

LOUIS: Body count? But we enter for da Microbe project. *Non*?

RAY: Microbe project? Jesus. Look at the war news. It's already been field tested. No. Yer the fuckin' project.

LOUIS: *Quoi?* I don't understand nothing.

RAY: Jesus Christ. It's you. You fuckin' moron. You're the goddamn project.

LOUIS: *Quoi?* Me? I am the project?

RAY: Social robotics, you fat fuck. Any job's a good job... *(bitterly)* Hell, you're the New Workin' Man.

LOUIS: *Non.* I am Louis Bob Lemaire.

RAY: No, you ain't. You're whatever I damn well want. Yeah. That's right. A pair of arms. A nail. A piece of fucking tubing. You're fuck all with no questions asked.

LOUIS: Bastard.

RAY: Figure it out. It ain't hard. Like today. Ha. Today you're a ticket... *(bitterly chuckling)* My ticket outta here... My last, best goddamned hope... *(lunging)* And you fucked me in the ass!

LOUIS: *(pushing off, backing away)* Get off your hand. Me. I am...I am... *(doesn't know; stumbling out of bar)* Cunt! You fucking rich. *Trou d'cul!*

RAY: I want her done! Ya hear me! I want her fucking done!

SCENE 7

We hear powerful crowd noises in the distance. Chanting. Singing. Shouting. Sally is in her alley, crouched over, gently tending to what seems to be a pile of rags; crying.

SALLY: Ah, Gene. What ya go doin' somethin' like that for? *(dabbing with cloth)* Here. Lemme get yer head, there... *(cloth comes away bloody)* See. It don't look so bad... Ah, Jesus... Here. Drink this... Fuuuck. It's comin' out the back... I coulda got away, Gene... Ya didn't have to... Bastards. Fucking bastards... Won't even send no ambulance... *(continuing to dab body; rags are soaked in blood)*... You shoulda seen yerself, bro... Leadin' the charge... Here lemme get that... Ah, Jesus, Gene...wasn't fuckin' worth it... Why'd ya go and do it?

LOUIS: *(coming out of a dark corner, very drunk)* Was he on his feet?

SALLY: We gotta get an ambulance.

LOUIS: Suppose to make all da difference, eh?

SALLY: *(near tears)* Ah fuck, man. Cops hurt him bad.

LOUIS: He always want to die on dose feet.

SALLY: It shoulda been me. But he put himself in the way.

LOUIS: Never put yourself in da way.

SALLY: Oh, Jesus. Just lookit. He needs a doctor bad.

LOUIS: *(looking at body, wincing)* Oooooohh… Fuuuuck.

SALLY: I'm beggin' ya, man.

LOUIS: *(plops down by Gene, looks again)* S'too late. No can do… *(sticks hand into pile of rags)* See dis? Gene brain.

SALLY: *(cries out)* Ahhh. Noooo. They killed ya, Gene. They fuckin' killed ya.

LOUIS: Hero of da Revolution.

SALLY: You piece of shit.

LOUIS: *Oui.* Everybody. Dey say dat.

SALLY: *(getting angry)* That's Gene lyin' there. He was one of us!

LOUIS: Us? *Non.* Dere ain't no us, Sally.

SALLY: There's a fuckin' us.

LOUIS: Bullshit!

SALLY: Maybe we ain't figured it all out yet. Who ta follow and how far ta go. But there's an us. Pullin' wire and pushin' paper. Makin' phone calls and fibreglass…and dyin' in alleyways. Don't you worry, buster. There's an us, all right.

LOUIS: So…What? …You were fucking dat guy?

SALLY: What?

LOUIS: *(with brain tissue on his fingers)* Guess he had more brain den me.

SALLY: *(attacks Louis)* You son of a bitch. I'll kill ya. I'll fuckin' kill ya… *(pushed down, anger into tears)* You son of a fucking bitch…

LOUIS: You want to kill me… I got to kill you… Cop already kill him… *Crisse, eh?* Everybody busy.

We hear upsurge of crowd noise, a pause.

SALLY: He used to tell me not to ride ya so hard. Said we was gonna need ya.

LOUIS: You say horseshit!

SALLY: Yeah?

LOUIS: Only one need me… *(scoffs)* Mr. Ray Fucking Bidwell. S'why I am here. Your ass to save his.

SALLY: You ain't gonna do it.

LOUIS: I do everything else.

SALLY: Gene said ya wouldn't.

LOUIS: Gene. He say bullshit. *Oui.* A man. He can do things.

SALLY: Yeah. What kinda things, Louis?

LOUIS: Thing… All kinda thing… Like dem two little guy. All dem year ago. Dey throw dem rock at us. Remember?

SALLY: What little guys?

LOUIS: When we go walking to work. At Dominion.

SALLY: Bernie's kids? Walt and Bill? What? You cracked? That was ten years ago.

LOUIS: *Oui. C'est ca.* Walt and Bill.

SALLY: What d'ya do, Louis?

LOUIS: Every fucking thing!

SALLY: Louis?

LOUIS: *(disgusted with himself)* Dey was in da boxes, Sally. Dat's what I done… Dey was in da fucking boxes. Ray. He say not to look inside… *(breaking down)* But me? I look. *Pourquoi?* Don't know. But I look inside. And it was dem. Da twin… Dey was just looking for work. So, I took dem over to da germ place. *C'est tout. C'est tout…* I didn't know about dose experiment. And the big furnace. I swear. I did not know.

Stupid. Stupid. Stupid...Just drop dem boy dere. No question asked. And den dey was in da boxes...looking up at me...dead and all dry up. All yellow...wit dese eye...dese big fuckin' eye...

SALLY: The fuckin' twins, Louis?

LOUIS: *(crying)* Sally...Sally...I do every fucking thing.

SALLY: *(stunned)* Fuuuck, man.

LOUIS: Oh, *Crisse.* Please. You help me.

SALLY: Yeah, well take a fuckin' number.

LOUIS: So, you take Number One too, huh? Like everybody.

SALLY: *(long pause, looks at Gene as Louis moans pathetically)* Ya still got yer truck?

LOUIS: ...*Oui.* I got it.

SALLY: I ain't leavin' him here. Like he was nothin'.

LOUIS: Yeah. You would leave me.

SALLY: Listen, Louis. He's gonna get a proper seein' to. All right? I'm askin' *you* ta help me.

SCENE 8

RAY: *(in white bathrobe, on cell phone, pacing, under pressure. We hear his children fighting, a loud TV upstairs)* Yeah. Yeah. Yeah... Ta hell with the pre-nup! Listen. She doesn't get the kids. She doesn't get the house. She doesn't get the plant! She don't get nothin'! Nobody runs out on Ray Bidwell. Ya got that! ...No. No. Wait. Don't tell her that. Jesus. Just tell her I love her. All right?... *(hangs up, still pacing while dialing)* Yer killin' me, Georgia. Yer fuckin' killin' me... *(while connecting with new call, he yells upstairs)* Hey! I'm tellin' you guys for the last time. Get to goddamn bed!... *(TV sounds go off, kids go silent)* Little pricks... *(he connects with next call)* ...Yeah. Award Committee? Bidwell here... Yeah. Yeah. Listen. Ya got it all wrong. He musta left her behind a dumpster or somethin'. It's just some kinda oversight... My man...he's like money in the bank... Listen. Give it a coupla days. That's all I'm askin'. Her body'll turn up.

Hey. What could go wrong? It's Social Robotics, man...hello?... hello?... Fuck... Fuck. Fuck. Fuck... *(cell phone rings)* Yeah. What is it?

SALLY: Oooo, Frederick. You sound so forceful.

RAY: *(frazzled)* Georg—? ...Brandy. Geez. What the fuck. Man, it's fuckin' time. Isn't it?

SALLY: And then some. Was startin' to think you found somebody else.

RAY: *(looking at watch)* No. No. Just had a few things to take care of. You know. You fuckin' know.

SALLY: Pressures, right?

RAY: Like a fuckin' vise.

SALLY: Well, the doctor is in, big boy. And she's got a free prescription. So why don't you just lay back. That's it. See if ol' Brandy's got what ya really need.

RAY: *(getting into his La-Z-Boy, preparing syringe)* Don't get me wrong, Brandy. I've really been looking forward to this. Just seems lately I haven't had any time to spend on my fuckin' self.

SALLY: You need a little *you* time.

RAY: Yeah. That's right. Me time.

SALLY: Well, Brandy's here now, baby. Just lay back. Take a deep breath. That's it. Just relax.

Ray sighs heavily.

Got the bag?

RAY: *(putting it on)* Yeah. I got it.

SALLY: I want ya to roll it down now. Nice and easy. That's it. Doesn't it feel smooth, Frederick? And tight. Just lay back, now. I got a little story for you, lover. A nice, sad little story.

RAY: We're close, Brandy. I just know it.

SALLY: Got the needle in?

RAY: *(jams needle in leg)* You don't know how long I've been waitin' for this. All right. What ya got, babe?

SALLY: You listen up good, Frederick. I wanna tell you about somethin' that shoulda happened a long time ago. About somethin' that maybe is about to come.

RAY: Okay, baby. Shit's kickin' in. Lay it out. I wanna come too. Lay it out… *(bag is now rolled down over mouth, Ray constantly gasping, slowly reacts to story with increasingly ecstatic mournful grunts and groans)*

SALLY: Tools were down for almost a week and the cops were crawlin' thick as flies before the fat asses from the union came down to squeeze out a deal. Grinnin', like they always do. But this time we wouldn't let 'em in. Didn't want 'em to get their fucking suits all dirty. That got 'em goin'. Said if we didn't come out, there was nothin' they could do. It'd be the cops' turn. Said they had fuckin' dogs. Ol' Bernie, why he just winds up with a wrench and clocks one of 'em right in the mouth. Fuckin' Bernie. That ended the conflab. Ya see, the way we saw it. We was strong. It was our plant, now… *(Ray moaning)* Well, that got things hoppin'. Cops start to shoot gas through the windas, but we're usin' the fibre fans to blow the shit back. It's touch and go now, man. The owner's jumpin' up and down and yellin' at the cops to do somethin', when outta the night ya see these strings of headlights comin' from every which way… And it's just folks. Cars and cars full of folks. With the Equalizers leadin' the way… *(by this time Ray is very excited)* …Hundreds first. Then thousands. They're drivin' round the blockades, fillin' up the parkin' lot. Throwin' up food through the windas. Hell, there's even a coupla fire trucks, fer Christ's sake, squirtin' the cops with their hoses. That got them pigs runnin'. Left the owner sorta just standin' there… *(Ray is very excited, suffocating, calling out "Brandy… Yeah… Daad?)* …All by himself… With everybody all around. All quiet. Just lookin' at him. He was cryin' now and screamin' and tryin to punch his way through the crowd. Callin' out to somebody. Somebody named Ray… *(Ray, gasping, calls out "Daddy!")* …But nobody came. He was tryin' to open the factory gates. Callin' out "Ray! Ray!"…But there weren't no Ray. Only the people. And they wouldn't let him… *(Brandy is now Sally in full form, Ray falls silent. He has suffocated)* Ya hear me, Ray? The people wouldn't let him. The people wouldn't let him!… *(throws cell phone away)* That's how it shoulda fuckin' been. That's how it's gotta fuckin' be…

Lights down on Sally. We hear two children giggling, footsteps on stairs, a creaky door opens. Lights abruptly down on Ray's corpse. We hear one of the twin's voices: "Dad?..." (then, in terror) "DADDY!"

SCENE 9

It is a few days later. The TV comes on, showing a mass crowd rally. Then the Drink Molson's-Labatt's sign comes on. The stage is slowly illuminated. We hear the instrumental opening of a song.

SALLY: *(aggressively singing a Nancy Sinatra karaoke)* These boots are made for walkin'. And that's just what I'll do. One of these days these boots are gonna walk all over you. I said, these boots are made for walkin'. And that's just what I'll do. One of these days these boots are gonna walk all over you—

A split stage effect begins.

LOUIS: *(outside, pacing in front of phone booth, getting up courage, talking to himself)* —*Âllo*, dis dem Equalizer? *Non. Non.* Not like dat. *Âllo*? Dis Louis Lemaire... *Non. Non.* No name... *Âllo*? Put me through to dat news guy... Yeah. Dat it. Just straight out... Let me talk to dat news guy wit da Equalizer... *Âllo*, let me talk to dat news guy—

SALLY: *(at microphone; loud laughter from crowd, then)*—Hey, Tommy. What's the B. stand for? Yeah. In Lester B. Pearson. That's just it. Nobody fuckin' knows... So. You guys seen the papers today. No, no. Not the skin page. The Ray thing. Jesus. I'm tellin' ya. What a crime. Phone bill alone woulda killed me... Bastard... Okay. So it's great to be back... *(holding up stump)* Well, most of me, anyway... Got a tip for ya. Say No ta Drugs. Believe me... Listen. I wanna get serious fer a minute. Got somethin' I wanna sing tonight. For Gene and maybe some of youse too... Kenny. Number 12—

LOUIS: *(now in phone booth)* —No. I tell you... No. No name... No. No... Den I don't... *Crisse*, I thought you Equalizer... Me. I don't got to do dis... Listen, you don't need to know who the fuck I am. *Comprennez!* ...No. Listen! I will hang up... Okay. Dat better. Meet me out in da back... *Oui*, da

Microbe place... Midnight... And bring a camera. I want to show something—

SALLY: *(singing from "Working Class Hero")*—As soon as you're born, they make ya feel small. By givin' you no time instead of it all. Till the pain is so big you feel nothin' at all—

LOUIS: *(walking, on cell phone)*—*Âllo.* Black Jack? Listen, *mon vieux.* I ask you to leave da door open tonight... To da incinerator... Eh? Who has died and made me...Ray, *idiot.* Ray has fucking died... *Oui. Oui.* Don't worry. For you, da same commission. Only tonight. You leave da door open. Got dat? ...And by da way, thanks for dat special job. Got ol' Gene back dis morning... *(hangs up)* Asshole!—

SALLY: —Keep you doped with religion and sex and TV. And you think you're so clever and classless and free. But we're still fuckin' peasants as far as I can see—

LOUIS: *(enters Canada House, sits down, takes shoebox out of booster coat)* Andy, *Cinquante... Oui. Cinquante* for everybody!

SALLY: *(moves towards Louis; opens box and sifts a handful of ashes)*—A workin' class hero is somethin' to be. A workin' class hero is somethin' to be. A workin' class hero is somethin' to be...

SCENE 10

Sally is sitting on a bench in a park; a ghetto blaster next to her; she pulls out a pill bottle, empties it on the ground, throws it away. She's smiling, talking to a shoebox on her lap. As Sally talks to shoebox, Louis quietly enters; listening.

SALLY: Ah, Gene. It was one of the nicest things ya ever did. My ma, she never got over it. There she was all weak and bent over by the cancer. Could hardly move, let alone drag that fuckin' oxygen tank they give her. Hard part, though, was when folks kinda just stopped talkin' to her when she stopped in for a drink. Like she was already dead. That really ate her up. Well, there you was, sittin' way down at the end of the aisle when she comes in the door. She's movin' like a fuckin' snail on Percodans. Draggin' that fuckin' contraption. Folks are tryin' not to notice, but goddamn, she's coverin' only about five yards by the minute. Blue Jays got a whole half innin' in the books before she pulls alongside yer table. And with everybody shiftin' in their seats and lookin' in their drinks, there you go yellin' out, "No runnin', Annie..." *(Louis starts laughing; so does Sally, hysterically)* No runnin', Annie... She's movin' like a fuckin' glacier. And old Gene yells out... *(more laughter).*

LOUIS: *(still laughing)* Da funniest thing dat I ever saw.

SALLY: *(still laughing)* Broke up the whole fuckin' bar.

LOUIS: *(calming down, still smiling)* Ah, *Crisse.* Dat day. I will never forget.

SALLY: Ol' Ma laughed about it till the day she died... *(smiling)* Think that's what killed her.

LOUIS: Ah, Sally...

SALLY: *(pause)* He liked comin' ta this end of the park.

LOUIS: Less dog shit.

SALLY: More quiet too... *(long pause)* Hey. Lookit. Butterflies!

LOUIS: *(takes a look, then nods with a new confidence)* Da Monarch.

SALLY: *(after another pause)* I seen the papers this mornin'.

LOUIS: I show dat guy da whole operation.

SALLY: Yeah. That ya did, Louis.

LOUIS: From soup to da nut.

SALLY: Yeah. We turned over a rock today... *(looks at shoebox)* The three of us.

LOUIS: Think da people. Dey will take some notice?

SALLY: Got to. Human need, not fat ass greed. A job and a place ta live. Don't bomb folks. It ain't rocket science.

LOUIS: Maybe. But dose big shot. Dey will not just give it up.

SALLY: Then we'll fuckin' take it.

LOUIS: Yeah? How come you so sure?

SALLY: *(pause)* 'Cause I know what folks can be, Louis. I know what folks can be…

Sally hands Louis the shoebox, turns on boombox. We hear an uplifting Mozart piece—Symphony No. 41 "Jupiter" Finale, 4th Movement.

C'mon. Let's send him out proper…

Sally slowly takes a handful of ashes and throws them into the air; as music builds she begins to throw ashes without a care. Louis joins in. Music continues. Actor playing Ray enters. All three take their bows.

The End.

STARTER HOME

KATHERINE KOLLER

Photo: Hannah Wensel

KATHERINE KOLLER

ABOUT THE PLAYWRIGHT

Katherine Koller lives in Edmonton, Alberta, and writes for radio, stage and screen. Her first plays were produced at the Edmonton Fringe Festival. Her plays for CBC radio include *Cowboy Boots and a Corsage* and *Magpie*. Jagged Edge Lunchbox Theatre in Edmonton produced three of her one-act comedies: *The Early Worm Club, Starter Home*, and *Magpie*, and Winnipeg's FemFest produced *Cowboy Boots and a Corsage* in 2003 and *Abby's Place* in 2006. *Coal Valley: the Making of a Miner* was commissioned and produced in Drumheller in 2005. *Perdu* and *Intimacy, Inc.*, were produced at Walterdale Playhouse in Edmonton and Alumnae Theatre in Toronto, respectively, in 2007. Katherine was awarded a self-directed writing residency and a production residency at The Banff Centre on *The Seed Savers*, a drama about the heroism of farming, forgiving and falling in love, which received its first public reading in Saskatoon. Katherine is currently working on a new play called *Lily of the Prairie*, about the power of one in cataclysmic times, in Workshop West Theatre's Playwrights' Unit.

PRODUCTION HISTORY

Starter Home was first produced by Jagged Edge Lunchbox Theatre in Edmonton, Alberta from March 6-31, 2001. It was directed by Alison Wells, and stage managed by Annabel Brophy, with set design by Mary Ann Forbes, and lighting design by Wes Gillis. Amy DeFelice was the assistant director. The cast was Lisa Newman as Vanessa, Ian Horobin as Wayne, and Wendi Pope as Betty-Lynn.

Starter Home was developed with the help of Alberta Playwrights' Network and the participation of Jessamyn Corness, Ian Horobin, Lisa Newman, Wendi Pope and Alison Wells.

Starter Home was published as a chapbook by the Playwrights Guild of Canada in 2001.

For production rights, contact Signature Editions, or the author at at kkoller@donovans.ca.

CHARACTERS

Vanessa — A dance instructor, early thirties.

Wayne — A computer programmer, early thirties.

Betty-Lynn — A landlady, fifties.

SETTING

The backyard of a cozy, well-kept bungalow in a friendly neighbourhood in a medium-sized city.

TIME

The present. It's a weekday evening, about 7 p.m., on a warm July day.

SET

There is a door to the house, and a window from the kitchen overlooking the patio, which is generously adorned with pots of flowers. There is ivy climbing the wall of the house, with a small bench. There is the suggestion of a fountain nearby. A path leads through the audience to the garage. A gate or an arbour leads to the street. On the patio, in the shade of a large tree, is a small table and two small chairs.

SCENE 1: THE GARDEN

Music: "Blue Heaven" by Dean Martin.

Vanessa and Wayne emerge from the house. They take time to look around, and then kiss each other, happily. Betty-Lynn observes from her kitchen window, victorious. She holds up a freshly baked pie.

VANESSA: This must be a dream.

WAYNE: I know. There's nothing to fix.

VANESSA: It's so clean!

WAYNE: It feels so big!

VANESSA: It smells so good in there. Like apple pie.

WAYNE: That could be a real estate trick.

Betty-Lynn sets a pie to cool on the windowsill.

VANESSA: I don't think so.

WAYNE: It's like the botanical gardens out here. With a pond, even.

VANESSA: There's so much care given. Every detail, inside and out.

WAYNE: How do you like the bedroom?

VANESSA: I love it. All that eyelet—and the cut flowers?

WAYNE: It's just like you.

VANESSA: It's not too old-fashioned for you? I mean, all in white?

WAYNE: Not as long as it's got you in it.

VANESSA: There's a little room that could be your study.

WAYNE: I don't think I'll be doing office work at home.

VANESSA: Oh? Then it could just be a . . . spare room.

WAYNE: We could put my computer in it. And your sewing machine. But we would probably be doing other things, you know, together.

VANESSA: At least we wouldn't have to strip wallpaper. And the paint looks like it's just been done.

WAYNE: The colours are okay.

VANESSA: There's nothing that would have to go right away.

WAYNE: And the furniture is all in place. That's a bonus.

VANESSA: Simple, nothing fancy. It goes with the few things I have.

WAYNE: The location is great.

VANESSA: I could walk to work.

WAYNE: I could bike.

VANESSA: And we're so close to the market. We could buy everything fresh on Saturdays, early, before I go to work.

WAYNE: I could take you to work, and then put away the groceries. And spend the day working in the yard or washing the car.

VANESSA: And when I got home, I'd cook for you.

WAYNE: And I'd cook for you.

VANESSA: Sundays, we could go for walks. Wave at the neighbours.

Vanessa waves. Betty-Lynn waves back.

Oh!

The fantasy is broken. Wayne turns Vanessa away from Betty-Lynn.

WAYNE: She's not an ordinary landlady.

VANESSA: What is she doing?

WAYNE: You told her we hadn't eaten yet.

VANESSA: I thought she was just making tea.

WAYNE: She's going to bring out that pie.

VANESSA: It's very sweet of her. Maybe just a tiny piece.

WAYNE: Aren't we going out for dinner? That new Thai place?

VANESSA: I know we said we would.

WAYNE: She's tempting you.

VANESSA: It's not exactly the apple in the Garden of Eden.

WAYNE: You told me: deep fried at any point in its history; crusts of any thickness; and dairy fats one percent and over are all out.

VANESSA: Wayne. This is what we want. Isn't it? Even if we have to eat a piece of pie? A home of our own.

WAYNE: I can hardly wait. No more getting up in the middle of the night to get home and ready for work.

VANESSA: Waking up slowly every morning together. That's what I want.

WAYNE: What if we could move in tonight? Think of that big white bed.

VANESSA: Then it really would be a dream.

SCENE 2: THE LANDLADY

Betty-Lynn brings out a tray of drinks and a plate of appetizers.

BETTY-LYNN: Here we are. So, how do you like the garden?

VANESSA: You've put a lot of work into this.

BETTY-LYNN: Oh! Not work! Fun! Fresh air! Exercise! It's what keeps me ticking! Me and my secret garden.

WAYNE: Why secret?

BETTY-LYNN: Well, nobody has seen it before you. Not a soul.

VANESSA: You mean you have never rented out this property before?

BETTY-LYNN: You would be my first victims! If you decide to take it.

WAYNE: No wonder it's so well kept.

VANESSA: So, why are you moving out?

BETTY-LYNN: Oh, I've lived in my present home now for many years. But this was my original home, I mean when I was first married. My starter home.

WAYNE: And you've kept it up all that time? Just so you could garden?

BETTY-LYNN: Well, yes. I thought my daughter or my son would want this home to start their own families. But my daughter, she is away at university and probably won't stop until she has five degrees and the university finally hires her; and my son, well, he is just not the settling down kind. Like you. Now, tell me. When is the wedding?

WAYNE: What?

VANESSA: Uh, we haven't decided about that yet.

BETTY-LYNN: Well, count me in to help out. I love weddings! The decorations, the music, the clothes! I love to cook, and I have this great low fat recipe for wedding cake.

WAYNE: Uh, we've both just started new jobs, and it will be at least a year until we can take time off.

BETTY-LYNN: The more time you have to prepare, the better. My wedding was a rushed affair. Edwin, my husband, could not wait. I didn't even have time to make a dress. I had to wear my suit. But if I did it all again, I'd go for the works. You young people today, it's easier. You can do things out of order, like move in together before you make the cake. Now, have a little something to eat.

VANESSA: These look delicious.

BETTY-LYNN: I thought you looked like a fresh fruit and vegetable girl.

VANESSA: I am.

BETTY-LYNN: I bet you are a dancer.

VANESSA: Yes! I'm a dance instructor. At the ballet school a few streets over?

BETTY-LYNN: I know.

VANESSA: You do?

BETTY-LYNN: I've seen you and Wayne coming out of the school, many times. And I think I may have a teeny tiny bit to do with you being together today. I mean, every time I saw you I'd say to myself, now that is a fine looking couple, I hope they stick together, and I sort of willed it, you know, that you would fall in love and then I thought, what could I do to help this lovely young couple? So I decided to rent my house.

WAYNE: Why do you go to the dance school?

BETTY-LYNN: My daughter Stacey went there! I bought her all the little things, you know, and I made her this sweet little bag, yes I did, but she only lasted two weeks. She didn't like her teacher. Too strict.

Stacey was always very shy. She would rather read, she said. That girl had her nose in a book all the time. I thought ballet would be perfect for her, to draw her out, you know?

WAYNE: But that must have been twenty years ago!

BETTY-LYNN: Yes. And now, Vanessa is the teacher there! I wish Stacey had you for a teacher. You could have changed her whole life.

VANESSA: Oh, I'm afraid I am very strict, too. Dance is a very disciplined art.

BETTY-LYNN: Stacey has discipline. She can read and study for hours at a time. She grew up speaking a whole different language. What does a girl need all that education for?

WAYNE: It sounds like Stacey is a born scholar.

BETTY-LYNN: Not you, though. I can tell. You're so down-to-earth. Reasonable. Honest.

WAYNE: I work in a law office.

BETTY-LYNN: When I saw you I knew you were going to rescue me. I'm very much in need of a lawyer right now.

WAYNE: I could recommend some. I'm actually the office manager. I handle all the machines, computers, maintenance, personnel, special events, that kind of thing.

BETTY-LYNN: That sounds like a good variety of jobs in one. I'll bet you're very handy.

WAYNE: I like fixing things, yes. I grew up on a farm. It's one of the reasons we wanted to rent a house instead of moving into one of our apartments. I like working in the yard. And I know how to look after a building.

BETTY-LYNN: Oh! What a find. Keep this man, Vanessa. I've always had to do all the repairs myself. My husband was never really involved in the house. He rarely even came out here. He's a front door kind of man. I once had a neighbour across the street who was the wife of a famous European scientist. They were only here a year before he was whisked away by an American university, but she told me that instead of a husband who could win the Nobel Prize, she'd rather have one who could fix the doorknob!

WAYNE: So . . . if there are any minor repairs to do around here, I could take care of them. But I don't see any. You've kept the place in mint condition!

BETTY-LYNN: A house, a home, is very important to me. I have loved this house and taken care of it because I knew that some day, it would go to some very fine young people. And I think I've found them.

VANESSA: You haven't had any other inquiries?

BETTY-LYNN: You are the only ones I want.

WAYNE: I'd just like to know why you are renting the house now, after all this time?

BETTY-LYNN: I don't like to say this in front of such innocents, as you are, soon to be married, but I'm sorry to say, Edwin is leaving me for a young Asian girl.

VANESSA: Oh, Betty-Lynn, I'm sorry.

BETTY-LYNN: It's very hard, because I was so happy here, and this house is my living memory album, but now it's time for me to let go. I updated all the furniture, and changed all the curtains and towels. I've tried to make it a blank book again, for you, so you can fill it up with your own memories.

VANESSA: Wow. Wayne, let's take it.

WAYNE: Okay!

VANESSA: We would be honoured to rent your house.

BETTY-LYNN: Oh! You are just what I wanted. So polite, so appreciative, so earnest. I am feeling a little overwhelmed.

WAYNE: Shall we draw up an agreement?

BETTY-LYNN: Oh! Yes. I have one. From the landlord and tenant board? I left it in my car. I'll be right back.

Betty-Lynn takes out the tray through the kitchen door. She is seen from the kitchen window briefly, again triumphant.

SCENE 3: THE AGREEMENT

VANESSA: Wayne?

WAYNE: Yes?

VANESSA: Are we really getting married in a year?

WAYNE: I don't know. We hadn't really gotten that far.

VANESSA: I know. But Wayne. I think we got a little farther just now.

WAYNE: What do you mean?

VANESSA: All of a sudden we're getting. . . organized. Our relationship is moving to a whole new plane.

WAYNE: Because she was watching us? Like some sick stalker?

VANESSA: She's going to make our wedding cake!

WAYNE: Forget it. After today, we'll probably never see her again. I can do anything that needs repairing, and the way this place is, we'll never have to call her, except for an act of God like a tornado or a flood. We'll postdate the rental cheques and that will be it.

VANESSA: How long are we going to rent for?

WAYNE: I was thinking six months to start.

VANESSA: Why only six months?

WAYNE: To make sure we like the place. I think we will, though.

VANESSA: Let's say a year.

WAYNE: Okay, a year.

VANESSA: It is like getting married.

WAYNE: For a year, anyway.

VANESSA: With the option to renew our contract.

WAYNE: Right.

VANESSA: With the option to make our wedding cake.

WAYNE: Vanessa!

VANESSA: Betty-Lynn seems kind of needy right now. I mean, I don't want her dropping in on us with her baby pictures, do you?

WAYNE: I've met this kind of lady before, at my aunt's in Vegreville. She just needs something to do.

VANESSA: What is she going to do without this house, then?

WAYNE: She'll have lots to do with her divorce. There's her other house. The money. Her kids. Don't worry. I've seen these domestic women come in the office bringing cookies in a tin and, by the time they leave, they're wearing full body armour, ready for mortal combat.

VANESSA: Then you don't think she's going to plan our wedding?

WAYNE: Oh, no.

VANESSA: No to the wedding or to her?

WAYNE: To her! Vanessa, we don't have to decide anything right now. Just: is this our house?

VANESSA: Let's go back to the six months.

WAYNE: Why?

VANESSA: I guess in six months, I'd like to know if we are getting married. Especially if I have a prototype of my wedding cake in the freezer.

WAYNE: Vanessa, what is this?

VANESSA: I thought it would just happen naturally. We're in love, we want to live together, and eventually we'll want to get married. Make it forever.

WAYNE: That's what I thought, too. Step by step. We don't want to rush. That's what Edwin and Betty-Lynn did, and look what happened to them! Let's give ourselves some time. We'll sign for a year, and make sure we at least talk in six months. I'm sure we will. It will happen naturally, like you say. Organically. We'll grow into a feeling, and then we'll talk about it.

VANESSA: If we don't talk about it in six months, we break the lease.

WAYNE: I'll mark my calendar.

Wayne doesn't, but Vanessa gets out her daytimer and circles the date.

VANESSA: I am so glad we discussed this.

WAYNE: It would have happened sooner or later.

VANESSA: Sooner is better for me. Thanks to Betty-Lynn.

SCENE 4: THE FINE PRINT

Betty-Lynn brings in the rental agreement and some pens.

BETTY-LYNN: Sorry! The neighbours called me over for a chat. They want you to come to the block party next weekend. And they want my Potato Salad for a Crowd again. Fun! I can introduce you to all the folks here. Now. So, did I mention the rent?

VANESSA: Yes. On your notice.

BETTY-LYNN: Well, how about we knock it down fifty dollars, just because I like you so much?

WAYNE: Wow. Okay.

Betty-Lynn strikes out some numbers and rewrites them.

BETTY-LYNN: And you are renting for how long?

VANESSA: A year.

WAYNE: To start.

BETTY-LYNN: I want you to be happy here. This is where I spent my best years, with the babies, wiping those dear little noses and bums. I have pictures . . .

WAYNE: Maybe another time, Betty-Lynn. We should get this done.

BETTY-LYNN: It just brings back so many feelings, seeing the two of you just starting out. Just look at you, so affectionate. It's why I couldn't leave when Edwin put this house up for sale. I got the agent to sell the house right back to me. I used my own money.

VANESSA: You mean, Edwin doesn't know you still own the house?

BETTY-LYNN: No. He doesn't need to. He's busy with his work, feeding the multitudes. He owns the five restaurants now. That new Thai one is his latest.

WAYNE: It's supposed to be good.

BETTY-LYNN: I'm sure it is. He spends all his time with his restaurants. The five continents, I call them. He has his five that need him full-time and I only had the two and they're grown up now.

VANESSA: Does your son still live at home?

BETTY-LYNN: When he's not in jail.

VANESSA: Oh.

BETTY-LYNN: The only time I get to talk to him is when I bail him out. It's usually assault, mischief or theft under a thousand. Then I have to drive him home. It's forty minutes from downtown to my new house.

WAYNE: Maybe we should get back to this house, and the papers at hand here. Everything looks in order to me.

BETTY-LYNN: Good. Then I'll sign here and here, and you sign there and here. Neat and tidy.

WAYNE: We should initial that rent change.

BETTY-LYNN: Of course. There and there. One copy for you and one for me.

VANESSA: Great!

WAYNE: Super!

BETTY-LYNN: Now that's done, let's talk about the details.

WAYNE: What details?

BETTY-LYNN: Well, summer is closing soon, and when it gets to autumn, the leaves from all these mature trees are going to pile up. There will be apples to pick, and a garden to dig over.

WAYNE: Don't worry. My dad's a farmer, and he wanted to make sure I was another son, so I was conceived with a shovel and a rake and a hammer under the bed.

BETTY-LYNN: Nevertheless, I've taken care of this yard myself for almost thirty years, and I don't really want to leave it to anyone who doesn't know it like I do.

VANESSA: I love raking leaves.

BETTY-LYNN: So do I! Oh, I know we're going to get along fine. So, I'll come over when it's time and get the yard all tidied up. . .

WAYNE: But we can do that. That's why we wanted to rent a house. I'm at a desk all day. I need the exercise.

BETTY-LYNN: Well, you can help. I don't like to fuss, but I won't sleep unless I know it's done right. And the crabapples: I'll be here to pick them and make them up into jelly for you to last the year. And the extras can be wrapped up for little hostess gifts during the holiday season.

VANESSA: I don't use jams and jellies, actually.

WAYNE: Me, neither.

BETTY-LYNN: Oh, but you'll love mine. Now, winter, there's the snow to clear. I've got a dandy shovel I bought off the TV from that K-Tel outfit? It works just great. But you've got to get out there right after it snows. Before the mailman and the schoolkids trample it all down and pack it up. So I'll do that, because you're both at work all day, and when you get home you can just pour a glass of wine and put your feet up. Especially you, Vanessa, with your toes in pointe shoes all day.

VANESSA: Oh, it's not like that. I adore the fresh air. I'm looking forward to the snow. And we'll do it, Wayne and I. We want to.

WAYNE: The flakes will hardly touch the pavement.

BETTY-LYNN: We'll see. Now, spring. I have an excellent vegetable garden out here. I plant it every year and give the produce to the Food Bank. But now, it will be for you! Oh, just think of the vitamins it will provide! Just in case, you know, there's a little somebody on the way by then! Oh, I can hardly wait for spring!

WAYNE: Now, hold on.

BETTY-LYNN: Then there's summer. Now you two will probably want to go off on vacation somewhere, so don't worry one whit about the house. I'll take in your mail and water the plants and stock your fridge just before you get home. And I'll keep up the garden, of course, and start on the preserving. Now I can tell a modern young couple like you would appreciate homemade salsa and antipasto. Oh! I'll have to look in some up-to-date cookbooks to see what healthy things I can make for you!

VANESSA: I think you're going to way too much trouble, really.

WAYNE: How will we know what season it is if you do all the work?

BETTY-LYNN: Well, I'll haul out the seasonal door wreaths at the appropriate times. I keep them in plastic wrap in the attic of the garage.

WAYNE: But, Betty-Lynn!

BETTY-LYNN: Don't worry. I won't let those farm-fed muscles go to waste. I'll have a list for you, and we can strike it off as we go!

WAYNE: A list?

BETTY-LYNN: But you might never get around to it! Now, I can tell by the way you opened the door for Vanessa and closed it, with that little touch you gave it after, that you love cars.

WAYNE: Well, yeah. I used to work in my uncle's garage.

BETTY-LYNN: Then you better check mine.

WAYNE: I bet it's as well organized as the house. I'll take a look. You'll leave all the tools for me?

BETTY-LYNN: Oh, yes. Everything you see as is.

Wayne exits down the path to the garage.

SCENE 5: THE HOOK

VANESSA: He loves to work with his hands. He's negotiated a week off to go home and help with the harvest.

BETTY-LYNN: And will you go with him?

VANESSA: I'd like to. I haven't met all his family yet. But I'll have to be at work.

BETTY-LYNN: You know, I'd love to help your dance school make costumes. I always dreamed I'd do that some day, and look! Here's another opportunity.

VANESSA: Well, maybe you could do some pearling. The costume department is already so busy. We could use someone to do that.

BETTY-LYNN: Oh! Count me in. I just love hand sewing. I think hand sewing infuses a garment with love.

VANESSA: With all your experience, we'd be lucky to have your help.

BETTY-LYNN: And I'd have some handiwork to help fill my hollow hours.

VANESSA: I know what it is to be lonely. I had lots of years, when I was very young, really too young, when I lived on my own and all I did was train. I was away from my family, and I just grew in another direction. I never really felt a part of a unit after that. I was pulled away too young.

BETTY-LYNN: The sacrifices we make.

VANESSA: Then I was always performing, and that was fun, and exciting, but you're not very centred when you're on the road; it wears you down. I didn't want to spend the whole rest of my life with my roots in a glass with my toothbrush, so I took this job and then I met Wayne and now I know just how I want to live.

BETTY-LYNN: How did you meet?

VANESSA: He came to the dance school one day to pick up his niece, because his sister had just had another baby, and it was like the lights just went on. He asked me to go to the Dairy Queen after work, and that was the beginning!

BETTY-LYNN: I met Edwin at a restaurant. I was eating alone. I had taken myself out for a lonely birthday. I was new in town, and I didn't really know anybody, but my dear departed mother always said, "Dress up and go out, and you'll feel better," so I did, and Edwin was the manager of the restaurant, and paid me all sorts of special attention. He found out it was my birthday and bought me dessert with a candle in it and had coffee with me once the customers had gone, and soon after we got married. But he didn't want to have children until we bought our house, and he wanted to own his first restaurant before anything else. That's my only regret: it took so long to get started. I was made to have a whole bunch of children.

VANESSA: This house is just what we need.

BETTY-LYNN: And you're just what I need.

VANESSA: The extra income will be helpful. I mean, if you've been paying taxes and utilities all this time. . .

BETTY-LYNN: Oh, it's not the money. It's the satisfaction. The sense of having done right. Of offering the opportunity. What I would have liked to give my own children.

VANESSA: What about your other house? I mean, now that this one is occupied?

BETTY-LYNN: A big black dog with no name lives in my backyard at the other house. Edwin gave it to me to keep me company. It has torn up the ground and made it a wilderness that I do not care to encounter.

VANESSA: But not the house.

BETTY-LYNN: It was no longer a family by the time we moved there. Stacey was already staying at school or the library until it closed; then she moved into residence at seventeen. Tom quickly joined a gang of affluent young delinquents in the new neighbourhood. If I hung around the house until eleven in the morning, I could have the pleasure of seeing my husband eat the same identical breakfast cereal while he read the newspaper. Since it's the only meal he was home for, I had on occasion tried to make something special. But he only eats Shredded Wheat. Every morning the same mush in a bowl. Just like the dog. I can hardly wait to get rid of it all: the dog, the house and Edwin.

VANESSA: So where will you live?

BETTY-LYNN: I'm going to be a homeless person.

SCENE 6: THE BONUS

Wayne comes back up the walk.

WAYNE: Now that is a beautiful thing.

BETTY-LYNN: You like it? It comes with the house.

WAYNE: You're joking.

BETTY-LYNN: No. Go ahead. It's yours.

WAYNE: What a deal!

BETTY-LYNN: I bought it for Edwin as an anniversary present, but I never gave it to him. I just parked it in the garage. I was so angry that he wanted to move upscale, to a neighbourhood where they've never even heard of block parties. But now, look, it's perfect for a young man like you: handy, appreciative of older things. It's the same vintage as my marriage.

WAYNE: 1970.

BETTY-LYNN: You're right. It matches the house.

VANESSA: Animal, mineral or vegetable?

WAYNE: It's a Cobra Mustang. Full race. White with blue. 350.

BETTY-LYNN: Now, it hasn't been driven since I parked it. And the man who sold it to me said it's not a winter car.

WAYNE: Oh, no. That is a beach car.

VANESSA: I haven't been to the beach in ages.

WAYNE: You would look good in it, Vanessa!

BETTY-LYNN: I thought a car to fix up would keep Edwin at home.

VANESSA: But you never found out.

BETTY-LYNN: No. I decided I didn't want him at home anymore. I decided that I wanted to start back at the beginning, in our little blue and white starter home, and do it without him. And I did.

WAYNE: Wow. Edwin really blew it.

VANESSA: Oh, Wayne!

BETTY-LYNN: Yes, he did. And he doesn't even know it. Yet. He's gotten on a bus without even knowing where it's going.

Betty-Lynn folds up the contracts.

Now, Wayne, Vanessa, there's one more thing.

VANESSA: Mmm?

BETTY-LYNN: There are times, you know, when I get quite lonesome for this house.

WAYNE: Not if you take on all those jobs through the year.

BETTY-LYNN: Now, no one knows this but you: Edwin is rarely home before morning; who knows where my son is at; and Stacey has her answering machine always on; and I get, well, so that I need the comfort of these four walls. So I sleep over. In the back room. I keep a little overnight bag here, with everything I need.

WAYNE: Now, hold on.

BETTY-LYNN: Oh, please.

VANESSA: Are you serious?

BETTY-LYNN: I'd call first. I would.

VANESSA: You would still want to, with us here?

BETTY-LYNN: Oh, yes. You and the Cobra.

WAYNE: How often? Once, twice a year?

BETTY-LYNN: Once a week. Minimum.

VANESSA: No way!

WAYNE: We're out.

VANESSA: We're leaving.

WAYNE: Come on, Vanessa. Let's go.

VANESSA: Goodbye, big white bed!

WAYNE: Goodbye, Cobra!

BETTY-LYNN: Okay. Per year. Please. Maybe just a visit. A little home visit won't hurt.

VANESSA: How about when we are away? That would be okay.

BETTY-LYNN: Yes! Yes! That will work!

VANESSA: Come on, Wayne. We love this place.

WAYNE: Well, it is good to have someone checking on the property while you're gone. Insurance companies like to have someone check every day.

BETTY-LYNN: Yes! And just think of the pies and casseroles and breads I could make while you were away! And soups? The freezer would be full of good things. And the laundry. I could get all the ironing done.

VANESSA: You would?

WAYNE: Vanessa.

VANESSA: I could handle that. It would be like having a fairy godmother.

BETTY-LYNN: Yes! That's it! And Wayne, you know those nights that Vanessa is out with her school performing, you could call me over for a game of cribbage. Or backgammon. Or whatever you play.

WAYNE: I like computer games. You don't need anybody else.

BETTY-LYNN: I could surf the Internet with you! Just think of the recipes we could stir up on the 'Net!

VANESSA: I think it's sort of sweet. Like having a built-in mom.

WAYNE: I think it's sick. I've got a mom, and she's got the sense to let me live my own life. Which I thought was going to be with you.

VANESSA: It is with me! Wayne?

Betty-Lynn rubs Wayne's back.

BETTY-LYNN: And, Wayne, you wouldn't have to worry about being lonely. I'd draw you a bath. I could give your sore, tired back and shoulder muscles an aromatherapeutic massage, rub your temples...

VANESSA: Now, wait a minute!

Vanessa takes over rubbing Wayne's back.

BETTY-LYNN: And you, Vanessa, I could do wonders for your feet. Soaks, rubs, pedicures: I can do all those things.

VANESSA: But, Betty-Lynn! Wayne and I only want to be together. We don't want anyone else.

BETTY-LYNN: I know. It's so beautiful.

WAYNE: We're moving in together so we can be—alone.

BETTY-LYNN: But I am in the house. I've poured myself into it. Everywhere you look, I will be there. Silent. Sturdy. Secure. Serene.

WAYNE: We'd want you to be invisible.

VANESSA: As in not here.

BETTY-LYNN: I spent the best days of my life here.

WAYNE: But it hasn't been like that for fourteen years.

BETTY-LYNN: You are just starting that magic time. I want to share it with you!

VANESSA: Why can't you leave us alone?

BETTY-LYNN: What's wrong with wanting to catch the laughter, to feel the love reflecting off the water, to trap a little warmth for a dark rainy day?

VANESSA: Wayne, let's go.

BETTY-LYNN: Oh, please.

WAYNE: I wish we could accommodate you.

BETTY-LYNN: But you can!

VANESSA: I don't think so.

WAYNE: I hate to give up those wheels. I mean, if you wanted to spend a few days each season helping with the yard work, that's okay.

VANESSA: But we talked about doing it together! Sharing the work, because it wouldn't be work if we were together.

WAYNE: I know. But Betty-Lynn has her preferences. And it would be okay to house-sit or whatever while we are away. But that won't be for a whole year.

BETTY-LYNN: What about when one of you is out for the evening?

WAYNE: Well, when Vanessa was out, I would be in the garage, obviously. I'd be out there every spare minute.

VANESSA: What?

WAYNE: Honey, that is a dream car.

VANESSA: So now all you care about is that snake! What about me? You're just like your dad and his horses! You told me that any time there's a plan to make or a problem to be solved, he takes off to the barn. I guess the apple doesn't fall far from the tree! And Betty-Lynn, you are a temptress!

SCENE 7: THE FALL

Vanessa exits into the house, teary.

BETTY-LYNN: Oh, dear.

WAYNE: Everything was so perfect. Too perfect.

BETTY-LYNN: Maybe she didn't get enough to eat.

WAYNE: We have never had a fight before. We've hardly had an angry word.

BETTY-LYNN: Maybe I should go talk to her.

WAYNE: No! You're trying to come between us.

BETTY-LYNN: I'm not! I'm just very attached to this house.

WAYNE: If you want to rent it, you have to let go.

BETTY-LYNN: I don't know if I can. Altogether. Let go.

WAYNE: You can't tie yourself up to us. We need our own space.

BETTY-LYNN: But what will I do?

WAYNE: Get a job.

BETTY-LYNN: I used to work in a travel agency. But that was thirty years ago.

WAYNE: Well, didn't you ever want to travel, yourself?

BETTY-LYNN: Not at the time. I wanted to set down roots, like Vanessa. And since I've had the house, well, you can't be away from a house very long, or it misses you. It heaves. Walls crack. Doors stick. A house needs the aromas of human life. The rush of air as you hurry to put the water on for tea. The variation in the light when you open and close the curtains. And the comfort of an outside light at night. I've installed one of those motion sensitive lights so the house can see if it's just a cat in the yard or if it's a lurker.

WAYNE: We'll be here. You can leave it.

BETTY-LYNN: Well, maybe after a year. Once we've been through all the routines.

WAYNE: I don't think Vanessa and I would last a year if you were always butting in between us.

BETTY-LYNN: I have never butted in. I am opening up my house and my heart and my arms to you two.

WAYNE: You remind me of my aunt.

BETTY-LYNN: Oh? I do?

WAYNE: I never thought she liked me much. She used to call me Plain Wayne.

BETTY-LYNN: You are not plain, Wayne. I think your parents named you after the Great One.

WAYNE: I don't know. Anyway, my aunt was always busy, busy, organizing this, organizing that. If anything, I thought I was in her way. And then she goes and dies and leaves me all her money. A nest egg, she called it.

BETTY-LYNN: Your aunt thought you were very. . .worthy, and so do I. Vanessa is so lucky to find you.

WAYNE: I found her. I had to pick up my niece at the dance school. Except I was late. I got a little lost. New in town. Finally I got there, and there's Vanessa, body of an angel, with my niece, who's, like, six, right? And Vanessa is laughing and talking with her, staying late so the little kid wouldn't have to wait alone. She's so good with kids. That's the first thing I noticed.

BETTY-LYNN: She will make a wonderful mother.

WAYNE: I know.

BETTY-LYNN: Wayne, you know, I could be your aunt, if you still want one.

WAYNE: My aunt always thought she would travel. That's what she was saving up for.

BETTY-LYNN: There's a point in a woman's life, when you feel you are finally free to go past your own garden gate and see the world.

WAYNE: You're free. What's holding you here?

BETTY-LYNN: No one.

WAYNE: If you were my aunt, and you could go anywhere in the world, where would you go?

BETTY-LYNN: I don't know.

WAYNE: Just pretend.

BETTY-LYNN: I'd go where there was colour and perfume and heat, like Indonesia.

WAYNE: Where else? Keep going.

BETTY-LYNN: And somewhere there was happy, laughing, dancing music, like Ireland.

WAYNE: Okay. Where next?

BETTY-LYNN: A place where I could touch the marble sculptures and taste the fruits of the earth.

WAYNE: Italy!

BETTY-LYNN: Yes!

Vanessa returns, upset, and tears up the rental agreements.

VANESSA: I know why you haven't rented this house for fourteen years. You're crazy.

WAYNE: Wait!

BETTY-LYNN: You're right. I am crazy to rent it.

WAYNE: Vanessa, we were making progress here.

VANESSA: Right now I feel very far apart, Wayne. My ribbons are loose. I'm stumbling.

WAYNE: No! Vanessa. This could work. Listen.

BETTY-LYNN: I'm prepared to offer you my home, for free.

WAYNE: What?

VANESSA: Why? Why would you do that?

BETTY-LYNN: I'll do it all. Make the meals, sort the laundry, take out the garbage, clean the bathrooms, change the sheets.

WAYNE: Betty-Lynn. That's not being my aunt.

VANESSA: I'm leaving.

BETTY-LYNN: No! I want you!

VANESSA: Sorry. We are not for sale. Or for rent.

WAYNE: Now, wait, Vanessa. We can work this out.

VANESSA: I don't think we're even together anymore.

WAYNE: Come on. We want this house.

VANESSA: I want our souls to be connected. I want total communication, complete honesty.

WAYNE: You've got that. When have I not been honest?

VANESSA: You want this house because of the car!

WAYNE: I like that car. But I love you.

VANESSA: For six months, maybe. Then what? I don't know about moving in together anymore.

WAYNE: Why not?

VANESSA: Maybe we're not ready.

WAYNE: We are. We talked about this.

VANESSA: Not really. It just happened. We saw the ad up at the dance school and we drove by this place, and we thought we'd ask. Like we were in a daze.

WAYNE: We never talked about a budget, that's for sure.

VANESSA: See? We were just going to let it happen. And for how long? And what happens if we don't like the place, or each other after a while?

BETTY-LYNN: Now, listen. You are perfect for each other.

VANESSA: How would you know? You don't exactly have a great track record. This house is probably bad luck.

BETTY-LYNN: No, no! Don't say that!

WAYNE: I didn't know you could be so fickle.

VANESSA: I'm being realistic.

WAYNE: You said this was your dream house. You wanted to move in tonight. I thought I was your man.

BETTY-LYNN: You are! She loves you! You're steady, and handy, and honest and strong. Vanessa, keep this man!

WAYNE: When I met you, I thought I had found a rare orchid growing out of the cement of this city. I didn't know that particular species could be poisonous.

VANESSA: I didn't know you'd ask me to share you with another woman in some freaky ménage à trois!

WAYNE: I don't speak French, and I don't want anything to do with any of the women right here right now!

BETTY-LYNN: Oh! Now. Oh, dear. Kids. These poor walls have never heard such disruption!

VANESSA: I'm going to call a cab.

BETTY-LYNN: No! No. Vanessa. He loves you! With you, he's not plain Wayne!

VANESSA: Oh?

BETTY-LYNN: He wants you to have his children.

VANESSA: You do?

BETTY-LYNN: He's seen you with those little kids at the school. You're so patient and loving. He wants a happy family. Don't you, Wayne?

WAYNE: Some day. But it's looking farther and farther away.

BETTY-LYNN: But why? You have each other. You have this house.

WAYNE: No. You have it.

VANESSA: I'm going.

WAYNE: I'll drop you off.

BETTY-LYNN: Drop her off? It sounds like a cliff! For ever and ever. Oh, no.

Vanessa and Wayne get up to leave. They pass through the gate.

Wayne, Vanessa, I want to be your auntie! I want to give you a nest!

WAYNE: You can't.

BETTY-LYNN: What if you could buy the house?

Beat.

WAYNE: You would sell?

BETTY-LYNN: Everything. Furnished. As is. The car, too.

WAYNE: It would be ours, then, not yours. You'd have no claim, no reason to be here.

BETTY-LYNN: That's right.

VANESSA: But you want to be our auntie.

BETTY-LYNN: I just want to send my postcards here, from the places I go, so somebody knows where I am.

WAYNE: Betty-Lynn wants to travel.

BETTY-LYNN: If I don't, then the world may lose a couple who were as meant to be as Adam and Eve.

VANESSA: I don't know. We're not in the same place we were when we came here.

WAYNE: No, we're not.

BETTY-LYNN: You are! You're just at the mouth of the tunnel. It's scary, I know, but you'll do it together! And this house will protect you.

WAYNE: It's a good house, Vanessa.

VANESSA: If it was ours, then we could . . .

WAYNE: Get started.

VANESSA: Do you still want to?

WAYNE: Do you?

BETTY-LYNN: I'll even sell it to you for what I paid Edwin fourteen years ago.

WAYNE: That's very reasonable.

VANESSA: Can we?

WAYNE: I can make a down payment from the money my aunt left. We'll get a mortgage. We'll make a budget.

VANESSA: I'm not talking about the money.

WAYNE: It's what we wanted. When we saw that bed waiting for us. And the flowers.

VANESSA: And the pie. If we buy this house, then it's suddenly permanent.

WAYNE: It feels a bit fast, but it feels all right. I like speed, when I know I'm going in the right direction.

VANESSA: If you hold my hand, then I'm ready to run. Even if there are tunnels.

BETTY-LYNN: You could move in tonight.

VANESSA: Oh, could we?

Vanessa and Wayne come back through the gate.

BETTY-LYNN: We'll settle the money tomorrow. Not here. Somewhere else. Your law office. Tomorrow at ten.

WAYNE: My aunt would be glad to see her travel money going to you.

BETTY-LYNN: I'll be gone as soon as I get it. Edwin won't notice until the next time the police call him about Tom. It's about time those two had a father-son chat. And Stacey, well, I've got her e-mail. Maybe we'll have an electronic relationship.

VANESSA: Where will you go?

BETTY-LYNN: First, I'll go to Indonesia. Where they scent the waters with floating flowers.

VANESSA: You won't have time for pearling ballet costumes any more.

BETTY-LYNN: I wish.

VANESSA: And all the chores of the house: you'll leave it to us?

BETTY-LYNN: All yours.

WAYNE: One thing. You'd have to be back for the wedding.

VANESSA: Oh, Wayne!

WAYNE: I think we should set a date.

BETTY-LYNN: I'll need to know. For the cake!

VANESSA: For everything! Wayne!

Vanessa kisses Wayne.

BETTY-LYNN: Don't worry about me. I'll let myself out. I just want to take one last look around.

Betty-Lynn picks up the ripped papers and exits through the path to the garage. Wayne and Vanessa watch her go.

VANESSA: Will she survive?

WAYNE: She'll have money.

VANESSA: She'll have freedom.

WAYNE: Independence.

VANESSA: No responsibilities.

WAYNE: She could meet new people.

VANESSA: She'll see the world.

WAYNE: Do whatever she wants.

VANESSA: And leave us alone.

WAYNE: In our very own house.

VANESSA: With room to grow.

WAYNE: Season by season.

VANESSA: We'll make it our own.

WAYNE: We'll come home.

VANESSA: Home.

Music: "Our House" by Crosby Stills, Nash & Young.

Wayne and Vanessa embrace as in the beginning and exit into the house. Betty-Lynn comes out with her overnight bag, sets it down, and takes the apple pie from the window ledge and sets it on the table. Out of the bag she brings pajamas, cosmetic bag, a glass with a toothbrush. She brings out a bunch of flower petals, and twirling, tosses them above her. She repacks the bag. Then she takes the house key from her bag and holds it up. She kisses it, then pokes it in the top of the pie. She takes her bag to a bench, unseen by Vanessa and Wayne, who look out the window. Betty-Lynn takes out another key, which is on a ribbon around her neck, holds it up, kisses it, holds it tight and smiles.

The End.

THREE DOGS BARKING

FRANK BARRY

Photo: Rhonda Pelley

FRANK BARRY

ABOUT THE PLAYWRIGHT

Frank Barry was born in St. John's, Newfoundland. He began working in theatre in 1977, when he appeared as a dancing fool in a Newfoundland Mummer's play. He was a co-founder of the award-winning theatre company Sheila's Brush. He has toured extensively on the Island and the mainland and is the author of numerous original plays and screenplays. He also appeared in the national television show "Gullages." He recently won The Newfoundland and Labrador Arts and Letters Competition for his screenplay *Kimono*. He lives and works with his love Rhonda in Old St. John's and is currently working on a new play for his Wreckhouse production company.

PRODUCTION HISTORY

Three Dogs Barking was first produced at the Masonic Temple in St. John's by Wreckhouse Productions in 2003. It was subsequently produced at the LSPU Hall in St. John's by RCA Theatre Co. in 2004, and at Waterfront Theatre Festival in Halifax by Richard Donat in 2006.

Three Dogs Barking premiered at The Masonic Temple in St. John's, Newfoundland, August 20, 2003, with Barry Newhook as Jim Larkin, Frank Holden as Constable "Big Ted" Coveyduck, and Frank Barry as Dr. John StJohn. The production was directed by Frank Barry, and stage managed by Erin Whitney, with lighting design by Victor Tilley, set design by Frank Barry, and props and poster design by Rhonda Pelley.

For production rights, contact Signature Editions, or the author at FRANKBARRY@yahoo.ca.

CHARACTERS

Jim Larkin — A petty thief.

Constable "Big Ted" Coveyduck — A police officer.

Dr. John StJohn — A criminal psychiatrist.

Scene. An office at police headquarters. It is undergoing renovations. Various construction materials are lying about, including a utility light on a long cord. There is a desk and four chairs. Dr. StJohn, a police psychiatrist, enters and goes through a file. Then Constable "Big Ted" Coveyduck enters.

COVEYDUCK: Dr. StJohn's, is it?

STJOHN: *(exasperated)* StJohn. StJohn.

COVEYDUCK: Whatever. He's here and I want to tell you one thing before we start. Don't believe a word that comes out of his mouth.

STJOHN: Pathological?

COVEYDUCK: That would be your word for it. I'd just say he's a fuckin' little liar. And I'll tell you something else. He's not stupid. In his opinion, he's a real genius. In my opinion, he's a little jerk-off who thinks the world is out to get him...from the Heights.

STJOHN: I'd prefer it if you didn't swear.

COVEYDUCK: So would I. But what the fuck can you do?

STJOHN: *(reading the file)* He attended the university for two years.

COVEYDUCK: *(grunts derisively)* Arts. Two years. Just enough. And the mother was a teacher. Apparently there were "books" around the house. You know the type.

STJOHN: And the woman that he has confessed to killing was a teacher.

COVEYDUCK: *(sizing him up)* Don't even go there. He didn't kill anyone. We've proven that beyond a doubt. He's a punk that never grew up, looking for attention.

STJOHN: He does have a criminal record.

COVEYDUCK: Yeah, but look at the crimes. Bit of dope. Break and enter. Shoplifting. Vandalism. A petty thief.

STJOHN: What's this *three dogs barking* business about?

COVEYDUCK: *(sitting on side of desk)* That was his first big caper. Landed him in the Whitbourne Boys' Home. He goes out one night, robbing the clothes off clotheslines on Waterford Bridge Road. Rich people's clothes. He'd sell them, see, and make a little bit of money. You'd see these unemployed fuckers—sorry—up on the Heights, walking around in Calvin Klein. Couldn't prove anything. But this night he goes on a real "crime spree" and steals from three different houses. Underwear. Anyway, he wakes up the dogs. Fucking mastermind. Each house had its own dog. The paper got a hold of it and for fun, I guess, prints THREE DOGS BARKING—THIEF CAUGHT. It stuck. At the Home they started calling him "Three Dogs Barking." Like, you know, he was an Indian or something. The little bastard loved it. Had it embroidered on his jean jacket? A real wiener.

StJohn: You seem to know a lot about him.

Coveyduck: Oh yeah, we go way back. I'm from the south side myself. As a matter of fact, *my* old man arrested *his* old man. We could be brothers.

StJohn: What happened to his father?

Coveyduck: Ah. Drunk. Nobody knew what the mother saw in it. Like I say, she was a teacher. Or was going to become one or something. In any case, she wasn't from there. Get this. Forest Road. Had it made. Until good old Jimmy Senior knocks her up. I mean, how did they ever even meet?

StJohn: What happened to him? The father?

Coveyduck: Dead. Jimmy boy lived with his mother. Until she died. Quit the books and took off to the mainland for a while, then he comes back and lives there in the house all alone. Real little weirdo. Capable of anything. Probably queer on top of it. If it had the guts, which it don't.

StJohn: Constable? I'm sorry.

Coveyduck: Coveyduck. Don't be. You're new here. Constable Ted Coveyduck. But everyone calls me "Big Ted." That's me. Constable "Big Ted" Coveyduck. It's there in the file. Arresting officer.

StJohn: I wonder if you'd mind taking a—non-participatory role? I'd like to see if I could get him to open up.

Coveyduck: Open up? Jesus, see if you can get him to *shut* up. He's a real motormouth. I'm sick of listening to him.

STJOHN: I'd like to compare his reactions. At first...

COVEYDUCK: Okay. I'm not going to tell you how to do your job. But. This one is just a head case looking for some extra attention. My advice is—you just let me haul the kid off for obstruction and let him think all about it for a couple of months down at Her Majesty's.

STJOHN: He's not a child anymore. He must be close to thirty years of age.

COVEYDUCK: Thirty-two. But, hey, we're men. Why bother to grow up?

STJOHN: It says here that he was a suspect and that you were planning to arrest him prior to his confession.

COVEYDUCK: Yeah, well. He worked for her. Odd jobs. He was handy like his old man. You know what they're like up there. Put the arse back in a cat. He was digging her a wishing well. You know—with the little roof over it?

STJOHN: Where they found her body?

COVEYDUCK: Yeah. So he was implicated. We talked to the neighbours. Usually you can't get a word out of those fuckers. They hate cops. But even they don't like him. So apparently he was always over there. At her place. The crowd figured they had something going on. A woman like her? Not a chance. She'd just bought the place and needed a lot of work done and, like I said, he was handy.

STJOHN: He lived next door?

COVEYDUCK: Handy as in hammer and nails.

STJOHN: How did she come in contact with him?

COVEYDUCK: She put a notice up in the local store. Looking for handyman. Of course about a hundred arseholes showed up. A whole fucking tribe of handymen waving their hammers. Pick me! Pick me!

STJOHN: But she picked him.

COVEYDUCK: So?

STJOHN: Well, looking at his picture here, I'd have to say that he was the least likely looking handyman that one could imagine.

COVEYDUCK: So?

STJOHN: Well. She moves into a strange community. She doesn't know a soul. And when she advertises for a handyman, she chooses one that looks like this *(shows him picture in file)* out of the hundred that show up. A handyman with a...what do you call them?

COVEYDUCK: Mohawk.

STJOHN: Mohawk. Why?

COVEYDUCK: Have you ever been up there? Mohawk? She probably chose that over ninety-nine mullets. They're the fucking Mullet Tribe. It doesn't really matter, does it, why she hired him? It wasn't him who killed her. Besides, I'm pretty sure the hairdo was gone by the time she arrived. That's from an earlier arrest.

STJOHN: What was the nature of that particular crime?

COVEYDUCK: It should be in there.

STJOHN: *(looking through file)* Break and entry. Nothing stolen. *(reading)* He left faeces at the scene.

COVEYDUCK: Faeces.

STJOHN: Excrement.

COVEYDUCK: Oh, I know what it is. I'm the one who found it. And if you'll read farther on you'll see that our little genius used it to write his name on the wall. And on the pews. And on the confessionals.

STJOHN: A church.

COVEYDUCK: That's right. The filthy little beast.

STJOHN: That's extremely interesting.

COVEYDUCK: Before you even start. Don't. Stop. Before you start flipping through your Freud or your Jung or whichever you got yours in? None of it applies. No big magic, no little magic. We're not dealing with a complex here. We're dealing with a simplex. It's this. SHIT—ON—YOU!

STJOHN: What did he use to write it with?

COVEYDUCK: What...

STJOHN: His signature. What instrument did he use to write it? His finger? A stick?

COVEYDUCK: His finger? A stick? His dick? There's his name in capital letters. Look at the pictures.

STJOHN: *(looking at the pictures)* Three Dogs Barking. With an exclamation point?

COVEYDUCK: *(taking the pictures)* That's it.

STJOHN: I've never seen anyone sign his name with an exclamation point.

COVEYDUCK: Yeah, well I guess he was pretty proud of himself.

STJOHN: Maybe.

COVEYDUCK: No, not maybe—definitely. And I know that because I went to pick him up. I should've rubbed his nose in it. Never denied a thing. Smirking all the while. It was his shit.

STJOHN: And there was nothing missing? Nothing taken from the church?

COVEYDUCK: Not really. There was some sacramental wine taken from the sacristy, but we didn't find it. But then, altar boys will be altar boys. I was one myself. Now and then a bottle or three would go missing. *(slipping into an Irish accent)* Father didn't mention it. The price of doing business.

STJOHN: Was he an altar boy?

Coveyduck just looks at him.

You said he never denied it. Did he actually confess to it?

COVEYDUCK: No. He's a tough little customer like that. We caught him at different stuff red-handed half-a-dozen times. Never confessed. Not once. And we do have our ways.

STJOHN: Not once—except for this last time.

COVEYDUCK: Yeah, the one time we know he's definitely innocent. He's a nut case. Just process him out and let me get on with my investigation.

STJOHN: And you're absolutely sure he didn't do it?

COVEYDUCK: DNA. It was human. Leaving him out.

STJOHN: Is there something personal between the two of you?

COVEYDUCK: Fuck, yes. Day after day, month after month, year after year, I have to waste my valuable time dealing with idiots like that one sitting down there, when I could be more usefully employed—otherwise.

STJOHN: So it's just a coincidence, then, that on, let me see, nine of the fourteen arrests of one Mr. Jim Larkin, you were the arresting officer?

COVEYDUCK: What can I say? I'm just lucky? But let's not get sidetracked here, Doctor Agatha. I'm not the one you're supposed to be questioning. Whatta ya say we get Citizen Jim in here? You can see for yourself what we're dealing with and then I can get on with the humble job of finding the real person that murdered June Newhook—the old-fashioned victim.

STJOHN: I wasn't criticising…

COVEYDUCK: *(sitting in chair by desk)* There's no need. I see it all the time. You don't even believe in Evil. Environment? The problem is—you can raise two mutts in the same cage. One will crawl on his belly and lick your hand. The other will escape or go for your throat. There's no real answer. But when the mutt that escapes jumps the fence into one of your backyards and tears the throat out of Mr. Wiggles, the pet bunny, in front of the birthday party full of *professional* kids? *(points to himself)* Dog catcher.

STJOHN: So you believe in Evil?

COVEYDUCK: I believe what I see. And so would you if you'd seen it.

STJOHN: I always thought it had to be felt.

COVEYDUCK: *(sizing up the doctor)* You're married?

STJOHN: Yes, I am.

COVEYDUCK: Any children?

STJOHN: Two. A boy and a girl.

COVEYDUCK: What are their ages?

ST JOHN: The boy is four and the girl is three.

COVEYDUCK: Close together. That's good. And your wife? She's beautiful—you love her?

ST JOHN: Of course.

COVEYDUCK: Of course. Well, let me prepare you, Doctor. What I'm going to say is going to upset you. But let's play a little game. Let's say... What are your children's names?

ST JOHN: Michael and Sarah.

COVEYDUCK: Nice names. And your wife's?

ST JOHN: Julie.

COVEYDUCK: That's nice too. So let's say, we're just playing a game. Let's say you leave your work here tonight. You drive home in your...whatta ya drive?

ST JOHN: Saab.

COVEYDUCK: Also very nice. You roll your Saab up to the door of your house. I'm sure it's a lovely one. With a hedge to keep the nosies out and a garage to put the Saab in. And there's something...not quite right. What is it? Ah, the front door is open. But? It's, say—January. And you get a funny little feeling—not much, but something. Something's not right. So you go in the house and you call out. Julie! Nothing. You call again. Julie! Nothing. You're starting to feel very uneasy. Then you hear a little moan. You stop. You think that maybe you should arm yourself. But there's nothing. You go into the bedroom and there, lying on the bed, is your sweet wife Julie. Her dress is up around her head and there's blood everywhere. You can't—but you do. You pull down the dress and there's her beautiful face all bashed in like a broken pie. You hear the moan again. You want to scream, but nothing will come out. You take off for your son's room. There he lies with the Swiss Army knife you bought him stuck in his throat. You hear that little moan again. You run into your daughter's room and there she is—the apple of your eye. Sarah. Naked and covered in blood. You pick her up. She's still breathing. There's a chance. But no. With one gentle, final gasp she expires in your arms. Now the question is,

Doctor. What has come to visit? The product of bad environment? Or Evil?

STJOHN: Neither. It was last week's episode of "Law and Order."

COVEYDUCK: Fact or fiction. It's still the same question. It's the perspective. Just imagine it happening to you and everything changes. Them dead. Raped. Brutally killed. And the killer, if he's caught, and it's always a he, is playing ping pong, eating three squares a day and watching cable TV in some maximum security retreat, never mind what they show you on HBO.

STJOHN: You seem to refer to TV quite a lot. Does it help you to form all of your opinions?

COVEYDUCK: Not all—but why not? It helps to form everyone else's. Even yours. And I like to know what everyone else is thinking. And just because it was on TV doesn't mean anything. I just used it to *illustrate* a point. That, and worse than that, happens every day of the week.

STJOHN: Yes, usually between the hours of prime time. *(looking at the file)* Why did he kill her?

COVEYDUCK: He didn't kill her.

STJOHN: I mean—why does he say he killed her?

COVEYDUCK: Oh, for that you'll have to talk to him. I'm not interested. He didn't do it. Wasting my time. I just want him put somewhere where nobody has to listen to him.

STJOHN: Well, it's my job to listen to him.

COVEYDUCK: That's right. And my advice is to do just that. Don't go looking for hidden meanings. Just listen to what he says. And I am sure that you too will come to the conclusion that this one's light is better off hidden under a bushel.

STJOHN: I might like *him.*

COVEYDUCK: Impossible. Some people have a chip on their shoulder? This one's got a wooden block big enough to carve the Trojan horse out of.

STJOHN: History Channel? *(Coveyduck gives him a look)* Perhaps we should bring him in?

COVEYDUCK: I'll go get him. Prepare to be underwhelmed. *(looking around)* They haven't installed the cameras.

STJOHN: No. It seems that your Emmy will be delayed.

Coveyduck gives him a look and leaves, and then the Doctor looks at his watch and exits. Coveyduck comes back with Larkin, in handcuffs, wearing prison fatigues.

COVEYDUCK: *(pointing to a chair)* Sit. *(Jim sits in the chair)* Stay. That's sweet. *(Coveyduck stands with his back to the door regarding Jim, who seems intent on a ceiling tile)* Well, Jimmy boy. You've gone and done her this time. *(long pause)* What would your mother think? She's probably turning over in her grave. Haven't got a friend in the world, do you, Jimmy? But you're probably thinking, *(slips into mocking hillbilly accent)* "Hey—maybe me and this Dr. StJohn can become friends. He's educated like me. Those two Psych classes I took just about make him and me colleagues. He'll understand me. Erhuh. Erhuh." Well, Jimmy—there you got it right. He's going to understand perfectly—just what a total waste of human skin you really are. He's going to understand that those two Psych 101 classes were just exactly enough to fuck you up. To give you some big ideas about your intellectual abilities.

Now don't get me wrong, Jimmy boy. I'm not saying that you're stupid. You're not. A real sleeveen so far as it goes. But how far can it go? You're ancestrally indisposed. I mean. So am I. But the difference is, dear James. The difference is. I don't pretend to be other than what I am. And what I am is—the DNA with the MTA. MTA. More Than Adequate. More Than Adequate to fulfill my role. Which is, luckily enough, also my destiny. And that role, Jimmy. That destiny, Jimmy boy. Is to make sure that little fuckers like you know who you are. That's it, Jimmy. I'm just here—to make sure—that you know—*who you are.* Whoever that may be.

LARKIN: *(short pause)* It's *whom*ever.

A look of pure hatred crosses Coveyduck's face. Dr. StJohn enters.

STJOHN: So we're getting along then?

No one answers. StJohn goes to his desk and sits down. Coveyduck takes a noisy slurp on his coffee. Jimmy imitates him and it's very funny. The Doctor has to keep from laughing. A rapport is established.

COVEYDUCK: What? Funny is it? Well, excuse me, Doctor, for interrupting this little vaudeville routine. But I'm a very busy man. Things to do? Places to go? People to see?

LARKIN: Don't take any wooden grindstones. *(Coveyduck stares at him)* Coveyduck? *(snorts)* You're a walking fucking cliché. From your big fat head to your big flat feet.

COVEYDUCK: You know—you might prove to be too great a temptation.

LARKIN: Really—well, Covey Ducky, for twenty bucks I'll let ya blow me.

Coveyduck looks at StJohn with exasperated resignation. You know he'd like to plough the little bastard but he really isn't worth it.

COVEYDUCK: I think it's time we got down to brass tacks.

LARKIN: *(feigning terror)* Oh no. No! Not that. Not—BRASS TACKS! Have mercy. Who's writing your material, Coveyduck? Because *whomever* he is, my advice to you is. Haul the fucker in here. Tie him to this chair. Handcuff him. And go at him with a pair of...brass tacks. *(laughing)* Too fucking much.

STJOHN: Mr. Larkin? *(Jim just looks at him)* Mr. Larkin? This is a very serious issue that we are trying to deal with here. James. And I think you should know that it is within my power to recommend to the court that— One. You are in control of all your faculties and are liable to be sentenced to a prison term for up to two years for obstruction of justice. Or two. You are mentally impaired and should be placed in an institution to receive the professional care that would lead to your rehabilitation. However long that takes. So I advise you, James, to take these proceedings very seriously.

LARKIN: Well coo coo ca choo. Do I ever feel chastised! Listen, you stuffed dummy. I'm here because I've confessed to murder. Do you think that I give a fuck about obstruction or hurting your professional feelings? I'm guilty. DO YOU UNDERSTAND ME?

STJOHN: We know you didn't commit this crime, James. And before we're out of here, you are going to confess to not committing it or you'll be...

LARKIN: What? That's the question. I think we got off on the wrong foot. The thing is—I'm *always* trying to make people laugh. It's because I don't have a sense of humour. If I go to a movie and the audience is laughing, I just sit there wondering what the hell they're laughing at. It's troubling. *(he stands up)*

COVEYDUCK: Sit.

LARKIN: *(he sits)* It's like I have this automatic reaction to everything that other people like. It feels like—if so many people like it—there must be something wrong with it. Something stupid. Imagine if an arsehole like Coveyduck liked you. Wouldn't that mean that you were as stupid as Coveyduck? It would have to. I know Coveyduck. And he doesn't like anyone that's not as stupid as he is. You should hear him and his pals downstairs going on about hockey. A real think-tank, let me tell ya.

COVEYDUCK: It doesn't even like hockey. It's barely human.

LARKIN: It didn't say it didn't like hockey. Hockey is a game. It has no problem with games. But unlike you, Coveyduck, *I* don't go in for the towel-snapping, bum-slapping, homo-erotic shower-room antics of you and your buddies in the ever-so-latent mercantile league.

COVEYDUCK: You see? This is why. This is why. This is why you could take it by the throat and squeeze until all the juice is gone.

STJOHN: Constable...please?

LARKIN: Ah, leave him alone. That's just his way of showing affection. I bet the little wifey gets a lot of affection, doesn't she, Covey? After a hard day of keeping society safe, a hero has to unwind. And what better way than a good hard-hitting game with the boys. Followed of course by numerous cold brewskies and a couple of lap dances down at Titty Titty Bang Bang's. Then a stagger home to the little mouse. Who—let's face it—doesn't quite stack up. Nope. Pamela Anderson she is not. And what about that bad call the referee fucker made and how ya lost the game to those firemen schmucks—our moustachios are bigger than theirs—and how you're not appreciated enough down at the old depot, and what the fuck is she just standing there for, get me a beer, woman, are you swimming in molasses or what?

And smack, that's for not having supper ready to go, and slap, here's for not having Pamela Anderson's tits, oh, I want to suck them, and bang, for the two little brats that mean I can never leave you and go live with Pamela in tit heaven where she's the captain of the cheerleaders and I'm captain of the team that always wins. And get on the bed, little furry mouse, and take it like a man, oops, I mean a woman. And the next days it's sunglasses at the supermarket and Oprah can't help and only the vodka because it don't smell and you can't tell and the bruises don't hurt so much and the diet pills are working it all together and oh dear god my life is hell when he comes home in one of those hockey moods with a bone on for Pamela Anderson.

COVEYDUCK: When do you think he might start to open up?

STJOHN: The delusion that's troubling us at the moment is the one that *you* are suffering from, James. Very soon. In a not very long while at all I am not going to lose my temper. And when that *doesn't* happen, what I suspect *will* happen is that I will just become bored. And boredom is a dangerous state, James. For you, I mean. Dangerous for you. My boredom is dangerous *to* you. If that happens, we'll just put you into a police vehicle and people who have some interest in that sort of thing will take you away for further observation. And I'm sure you'll prove to be as interesting and deep a subject as you are so painfully attempting to appear. Now, once again, I suggest that you take these proceedings very seriously and explain to me why you are lying about the death of June Newhook.

LARKIN: If you'll do just one thing for me?

STJOHN: Which is?

LARKIN: Bite me. No no. I just ask that you listen to my side of the story without prejudice. Pretend that you know nothing about me and Coveyduck here hasn't filled your ears with all that bullshit. Try to forget...where did you grow up?

STJOHN: Forest Road.

LARKIN: Forest Road. No shit. There ya go, see. My mother grew up there. Downstairs—but still. We could be brothers. But if you do this for me? I will prove to you beyond the shadow of a doubt. If you will pull that silver spoon out of your ass for just a second...I will tell you all you need to know. Forever. But before I do, I wonder if it would be possible for comrade Constable Coveyduck here to loosen these handcuffs a smidgen? I'm starting to lose the circulation. *(holds up his hands)* Feel them.

StJohn goes over and feels his hands.

STJOHN: They're icy. Constable? I'll take full responsibility.

COVEYDUCK: *(while undoing the cuffs)* I'll take them off for a minute and then they're going back on. Don't fuck around.

LARKIN: Why would I fuck around? I'm the one that's trying to convince you. You stupid fucker.

Just at the moment Coveyduck undoes the cuffs, Jim knees him in the nuts and manages to grab his gun when they go down together. He immediately strikes the groaning Coveyduck across the head, rendering him semi-conscious. He cocks the gun and points it at the doctor, indicating he is to put the handcuffs on Coveyduck. StJohn does as he is bid, then backs away.

There is nothing. And I repeat. Nothing. Like a kick in the nuts. Believe me I know. And do you know how I know? Because that fucker right there. *(he goes over and stands over Coveyduck)* Taught me. *(he kicks Coveyduck)* Just like his old man taught my old man. And now. *(he kicks him again)* I'm the teacher.

STJOHN: This is...improbable...

LARKIN: Wrong. This is happening. I've been waiting for that fucking moment for years. I knew that if I kept my cool long enough, he'd drop his guard. And bang. Gotcha. It's not like in the movies. Someone gives you a kick in the nuts, you're going down and you're staying down. This is how it happens? Suddenly? You're not dreaming. This, friend, is real. This is a gun. *(he goes over to StJohn, shows him the gun, then pokes him sharply in the ribs hard enough to break one)*

STJOHN: Ooh.

LARKIN: Ooh. *(he starts screaming and carrying on like a chimpanzee)* Ooh. Ooh. Ahh. Ahh. *(ad libbed)* Purpose from the tool?

STJOHN: I…

LARKIN: I. Dot dot dot. Not I. Me. *(he moves towards StJohn, backing him up and onto his chair behind the desk)* Have you got any idea how many of you fuckers have been walking around with their flashlights inside of my head? Shedding a little light here. A little light there. Illuminating the darkness. Well the thing is—is—that all they ever really did was cast…shadows. DOUBTS! So maybe today we will illuminate. We will remove all doubt. No more shadows.

STJOHN: I can help you.

Jim takes deliberate aim at the Doctor's head.

LARKIN: I will kill you. I am so fucking fed up that I would kill you. Then I will kill him. And then I will kill me—maybe. That's how fucking fed up I am.

STJOHN: What…?

LARKIN: What? Yes—what. What are you wondering?

STJOHN: I…

LARKIN: I..? I..? Aye fucking aye, Captain. Are you hungry? I'm starving. They haven't given me a bite all day. Do you want a pizza? A fucking gun. Let's order a pizza. 722-6969. Pizza Boy. Best fucking pizzas in town. They take longer but that's because they're so goldarn delicious. Extra large. Because you know as sure as there is shit in a cat, when "numbnuts" wakes up he's gonna want some. Extra-large combo with extra Italian sausage. That's the one. And cola. Coca-fucking-Cola. Bomb. Do it. 722-6969. Oh, and something sweet. Apple flip. Loves them I do. We'll have a picnic. Do it. 722-6969. That's a lot of 69.

StJohn picks up the phone and dials the number.

STJOHN: Yes, I would like to order a pizza, please. What? Yes. Delivery. That will be fine. Yes. Um, an extra-large combination with extra Italian sausage. Yes. No. Wait. Cheese crust? *(Jim sticks his fingers in his mouth miming puking)* No. No. Apparently no cheese crust. Yes. And a two-litre container of Coca Cola. A bomb, yes. And an apple flip. They don't have any apple flips.

LARKIN: Cocksuckers. Oh Henry.

STJOHN: And an Oh Henry. Yes. Yes. I would like to have that delivered to Dr. John StJohn's office at Fort Townsend. That's right. The police station… No, I'm not *fucking* around. Just have the deliveryman tell them at reception. They'll point the way.

LARKIN: They'll point the way. *(shakes his head)* Ask how long.

STJOHN: When should we expect it to arrive? That's good then. Thank you very much. *(he hangs up)* Forty-five minutes to an hour.

LARKIN: That's good then. Forty-five to an hour? What are they doing—growing the bacteria for the cheese? It's pending. Pending. Isn't it great when there's something pending? Something is beginning to pend. Pizza pending. Pizza pending. It's just a pizza pending. But, still. That's something. There was nothing. And now. It's pending. *(lisping like Sylvester the cat)* Do ya feel the pense the pectation?

There's a long silence when the phone rings, startling both men.

STJOHN: *(answering phone)* Perhaps I should reiterate. *(screaming into phone)* NO, I AM NOT FUCKING AROUND! *(hangs up. Looks at Jim, who is crouching with gun aimed at telephone)* I believe there's a great deal more than a pizza *im*-pending, James.

LARKIN: Oh, I'm not talking about the unknown. The unknown can't be pending. Like whether or not I'm going to blow my brains out and take you two with me?

That's not pending. The pizza is pending. The time of your death is unknown. You don't think about your death as pending. Speaking of which. *(he jumps up and points the gun at the Doctor, who screams)* Humiliating, isn't it? Humiliation is a dangerous weapon. It's a fucking boomerang is what it is. Isn't it, Coveyduck? Personally? I think that humiliation is grounds for justifiable homicide. Some people, probably yourself—wouldn't call it a crime of passion.

But maybe that's because you don't know what real passion is. Most people think it's like in the movies. Two movie stars fucking on the floor. *(like the voiceover in a movie trailer)* TWO MOVIE STARS! ONE FLOOR! MICHAEL DOUGLAS AND SHARON STONE. GRUNTING LIKE PIGS. Enough to turn your fuckin' stomach. Real passion is like a long slow fuse burning in the mind. Humiliation sparks that fuse and later on when everyone else has gone away and forgotten even that there was an insult: BOOM! Murder. All humiliations breed thoughts of murder. And where there's thought?

STJOHN: We know you didn't murder that woman. But now—this?...is kidnapping and assault. If you give up that gun now, I'll see to it that you get help. I'll personally see that...

LARKIN: You don't see fuck all. Is that my file?

STJOHN: Yes.

LARKIN: Slide it over to the side of the desk and step back.

STJOHN: I...

LARKIN: Shut up. Get up. Up. *(StJohn gets up and moves away)* Sit. *(he indicates chair next to the desk. He riffles through his file and discovers an old news clipping)* Three Dogs Barking. *(shaking his head)* This town? *(points to picture)* My girlfriend. Cute, huh? They don't mention her here. But I was stealing the underwear for her. Panties are expensive. And those rich slutteos on Waterford Bridge Rd. wouldn't even miss 'em. Three Dogs Barking. I hated it at first, but after a while I got to like it. My girlfriend loved it. She embroidered it on a jean jacket for me. I don't know what happened to it. Maybe she took it with her. *(gets up from desk)* She got a job serving pink rich pricks in a fancy restaurant and all of a sudden her shit don't stink. You ever notice that? You take some poor thing and give them a job serving rich fucks and all of a sudden they start acting like them. They get very protective. Their top lip gets really tight.

(he does a tight top lip) May I help you? May I help you? May I help you? They're just their fucking servants. Going around like butlers. But she became a hostess. Class betrayal, I think it's called. But it's not really. It's just auto-suggestion. I'm with them. They're better than you. I'm better than you. I'm with them. They're better than you. I'm better than you. But if you want to see a real example of class betrayal, just look at this slug over here. *(he sits on top of Coveyduck)* His whole family. His grandfather was a strikebreaker for Hickman's, back when the longshoremen were trying to set up the union. He'd travel outside St. John's and hire big buck baymen as scabs. Come in to break the strike. That's how Coveyduck's old man ended up on the force. Making sure Mr. Hickman and Mr. Crosbie *and* Dr. StJohn Sr. got their fresh oranges.

Anyway. His grandfather *bit off* my grandfather's two middle fingers when they were fighting to break the strike. A week later Pop was waiting for him with a big No. 9 coal scoop. When he came around the corner of a shed, Pop let him have it. *(acting it out)* Jesus. Get down. Right in the mouth. Cut all his top teeth away at the gums. Coveyduck's grandfather was down picking his teeth out of the snow. *(pretends to be Coveyduck's grandfather looking for his teeth)* And the red blood everywhere. Pop said they looked like ivory dice. Pop was gonna let him have it again with the big steel coal shovel but he took pity on him. *(looking over at Coveyduck)* You know something? *(goes back and sits at the desk)* Years later those two old fuckers used to sit down and drink a bottle of rum together. Wouldn't happen now. *(looking over at Coveyduck, who is groaning)* We go way back. How's he doing anyway? Let's get him up and happening.

STJOHN: So this is just revenge?

LARKIN: Just? Just revenge? *(getting up from desk)* You fucking guys kill me. Look at your fucking loafers. Prancing through life in a pair of loafers. *(does a mincing little prance while singing)* I'm off to see the Wizard. Jesus Christ, *John*. Pronouncing on who's sane and who's insane while wearing a pair of loafers.

STJOHN: *(looking at his shoes)* I'm not wearing loafers.

LARKIN: *(agitated)* In your *mind.* In your fucking *mind.* The loafers in your fucking *mind.* Resting in your recliner. Your La-Z-Boy. Making decisions. Absurd? And the watch? Don't think that beauty escaped my eye. Rolex.

STJOHN: It's a Timex.

LARKIN: In *my* mind? In *my* mind? A Rolex in *my* mind? I was a thief. And if you're gonna rob a grocery store—get the steak, not the sausages. But you wouldn't know about that, would you, *John*? You never had to hide behind the filthy yellow curtain when the landlord came with the sheriff. You never saw all your poor miserable second-hand furniture thrown out on Queen's Road in the middle of January. In the daylight, with all the stains showing to the traffic driving by. You don't know STAINS. The kids being hauled off by Social Services. Daddeeee! *(pointing at Coveyduck)* While the bulls sat in their nice warm patrol car smirking their fucking faces off. I JUST don't think so, John.

STJOHN: A lot of people have had hard beginnings and...

LARKIN: Dot dot dot, John. Dot dot dot. Beginnings. *(he climbs up on the desk)* In the beginning was the shoe. I was crawling along the floor. And I came upon a pair of my father's black leather shoes. *(he jumps off the desk)* They were in the porch by the front door. It was summer and the front door was open and the porch was full of sunshine. The shoes were grey with dust from the dirt road. In the summer, passing cars would stir up the dust. It poisoned everything. The curtains, the chesterfield. For some reason, I began to lick the shoes. The velvety texture of the dust, I suppose. My tongue wanted to feel it. And wherever I licked them, that spot would become shiny. I kept on licking the shoes, but as I continued, I saw that the spots were drying. They'd dry and become dull. I'd begin all over again. And of course...the same results. Pain stabbed my brains, John. It was the entering of the knowledge of the futility. I knew that before I knew myself. And I know *that* because as I was kneeling there, with my tiny swollen tongue, thinking about death—a taxi stopped on the road. It came to a stop in a cloud of golden dust and a figure emerged. He was wearing a white shirt and the sun blazed down on it making it almost painful to behold. I was transfixed. It was my father coming home from work. He came down the wooden steps from the road, and through the dust charged with sunlight. A million golden motes were torn asunder. He reached down and scooped me up. *(acting it out)* He carried me at arm's length into the house and passed me to my mother, who had come out to greet him. She took me at arm's length and spun me around and around. The fridge the stove the window to the outer world. I saw them all as if I was looking at them from a merry-go-round. And right then, right at that precise moment—I knew for the first time that I wasn't my mother. I wasn't my father. I wasn't the chair or the cat asleep on the chair or the window or the table or the budgie bird that lived in a cage above the table. I wasn't any of that. I was...I. And...I was outside.

Outside of everything and everyone else. And I have never been able to get back in. *(Coveyduck groans)* Get him up. *(the Doctor gets Coveyduck up onto the chair, where he sits with blood trickling down his forehead. The Doctor takes out his handkerchief and tries to deal with the wound)* Don't touch him. Let the fucker bleed like the Judas he is.

STJOHN: *(helping Coveyduck into a chair, then going to chair at end of room)* He needs to have that wound attended to...

LARKIN: He's all right. He's got worse than that, haven't ya, Covey? *(goes back to file)* Oh! Oh! Look at this. I can't believe this. You got *this* in here. *(he gets up and goes over to Coveyduck and whacks him across the head with the file. The Doctor jumps up and Jim points the gun at him)* Sit the fuck down. *(StJohn sits and Coveyduck struggles to his feet. Jimmy punches him in the stomach. Coveyduck falls back in his chair. When Coveyduck quiets down, Jimmy lets him go and goes over to the desk, puts down the file and holds up the picture of his name written in excrement across the wall of the church)* This. This...is fucking blasphemy. You want to hear the true story behind this, Doctor? I bet you were getting all excited and ready to trot out some regression theories. The fact is, that's not my shit. It's his. *(pointing to Coveyduck)* Or one of the priest's other bumboys. Oh, yeah. Let me tell ya. *(he goes over to Coveyduck and shows him the picture)* Whose work is this, Coveyduck?

COVEYDUCK: *(looking at the picture)* Yours—ya little prick.

LARKIN: *(mashing the picture into his face)* How's that feel? I just wish it was the real thing. Coveyduck was a spiritual child, weren't ya, Covey? Head of the altar boys. Anything church. Covey was mad for it. Especially the Bingo. Cah ching. But we'll get to that in a minute. Oh, yeah. The good Father loved little Covey. Took him to Ireland one time, didn't he, Covey? And get this—bought him a fucking motorcycle. Jap scrap, but still. Then, with the good word coming from all around, young cocksucker Coveyduck becomes young Constable Coveyduck. But he doesn't give up his good works, no. He becomes sort of like a recruiter for the good father. There was a fucking gang of them. The Altar Boys. Vicious little fairies. Run of the parish. Drove the priest's car. Used the priest's house for a clubhouse. Booze. Parties. It was sold as a sort of informal social club. Very exclusive membership. Coveyduck was the oldest. By a long shot. Couldn't let go. No girlfriends, though, one couldn't help noticing.

COVEYDUCK: Fucking little liar.

LARKIN: *(laughing)* But one day they went too far. O'Father was away on O'business for O'while and these guys were put in charge of running the franchise. Money went missing. Bingo money. A lot of it. Seven grand. Kept in a safe in the sacristy. When Father comes home the little fuckers get scared, and this is what nobody knows. I used to rob wine out of the sacristy. The priest found out about it and hauled me in. That's when I found about his *prelickydicktions.* But the boys cook up this plan to blame the money job on me. I was perfect. I was always getting in trouble for graffiti. And one time I robbed a summer house and left a stack of shit on the dining room table. They knew all this. Everyone did. I mean, it's this fucking town.

So they write my name in shit all over the church. The stupid little wimps weren't real crooks. They went around bragging about it and spending money on clothes. Clothes? A dead giveaway. The Father 100% cottoned on pretty fast, so they withdrew the theft. Say—nothing is missing. But they stuck me with the B and E, otherwise Coveyduck here would have been up shit creek. No pun intended. Anything wrong yet, Constable?

COVEYDUCK: You're such a fucking little liar.

LARKIN: Oh, I'm not finished yet. There's an epilogue. And it's a doozie. The boys are starting to get a little hairy-arsed for Father's taste so he starts to shove them out. Curtail their privileges. And what with "buggering brothers" in the news every second day, maybe he thought it was time to cool it. But the boys didn't like this. So they, get this, accuse the priest of molestation. And the officer they bring it to? You got it, Doctor—Holy Dovey Covey. Poor fucker homosexual Father Irishname was dragged through the mud. Now don't get me wrong. I'm not saying what he did was right. But if that gang of teenage vampires were sexual innocents I'm St. Francis of fucking Ass-isi. Talk about a Judas. Covey here is what you'd call an opportunist. You can be sure that when this happened in my neck of the woods, Covey's lightbulb lit up hot and red. Like a neon sign flashing out—Three Dogs Barking.

COVEYDUCK: You were at her house. You had a record.

STJOHN: Do you know what a persecution complex is, James?

LARKIN: Yeah. It's what overpaid, overfed, undersexed cunts like you call it when someone like me identifies the ranks of natural enemies that are lined up against him. Sorry. Any minute now you're going to say that you're on my side. Well, I'm over here on my side and guess what? Guess wha? Guess wha? Guess wha? Guess wha?

STJOHN: *(screaming)* Wha?

LARKIN: You're not here. And as usual you never ask the right questions. Why don't you ask him what happened to my old man?

STJOHN: He said he died.

LARKIN: Died. He died. He dead. Details?

STJOHN: No.

LARKIN: Well, he died—he died, Doctor—at the lockup. He was choked to death. Resisting arrest. And guess who the choker was? None other than Constable "Big Ted" Coveyduck Senior. Poppa! This is back before the days of video cameras. So it was their word against nobody's. But their story was that he was drunk. Resisted arrest and they put a chokehold, now illegal, on him and he succumbed. A tragic but yet somehow inevitable end to a life badly lived. Now why don't you ask him what happened to my mother?

STJOHN: He said she died.

LARKIN: She died. Did he tell you that at one time she was engaged to *his* father?

COVEYDUCK: That's a load of bullshit.

LARKIN: Shut up, you fucking ape. I'm in charge now, fucker. *(he looks at him for a second, then he steps behind him and puts him in a chokehold)* See, Doctor, this is a chokehold. See, Doctor, this is how ya does it. I learned it the hard way out at Whitbourne. Are his eyes popping? It feels kinda good just before ya pass out. *(stops choking Coveyduck. Goes to chair by desk and puts his head in his hands, breathing heavily)* And a beaut she was too. Mother. On her way to the teachers' college, don't ya know? However, between the jigs she meets Big Ted Senior. Young constable on the beat. Beat being the operative word, it turns out. Engaged. Ring for all the world to see. But there was one little problem. Wasn't there, Covey? *(mimes drinking)* GUKK GUKK GUKK. And when in the cups he liked to get a little rough. *(jumps up and does some shadow boxing)* One night he blackened her eye. Not a big deal. *(jabs at StJohn)* Love tap. *(goes back to desk)* But she could see it *all* coming. So take your ring and stick it up your arse! The fucker went mad. This back in the days when there were no such things as stalkers. He followed her everywhere. But she married Mr. Larkin. A nobody from the Heights who worked on the docks but *didn't* beat her up. But Big Ted Senior got his back, didn't he? One night in the lockup.

COVEYDUCK: He was a fucking drunk and a troublemaker.

LARKIN: *(lies out on desk. Dreamily)* They all used to drink. Work and drink and work. Then the longshore went away to nothing. Then the fish plant closes down. Railway gone. Finished. So now there's no work and all that's *left* is the drink. Or up hauling the guts out of cows for Maple Leaf in Edmonton. A crowd of fifty-year-old men sitting around the bar wondering where the fuck payday went. Not even cheap labour.

COVEYDUCK: Three Dogs whining.

LARKIN: That's pretty good. Night. Racket breaks out. Up shows Constable Covey Senior and the boys, and lo and behold. *(goes over to Coveyduck and starts to choke him again)* Spite. *(still choking. He stops abruptly)* Kills. Everything is different when you have the power. The power to ask the questions and demand the fucking answers.

STJOHN: Hardly a proud day for your mother and father, I wouldn't think. James.

LARKIN: You fucking quirk. Tell me, Doctor, have you ever really helped anyone? Anyone but yourself, I mean. Think about it. I'm not talking about drug prescribing. I could do that, for fuck sake. But real desert-island battlefield nothing else to be done must help someone help someone? Answer me. And don't lie. I'll know if you're lying and I'll...I'll blow his foot off. Answer me. *(pulls his ear)*

STJOHN: I don't know.

LARKIN: Don't know. *(lying on the floor)* Auntie Shirley had an obsession with cleanliness. A lot of women on the Heights had it to varying degrees. Comes from being called dirty sluts. Nuts. Scrub scrub scrub rub rub rub—couldn't get it clean. *(to the Doctor)* A classic...?

STJOHN: Obsessive compulsive.

LARKIN: Exacty-mundo. Opening the door to that house was like screwing the stopper off a bottle of Jeyes' Fluid. She used to collect all these little glass animal figurines. Hundreds. She talked to them. In front of people. Does Mr. Horsey want to take a bath tonight? *(makes screwy motion with finger to temple)* Like I said. And all the while—scrub scrub scrub rub rub rub. *(jumps up)* Now her husband, and this is the thing, worked delivering coal. He was a fucking coal man! The last of the coal men. So you can well imagine what she saw when he came home from a hard day in the coal dust down to Harvey's. A six-foot-two-inch statue of dirt. So nag nag nag dirty dirty dirty scrub scrub scrub rub rub rub. This behaviour of hers was slowly driving him around the bend.

She used to make him undress out in the porch. I mean the guy was after heaving coal for the past fourteen hours. So every now and then—when he'd get a few in—he'd flip out and bust up all the little fucking glass Red Rose animal figurines. Like you would, right? But. After a few times she called the Black Mariah and the bulls would come and haul him off. But I guess someone got wind of what it actually was that he done. A great big longshoreman taking it out on a bunch of little glass animal figurines. Then. One of you guys got involved.

Hauled in for psychiatric examination. The upshot is—they put him in the nut house. And by him I mean not her. They started drugging him up. But when the drugs would start to wear off he'd try to escape. One time they found him hiding in the swan house in the Bowring Park duck pond. Not Steve McQueen. Time to escalate the proceedings. Electro-therapy shock treatments. *(demonstrates on Coveyduck's head using his thumbs as electrodes. Coveyduck screams)*

STJOHN: Stop it. That technique hasn't been used in years.

LARKIN: And now his brain's so burnt-out he's safe to go home. Cured. You'd go up there and there he'd be—this big bloody six-foot-two longshoreman sitting there on the couch with his mouth gaping open and the TV blazing. And I swear to God, she used to dust him. With a feather duster. *(demonstrates on Coveyduck)* Pitiful. For all I know, she's probably still babbling to her collection of little glass animal figurines. Probably worth a fortune. And that's the first time I ever heard of you guys. I was pretty young but I sensed...something. I'd sit there across from him, eating a stale ginger snap, her speciality, and look into those eyes. Like two lumps of coal burning at the bottom of a well. Haunted is the only word. So the answer to my question is—no. A doctor who actually causes more suffering than he stops, since obviously there is no question of the prevention of insanity, only the prevention of treatment. A little electro-shock therapy, John? Think we could cure Ol' Covey here of his crypto-homo-fascist blues? *(he puts his thumbs on Coveyduck's temples and simulates electro-shock treatment, while making electric sounds and screaming)*

STJOHN: For God's sake, stop it! For God's sake! For your information, it did, and with quite a few modifications still does, in fact, relieve quite a deal of suffering.

LARKIN: Well, for God's sake, I suppose. Since there's nothing left to suffer with. Now you got everybody on the happy pills. Maybe we should be depressed. Maybe there's a lot to be depressed about. *(with great and awful sadness)* Do you know that rebel soldiers are eating the little forest pygmies in the Congo? Raping the little pygmy wives and eating the little pygmy husbands. *(Coveyduck chuckles)* Shut up, you. I'm going to enjoy this. *(smack)* He always managed to get the little smack in. Didn't ya, Coveyduck? *(he smacks Coveyduck across the head with his file)* You know, and I think this is probably ironic, he used to slap me across. *(he slaps Coveyduck)* The face. *(he slaps Coveyduck)* With this. *(he slaps Coveyduck)* Very file. Yeah, this is it. Brown file. Caca brown. Standard government issue. And it hurts. *(slaps Coveyduck)* Doesn't it, Coveyduck? To be slapped across the face with the history of your life. As it has been written in large part by the slapper himself. *(slaps Coveyduck across the face)* Or are you missing the irony of the situation, Constable Coveyduck, formerly cocksucker Coveyduck? *(slap)*

STJOHN: For God's sake, stop it!

LARKIN: *(mimicking him)* For God's sake, stop it! NO! I want to have some more fun.

COVEYDUCK: Fucking little coward.

LARKIN: Fucking little coward. Coward, is it? Tell me, John, did you ever see the display of RNC billy knockers that used to be at the museum? Yeah, they were there, on the wall, in a glass case. The old ones were the size of newel posts with square edges. They got smaller and rounder as the years wore on and the natives got subdued. A fine history of social conditioning, wouldn't you say? *(he puts the gun to StJohn's head)*

STJOHN: Please. Stop this. I believe you. I think you are capable of killing. And I think I know why and I can help you. I believe that you say you killed her because there is something else. Something else that you want to confess to. Some sexual shame. The priest, perhaps?

LARKIN: You stupid bastard. You'll say anything now. Now that fear has entered into it. But you're wrong. Shame? Just the shame of being human. Being pygmy. *(kneeling and imploring)* You see, you don't fucking listen. You never fucking listen. Someone is pouring out their melting heart to you and you're what? Admiring the tassels on your loafers?

STJOHN: *(inwardly seething)* Yes. I believe we're on to something here. There was something in your file. *(he gets the file)* Something that connected. Here it is. The picture of you after your arrest. You're wearing the jean jacket. The one that your girlfriend had embroidered. Right there, on the right shoulder. See. "Three Dogs Barking" with an exclamation point. *(pause)* It was you who covered the church in faeces. Who wrote your name over everything. *(pause)* You know, James, it is quite common for criminals to leave their faeces at the scene of the crime. We believe that it's an unconscious clue. You see, it's themselves they leave behind. *(pause)* He rejected you, didn't he? The priest. You wanted to belong. With the others. The Altar Boys. They didn't want you. They were good-looking boys, weren't they? But you were odd. Strange. Strange-looking. You wrote your name on those church walls. You wanted love. The love that the other boys had. You're still looking for it. It's why you say you killed June Newhook. The teacher. Your mother was going to be a teacher. James? Did she withdraw? Offer, and then withdraw? How did that make you feel, James?

LARKIN: Faeces. *(dangerously quiet)* One world where there's "faeces"— and another world where there's only shit.

STJOHN: Answer my question, James.

LARKIN: I never said I killed her. I said I was guilty of killing her. Even if I'd never laid eyes on her, I'd be guilty of killing her. Coveyduck was going to arrest me. And when everyone saw me on the six o'clock news? That's him. And if it turned out that I was innocent I would still be guilty of killing her and it was only chance that I hadn't killed her because, given the chance, I certainly would have killed her. *(he's getting very worked up)* We all killed her. We're all eating pygmies. Stand him up. *(the Doctor hesitates)* Do it, or I'll shoot him in the face. Do it!

COVEYDUCK: Fuck you.

STJOHN: This is outrageous.

LARKIN: I'll say. That's what I kept telling them the thirty or forty times it happened to me. The very word. Outrageous. Outrageous, I'd scream. Do it, fucker.

The Doctor goes to assist Coveyduck.

STJOHN: This man needs to see a doctor. A medical doctor.

LARKIN: Yeah, because when it comes right down to it, you're just about as useless as tits on a turtle, aren't ya?

STJOHN: I'm not going to answer any more of your rhetorical questions.

LARKIN: You're going to do exactly what I tell you to do. Your time for deciding who's nuts and who's not is over. You little god. Your reign is done. Because if you don't… *(he slaps the Doctor across the face)* Study me now, fucker. Up. You and that…get him up on the desk.

The Doctor struggles to get Coveyduck up on the desk. Jim turns off the overhead light and switches on the utility light. He shines it on the two men, casting huge shadows across the wall and ceiling.

Now, fuckers. Looking down? Looking down now? Pillars of the community? Towers of strength. Okay. Right turn! *(the two men slowly do a right turn. Jim is losing it)* How big are we now? How big are we now? *(he's pointing the gun and revving himself up to shoot them)* WE ARE TUMBLING DOWN! First you, Coveyduck, you fucking pig. Then you, Doctor Loafers. And then… *(he puts the gun to his own head)* And then…Eeeny Meeny Miney Mo. Catch a piggy by the toe.

He's pointing the gun alternately at the Doctor, Coveyduck and himself and whispering the rest of the words while backing towards the door. Just as his back touches the door there are three abrupt and very loud knocks. BANG! BANG! BANG! The noise startles Jim and the gun goes off, shooting him in the temple. He falls forward, extinguishing the utility light. Darkness. The door opens and the pizza delivery person is silhouetted against the light.

PIZZA BOY: Pizza?

Lights out.

The End.

PURITY TEST

SCOTT SHARPLIN

Photo: Tyler Bindon

SCOTT SHARPLIN

ABOUT THE PLAYWRIGHT

Scott Sharplin is an Edmonton-based playwright, director, and educator. His scripts have been produced by Calgary's Lunchbox Theatre and Shakespeare Company, as well as Edmonton's Theatre Network, Sound & Fury Theatre, Theatre Squared, and Walterdale Playhouse. Previous publications include "Burnt Remains," in the anthology Staging Alternative Albertas (Playwrights Canada Press, 2002). Scott is the former Artistic Director of Walterdale Playhouse, and has served as Alberta Playwrights' Network's Vice-President North. He teaches English, Drama, and Creative Writing at Grant MacEwan College.

PRODUCTION HISTORY

Purity Test won the Alberta Playwrights' Network Write To Win Competition in 2001 and was awarded First Prize in the Alberta Playwriting Competition in 2002, receiving dramaturgy by Sharon Pollock and a showcase reading at Alberta Playwrights' Network's PlayWorks Ink festival.

It was first produced by the Chill Room Co-op, at the Edmonton International Fringe Festival (August 2006). This production was directed by Vern Thiessen, and featured Belinda Cornish (Kat), James Hamilton (Robin), and Vanessa Sabourin (Maude). Kerem Cetinel was the production designer, Michael Cowie was the sound designer and publicist, and Theresa Kind was the stage manager.

For production rights, contact Signature Editions, Playwrights Guild of Canada, or the author at scott.sharplin@gmail.com.

CHARACTERS

Robin Sweers — Mid-twenties, anglophone. Dresses counter-cultural.

Kat Champagne — Mid-twenties, anglophone. Dresses sexy, transcending fashion.

Maude Moulier — Early twenties, francophone. Dresses like a starving student.

SETTING

Montreal, January 1998. Multiple settings (established through dialogue).

Note: Throughout the play, the characters will address the audience directly. For the most part, these asides and monologues should be self-evident; at possible points of confusion, the stage direction "out" has been included to clarify.

ACT ONE

In the darkness.

ROBIN: I reach out in the darkness.

KAT: I can't breathe.

MAUDE: My hands are sweating.

ROBIN: I can feel a spine. Her—

MAUDE: Hands.

KAT: I've left my body.

ROBIN: Something to hold on—

MAUDE: Whose hands?

KAT: So many bodies.

ROBIN: Have to count.

KAT: I lose myself.

MAUDE: Hands on hands on hands on hands on hands on hands—

ROBIN: *(on third "hands")* If I can count, if I can know for sure—

KAT: I'm in there somewhere.

ROBIN: Seventy-five vertebrae...

MAUDE: Twenty-four fingers and six thumbs...

KAT: Six lips surrounding eighty teeth...

ROBIN: And four breasts...

KAT: A thousand heartbeats...

MAUDE: Crackling, electrical—

R & K: —You can't tell which is which—

M & R: —And where you end and where the others start—

KAT: It's crazy.

MAUDE: It's intense.

ROBIN: It's like a nightmare.

Lights start to fade up on Robin, Kat, and Maude, in separate spots.

KAT: Heeere we go!

ROBIN: Ten...nine...eight...

MAUDE: *(overlapping) Huit...sept...six...*

KAT: *(overlapping)* Six...five...four...

R & K: Three...two...one...

MAUDE: *(overlapping) Trois...deux...un...*

R & K: Happy New Year!

MAUDE: *(overlapping) Bonne Année à tout!*

KAT: Now, watch them go, all roaring shouting screaming.

MAUDE: Everyone lets go of who they are, just for a flash.

ROBIN: Nineteen ninety-eight. Countdown to Apocalypse.

KAT: It's feeding time at Purgatoire. The whole club's into it, the French, the Anglos, Catholics, Protestants, jocks and drag queens.

MAUDE: I feel dizzy. All these people, smoke, this music. Why did I come here?

KAT: Everybody's making resolutions.

ROBIN: And I had a plan. Oh, right.

KAT: Kat's resolutions. Fix the broken things inside of me.

MAUDE: Forget myself.

KAT: To walk a straight but gorgeous line, to shed my skin, and breathe the air, and let the sunshine in. To make love to an angel and be carried off to Heaven.

ROBIN: I resolve to score some weed ASAP.

KAT: Is there an angel in the house?

ROBIN: I scramble up the metal tiers that make up Purgatoire. Down in the Pit, depravity's the norm. Bump and grind, a thousand eyes shoot arrows into orifices. I'd stay to document the orgy, but a greater fate awaits me.

MAUDE: That girl, she's watching me.

KAT: I've seen that face before.

MAUDE: So stupid. My whole future on the line and here I am.

KAT: Those eyes.

MAUDE: In three days, I will meet them. And I have to tell them, no, don't kick me out. I deserve to be an actress, still.

KAT: It can't be. Holy fuck. It is.

MAUDE: It's probably a lie.

KAT: I've seen those eyes a million times. Thérèse à Trois.

MAUDE: She's still—oh, *tabernac*, she's coming over!

ROBIN: In the cage beside the DJ's booth, Rafal the dealer holds court. This guy's amazing: rumour is, he was conceived during the October Crisis. Now he's like this uber-separatist, except he sells his weed at cost to Anglos, 'cause he says it keeps us torpid and unmotivated. So, *Vive le Québec libre.*

This time, he's got this multi-coloured cockatoo he's showing off to everyone. "He is a symbol. In the revolution, they will all fly free."

I'm like, "Yeah. My cat keeps trying to sneak out on my fire escape."

He goes, "Your cat is wise. He should get out before the shit is hitting. Unless, of course, he is a francophone."

KAT: Happy New Year.

MAUDE: *Pardon?*

KAT: Happy New Year. I know who you are.

MAUDE: You do?

KAT: Don't worry. I won't blow your cover.

MAUDE: How do you know me?

KAT: Your work. I'm an admirer.

MAUDE: You've seen me act?

KAT: You call it acting, but it's more like *channeling.* All our desires and urges, God—like, like in *Angel of Seduction*—

MAUDE: I think you have mistaken me.

KAT: I heard that you can cure a medically impotent man in under three minutes, just with— *(hand gestures)*

MAUDE: *Pardonnez moi.*

KAT: No, wait! *(out)* I'm such a slut, she came here to escape all that. *(to Maude)* Look, forget that shit. Let's drink.

MAUDE: I do not drink.

KAT: Oh. Oh, that's a resolution. I can tell.

MAUDE: A what?

KAT: I believe this is a holy time, you know, a time to fix the things inside ourselves.

MAUDE: It would be nice.

KAT: Let's do one now. Together.

MAUDE: You go first.

KAT: I, Kat Champagne, resolve to make love to an angel and be carried off to Heaven.

MAUDE: Beautiful.

KAT: Your turn.

MAUDE: I guess it would be for how I have to try things more.

KAT: Try things more.

MAUDE: I mean to be more *out.* I hide too much, inside myself.

KAT: Surprised there's *room.*

MAUDE: *(out)* I'm talking wrong. *(to Kat)* This is what they tell me I must do. To be an actress.

KAT: You are an actress.

MAUDE: I just want it to feel true.

KAT: Of course you do!

MAUDE: But now, to feel true, I guess I have to go outside myself. Become somebody else.

KAT: Oh, God, exactly!

MAUDE: Do you think that I should do that? As an actor?

KAT: Hon, I have to do it to feel *human.*

MAUDE: It all feels so wrong sometimes.

KAT: *(out)* This is amazing. Look at her.

MAUDE: *(out)* I don't even know this girl.

KAT: *(out)* Some kind of porn star ingenue—

MAUDE: *(out)* Why is she looking like that?

KAT: D'you wanna dance?

MAUDE: No, thank you, I should go.

KAT: Let's go together.

MAUDE: What?

KAT: Back to my place.

MAUDE: What for?

KAT: *(laughs)* What for? Uh, wow. Okay.

ROBIN: I'm uncrinkling my cash when Rafal goes, "I hear you are a writer of some kind." "Yeah, the unpublishable kind," I say. "Ah, *magnifique*," he says, "I want to make a magazine, for underground. The real Montreal. I think, I pay you pot, you write a piece for me. Okay?" "Okay, but, man, I write in English, see?" Rafal shrugs. "If it is good, we have it translated. If it is shit, we let it stay, for now. Just like you Anglos, henh?"

Kat whispers something in Maude's ear.

MAUDE: I have to go now.

KAT: Or we could just talk. I mean—

MAUDE: I'm sorry.

KAT: *Fuck!* It's me.

MAUDE: No, please, I—I was wrong impressioned—

KAT: This is what you do. I thought—

MAUDE: I think...I only like boys.

KAT: You like *boys?*

MAUDE: To, yes. You know. To do things with.

KAT: To...*things?*

MAUDE: To f— ... to f—...uck.

KAT: You're not Thérèse à Trois.

MAUDE: My name is Maude Moulier.

KAT: Oh my God. I am an utter slut.

MAUDE: No, no, it's—really, it's okay.

KAT: I'm treating you like Miss Porn Priestess, but you're really—

MAUDE: I am not insulted.

KAT: Normal.

MAUDE: I am—really, I am flattered.

KAT: I must make you sick.

MAUDE: No! I came tonight to look for people like you. Different from myself. But not to—I don't mean, to get picked up.

KAT: You sure you're not Thérèse? I'm sorry, just, your eyes—

MAUDE: I'm nobody. I'm not even an actress.

KAT: You said you were.

MAUDE: In school, I am. But now they say they have to kick me out, maybe.

KAT: I'm an almost-actress too.

MAUDE: You are?

KAT: My last role was a girl who really loved perfume. And recently I played a girl who really loved her underwear.

MAUDE: A model.

KAT: See, we're not different. We both have to swallow the same shit. We both have to lie.

MAUDE: If that's really all there is, why do it?

KAT: For those rare, pure moments. 'Cause if something's truly pure, then it's worth sinning for.

MAUDE: I don't think that makes sense.

KAT: You haven't been there yet, is all.

MAUDE: Please stop.

KAT: I can't. I made a resolution. "Make love to an angel…"

MAUDE: I am not an angel.

KAT: But you said you want to try new things.

MAUDE: But not like this.

KAT: Just let me kiss you. One time. New Year's kiss.

MAUDE: I—it would not be true.

Awkwardly, Maude reaches out to touch Kat's face, but can't bring herself to connect. She steps back into darkness.

ROBIN: I squeeze outside of Purgatoire and head up Mount Royal to celebrate. The air is weird and quiet but I know it's just the calm before the storm. I squat beneath the huge electric cross that crowns the mountain and look down at the city.

Lighting his joint.

There lies my readership. A thousand points of light, their sins electrical, like fireflies humping in the dark. Rafal be damned, this article is gonna kick some ass. I'll bypass politics and aim for the sex. Yes, sex, perversion, sixteen different flavours of vice, for vice is the currency of Montreal, the lube that oils the wheels of the apocalypse machine. I shall rob from the rude and give to the pure.

Fireworks in the distance. Robin howls, then sings.

Three, two, one, blast off!
Band of brothers, marching together,
Heads held high in all kinds of weather.

At the sight of Robin, take your stand
With the gallant leader of our band.
Send a joyous shout throughout the land
For Rocket Robin Hood!

Light's change.

KAT: *(out)* The next day hits me like a fist of shit. What is that noise?

ROBIN: *(out)* Where am I?

KAT: *(out)* Fucking phone.

ROBIN: *(out)* Track back. Last night.

KAT: *(out)* Goddamn! *(gets up)*

ROBIN: *(out)* I got my weed...

KAT: *(out)* Where is it?

ROBIN: *(out)* My assignment from Rafal...

KAT: *(to phone)* Hello?

ROBIN: *(out)* Climbed up the mountain…

KAT: *(to phone)* What? Melania.

ROBIN: *(out)* The fireworks...

KAT: What time is it?

ROBIN: *(out)* I came back down.

KAT: *(to phone)* One-thirty, well, what moron would be calling people up one-thirty New Year's Day? Yes, happy blah-blah, now I need to find my clothes.

ROBIN: *(out)* And then I think I went back into Purgatoire.

KAT: *(to phone)* Excuse me, I'm insulted.

ROBIN: *(out)* And then there was this girl.

KAT: *(to Robin)* Get up.

ROBIN: Zoinks!

KAT: *(to phone)* What makes you think I did that?

ROBIN: *(out)* There she is.

KAT: *(to phone)* Well, Melania, not that it's your business, but it's no longer my style to bring home slack-off drunks for one-night stands. *(to Robin)* Off you go.

ROBIN: I came home with you last night!

KAT: That's awesome, Sherlock. *(to phone)* Why? Because I changed, that's why. I made some resolutions.

ROBIN: Did we do it? Oh, God, tell me that we—

KAT: Look, buzz off, okay? *(to phone)* Oh, this and that. To fix the broken things inside myself, to walk a straight but gorgeous line— *(to Robin)* Don't make me call the cops. *(to phone)* Not "straight" like "straight," I don't mean—never mind. Why did you call?

ROBIN: *(out)* I don't remember any of it. This is catastrophic.

KAT: *(to phone)* 'Kay, Melania...

ROBIN: Look, ma'am, d'you think you might be able to refresh my memory? There's gappage.

KAT: *(to phone)* Yeah, y'know, this gossip shit is painful when I'm *not* hung over, so—

ROBIN: It's actually a kind of research. I'm a writer, see, a journalist. I've got this article, this very major—

KAT: *(to phone)* I don't really care who's fucking who this week—

ROBIN: Who's fucking *whom.*

KAT: *(to Robin)* Out of my apartment, now.

ROBIN: Just one more thing.

KAT: *(to phone)* So, babe, remember last year when you said you met Thérèse à Trois?

ROBIN: One question: did you achieve orgasm?

KAT: *(to Robin)* Fuck off. *(to phone)* Yes. Her.

ROBIN: From one to ten, I'm, what, an eight?

Kat pushes Robin onto her fire escape and shuts the door. He opens it.

KAT: *(to phone)* You think that you could track her down again?

ROBIN: A six? A five point nine?

Kat shuts the door.

KAT: *(to phone)* It would be fun, is all. I want to meet a porn star. To compare.

ROBIN: *(opening door)* Did you say that *I* compare to porn stars?

KAT: *(shuts the door. To phone)* So come and pick me up, okay? Yes, now, today.

ROBIN: I think your latch is busted, here.

KAT: *(to Robin) FUCK OFF!* God damn it. *(to phone)* See you soon, 'kay? That's my baby.

Lights change. Robin writes.

ROBIN: The scoop: she picked me up. We had the best sex of my life, if not hers. Then, when the sun illuminates our sins, she goes bipolar, kicks me out. The second phase of the whole Catholic horny-guilty cycle.

KAT: *(out)* I can't believe I brought *that* home.

ROBIN: That girl is Montreal epitomized.

KAT: You slut.

ROBIN: The Muse has handed me the perfect subject.

MAUDE: I'm at work, at the café.

ROBIN: Go home and shoo Houdini-cat inside the fire escape.

MAUDE: I have to concentrate.

ROBIN: I'm hyped. I have to write the quintessential piece.

MAUDE: "Too much inside myself," they said.

ROBIN: I'm gonna need some coffee.

MAUDE: The club girl, from last night. She'd know.

ROBIN: But first I have a toke. Also, a cigarette, some ibuprofen, some ephedrin, and a Saint John's Wort. The perfect piece requires the perfect high.

MAUDE: She picked me, and she just...came out.

ROBIN: My memories of last night are dissolving. Time is crucial.

MAUDE: So do it. Pick somebody, study them, and they will let you in.

ROBIN: Only caffeine can save me now.

MAUDE: But who do I pick? Somebody alive.

ROBIN: *(to Maude)* Hello?

MAUDE: *(out)* The redhead with the scarf, back in the corner.

ROBIN: Excuse me? Hi?

MAUDE: *(out)* Or the greasy man who's talking on his cell—

ROBIN: *Un café, s'il vous plaît? Aujourd'hui?*

MAUDE: *(to Robin)* I'm sorry.

Robin digs for his wallet.

ROBIN: *(out)* Now, which journalistic hat to wear? Exploitational? Objective.

MAUDE: What did you want?

ROBIN: Coffee. Please.

MAUDE: What kind of coffee?

ROBIN: Coffee. Just a non-espresso, non-grap-ap-accino, caffeinated coffee! Jesus!

MAUDE: Fine. *(out)* And fuck you too.

ROBIN: *(looking at his coffee card)* Ah, shit.

MAUDE: A dollar twenty.

ROBIN: Thanks. Sorry 'bout before, okay?

MAUDE: *Ça va.* Dollar twenty.

ROBIN: Here. *(gives her the coffee card)* I like your apron thing.

MAUDE: There is one left.

ROBIN: Say what?

MAUDE: One left, to punch.

ROBIN: It's free. The next one.

MAUDE: After one. See? Punch, punch.

ROBIN: That's punched. Or dented.

MAUDE: Dollar twenty.

ROBIN: Look, hey, tell you what. I've got this predicament.

MAUDE: This what?

ROBIN: See, I'm a writer, and I've got a major, major article that's due—and, well, I really need some coffee, sort of get my brain in gear?

MAUDE: Okay. A dollar—

ROBIN: Yeah, but I just spent my last ten bucks to feed another nasty habit, and I thought I had a freebie coming, but I guess, heh heh, punch, punch.

MAUDE: I guess. *(goes to take the coffee away)*

ROBIN: No, hang on. I'm asking for a favour, here.

MAUDE: What favour? *(he indicates the coffee card)* Oh, you want me to lie?

ROBIN: Who said lie? You don't have to say a word, you just *slip*. Whoops, punch, punch, Happy New Year.

MAUDE: Why should I lie for you?

ROBIN: It's not lying!

MAUDE: I don't even know you, and here you want me to punch, punch—

ROBIN: Oh, you do! You know me! We, we, look. Who made that hole? And that one?

MAUDE: How do I know?

ROBIN: This one up here, that was a *great* one. See, we have a whole *history*, we have a *relationship*.

MAUDE: A relationship of holes.

ROBIN: All I'm asking is, we take it to the next level.

MAUDE: From punching to slipping.

ROBIN: And from there, who knows? The sky's the limit.

MAUDE: I could lose my job.

ROBIN: But think of all you'd stand to gain.

Watching Robin, Maude takes the coffee card.

MAUDE: I'll do it. But you have to let me watch you.

ROBIN: Watch me what?

MAUDE: Whatever. Just observe.

ROBIN: Hang on. This is a really crucial article. I get all, like, self-conscious, lose my focus…?

MAUDE: I'll give you coffee till I'm off my shift.

ROBIN: Free coffee?

Smiling, Maude punches the coffee card twice. Lights change.

KAT: Before I can say "hi," Melania's tongue is in my throat. Melania's a model, one of those, you know, a "lipstick lesbian," oversexed and underfed, the kind of chick with "touch me!" eyes, but if you tried she'd break like glass.

"I met Thérèse just once, and hardly even then. And why you'd want to find an ugly skank like that..."

"She's not a skank," I say. "She's pure. She's got a spark."

"Well, anyway, it's just a waste of time. You think of all the things we could be doing. Tripping off to La-La Land."

She's always talking shit like this, about the two of us, we'll drop the model biz and fly to L.A.—"La-La Land"—and I'm like, *right*, of *course* we will. As if she'd ever have her shit together for a break like that.

Eventually I get it out of her she met Thérèse outside this downtown drug den. "We practically collided on the stairs."

And I go, "Yeah? So what'd you say?"

She's like, "What do you say to a porn star? I asked her to sleep with me."

And I'm like, *God.* "So what'd she say?"

"She told me to fuck off."

"See, that's the wrong approach. For girls like her, you need to think outside the box."

Robin is rolling a joint in the park. Maude is watching.

ROBIN: ...And here, I try to leave a bit of space, to grip it when you shake it down.

MAUDE: *(out)* I'm learning lots.

ROBIN: And then you twist the end off, and it's done. *Voilà.*

MAUDE: So why do you do it?

ROBIN: Roll them?

MAUDE: Smoke them.

ROBIN: Thought you said you were an actress.

MAUDE: Yes, but they don't think that you should smoke or drink. It interrupts your studies.

ROBIN: You always do what they tell you to?

MAUDE: If I want to stay in school.

ROBIN: *(moistens his joint)* Hardly what I'd call a liberal education.

MAUDE: You're smoking that here, in the park?

ROBIN: Are you from Montreal?

MAUDE: Trois-Rivières.

ROBIN: And that is why you fail.

MAUDE: I'm only observationing.

ROBIN: Well, how long will it take? Because you're staticking my writing vibe.

MAUDE: In class, they say you can become a person just by studying them.

ROBIN: That's all I need. An evil twin.

MAUDE: I'm not the evil one. *(indicating his joint)*

ROBIN: Come on, what's evil? This little guy's one hundred per cent natural. Like tofu.

MAUDE: But to smoke it in the park, like this, you know it's wrong.

ROBIN: Only to a virgin's eyes.

MAUDE: To what?

ROBIN: A virgin. Never smoked?

MAUDE: Oh, you mean pot.

ROBIN: Yeah, what, you thought I meant—

MAUDE: Never mind.

ROBIN: 'Kay. What's the worst thing that you've ever done?

MAUDE: I don't—

ROBIN: No, this is part of your crusade for knowledge. Think. Your cardinal sin.

MAUDE: My carnal?

ROBIN: Cardinal. Or carnal, cardinal, whatever, take your pick. You ever screw around behind somebody's back?

MAUDE: No.

ROBIN: Ever slept with somebody off-limits, like your doctor or your teacher?

MAUDE: No!

ROBIN: Ever do it when your folks were in the house? No? Dogs? Cats? Hamsters?

MAUDE: Sorry.

ROBIN: C'mon, you're French! It's in your blood!

MAUDE: Well, there was one thing.

ROBIN: Well, serve it up.

MAUDE: Once, I...punched two holes.

Pause, as Robin figures it out.

ROBIN: Fine. Be that way. Virgin. *(she gets up)* Hey, where you goin'?

MAUDE: Thank you for your time.

ROBIN: Ah, chicken. *(out)* Virgins make shitty sidekicks.

KAT: Melania drives up to Purgatoire. "We have to go in there?" I say, but still I head into the hollow metal bunker of the club, and up the spiral stairs to meet...Rafal. The room is packed. Their cocks, like compasses, all swerve in my direction.

I ask him for the strongest weed he's got. He grins, eyes dancing in the candlelight. He reaches underneath his throne and flourishes a thorny-looking ounce. "*Ça,*" he says, "*Ç'est* Zombie Orgy, from Jamaica. It will put your pretty body on the floor."

The cocks all laugh. "I'll take the ounce," I say. *(counting out her cash)* "And one more thing...tell me everything you know about Thérèse à Trois. Porn star? French? An angel's face? And body."

They play dumb. I rest my hand on his. It feels like ice. His eyes are cocks, but still I lock his gaze till recognition dawns.

ROBIN: I'm not obsessed.

KAT: "Thérèse... *The Angel of Seduction.*"

ROBIN: So it isn't stalking, 'cause I'm not obsessed. It's scientific research. And when I let myself inside her pad? It isn't B and E. Because her latch is busted. Just trespassing. A minor misdemeanour in an age of carnal sin.

KAT: Back in the car. I'm like a time bomb.

ROBIN: I'm looking maybe for a secret S & M shrine, or a giant photograph of Daddy—anything to see what makes her tick.

KAT: My hand burns, where he touched it.

ROBIN: It's all vanilla, though.

KAT: But he remembered.

ROBIN: Maybe I'm way off about this chick.

KAT: I have an address, now. I have a lead.

Robin finds Kat's diary beneath her bed.

ROBIN: Hello! What have we here? My Rocket Robin sense is tingling.

KAT: I tell Melania to drive me home so I can puke.

ROBIN: *(skimming)* Jinkies.

KAT: All those sleazy vibes have made her horny.

ROBIN: This is pay dirt.

KAT: I'm just numb and ugly, like the sky.

ROBIN: Blow jobs...

KAT: She escorts me up the stairs.

ROBIN: Sixty-nines...

KAT: "I think I need to go to bed."

ROBIN: Bondage...

KAT: She's like, "I can tuck you in."

ROBIN: This is terrific. She's a walking purity test.

KAT: I guess I owe her something.

ROBIN: I hear the lock click. Fuck. I'm trapped, I'm busted. Think. The closet, right, I'll—wrong. The bed. Yes, just the bed, reclining, Casanova. 'Cause she finds me in the closet? I'm a stalker. But she finds me on the bed, then there's a chance, however slim, I'll be a "wonderful surprise."

KAT: *(entering the bedroom; to Melania)* Just chill, okay, I gotta make the...bed...

ROBIN: Uh. Hi, there, sweet...heart.

KAT: Hi. You. What a...wonderful surprise.

ROBIN: *(out)* She's panicking.

KAT: *(out)* Who is this guy?

ROBIN: *(out)* I smile the smile of one who's never heard the words, "restraining order."

KAT: *(out)* He's the cock from last night.

ROBIN: *(out)* Now she's looking at her skinny friend, who looks a little pissed, and then she's back to me and suddenly...

KAT: *(all smiles)* Melania, this is...

ROBIN: Robin.

KAT: He's...one of mine.

ROBIN: *(out)* Why's her friend so pissed?

KAT: *(out)* Perfect.

ROBIN: Actually, I'm here on business. Research, for a piece I'm writing. I'm a writer.

KAT: Oh, yeah.

ROBIN: Scientific.

KAT: Hands-on stuff.

ROBIN: And strenuous activity. Leg work. Lots of—

KAT: *(out)* "Well," she says, "I'll leave you to it."

ROBIN: *(out)* Skinny chick shoots daggers at me, and I start to get the reason she's so pissed.

KAT: *(out)* Out she goes, a cloud of ice. I'm spared.

ROBIN: *(out)* This woman is amazing.

KAT: *(out)* That's one down.

ROBIN: *(out)* What *doesn't* she do?

KAT: *(out)* And one to go.

ROBIN: *(out)* I'm in for the ride of my life.

KAT: Get out.

ROBIN: Hey, whoa. Come on.

KAT: I'll call the cops. Fucking stalker.

ROBIN: What happened to the "wonderful surprise?"

KAT: It wore off.

ROBIN: Just, okay, a couple questions. It's—

KAT: Fuck off.

ROBIN: Scientific—

KAT: Now.

ROBIN: I think you owe me something, lady. I mean, I did just extricate you from an awkward situation.

KAT: *(on "from")* If you don't get out now then you can extricate yourself from your own ass.

Shuts him out on the fire escape.

ROBIN: *(out)* Still Number One with the ladies.

KAT: *(out)* God, Melania.

ROBIN: I watch her retreat into her lair.

KAT: All that ugly lust...

ROBIN: And then I realize...

KAT: The things she would've made me do.

ROBIN: I shoulda picked the closet! Oh, god, I shoulda picked the closet! *(he falls to his knees in mock despair. Kat's diary, tucked beneath his coat, falls out)* Hello.

KAT: Where's my...?

ROBIN: It's not theft. It's...accidental borrowing.

Lights change.

MAUDE: In the café, watching people. Try to see inside them.

ROBIN: *(reading)* "March the first."

KAT: It's gone. That's good.

MAUDE: I try to see the sins he thinks are everywhere.

ROBIN: "Guy named Luc. Kept clothes on. Tear in panties."

KAT: Empty, now. No past. I'm starting over.

MAUDE: Watch until I turn transparent.

KAT: When I find her, all that shit won't matter.

ROBIN: "April seventh. Guy in *Foufoune's* coat room. Standing up."

KAT: She'll make me pure.

MAUDE: Their stories flow inside me.

ROBIN: "April ninth. Blew fat guy on the Metro."

MAUDE: Fill me up.

KAT: Thérèse.

MAUDE: The redhead on her cell phone. The big bearded man, he's looking in the phone book. The couple with the mochaccinos. He licks the whipped cream from his finger. He would like to lick the whipped cream from her skin.

ROBIN: *(to Rafal)* "May fourteenth." Can you believe this stuff?

MAUDE: Did I just think that?

ROBIN: *(to Rafal)* "May fourteenth. Brought home Marie-Laure. Six piercings in her face. Like kissing a wire brush." Gold mine. Hey, man, are you even hearing this? *(out)* I'm trying to tell Rafal about my find, but he's all been-there, done-that. *(to Rafal)* Here, read this part. August ninth. Your brain will spooj.

MAUDE: Maybe they are going home to put whipped cream all over. The redhead with the cell is going, "Baby, let's get out the ball-and-chain and all those things that people do." *(giggles)*

ROBIN: You see? Spooj city.

MAUDE: And the hairy man is looking for a store with fur, because he is a, what is it? A "fuzzy." This is fun.

ROBIN: Rafal is also holding back the weed he promised me. "You should not write about her. It is rude."

MAUDE: I feel dirty.

ROBIN: That's the point.

MAUDE: It feels good.

ROBIN: "In Montreal, nobody wants to read about the slutty girls. They're everywhere, like licorice in jelly beans. Too many. Throw them out."

I'm like, "Okay, then what's the best flavour? The one you dig for?"

He grins back to his ears, and says, "It's cherry."

Lights change.

KAT: It's grim and glassy as I cab to the address Rafal gave me... It's way out in Laval, the driver thinks I'm nuts. "Dressed up for a neighborhood like this?" But I don't care. Once I find Thérèse, our eyes will meet, her pure spark. Then she'll let me touch her face, and it'll feel like baby's skin.

We pull up to a warehouse with the windows boarded up. The driver wants to wait for me, I tell him scram. The door has a grate on, locked, and so I hammer with my fist until I hear someone inside.

Some guy with fish-bug eyes opens up. I push right past him, letting his lap get most of the shove. "I barely found the place," I say, "Thérèse might be an angel but she gives the *worst* directions. Don't you think?"

Inside, there's carpets. Couches. Past some screens, I hear the sounds of camera crews, and catcalls, climaxes. I'm in the right place.

I'm like, "She *is* here, isn't she?"

"The fuck are you?" goes Fish-Bug.

"My name is Kat Champagne. Close personal associate of Thérèse à Trois. We have a lot of business to discuss. We two might be collaborating on some *très* artistic projects."

He laughs. "Thérèse, *henh?* That name doesn't get you much action round here."

(opens her bag and dumps the Zombie Orgy weed onto the table) "And what sort of action might this get me? *Henh?*"

ROBIN: *(reads)* "August twenty-seven. On display."

KAT: His grin unpeels. He shouts out something and the room fills up with...bug-eyed buddies.

ROBIN: "Fuck you with their eyes."

KAT: We smoke until I leave my body.

ROBIN: "Till they get inside you. Then they shut them."

KAT: They pick it up, my body, where I left it.

ROBIN: "They dump their shit in you. Their sicknesses."

KAT: I try to see if I can spot Thérèse, but everything's so dark.

ROBIN: *(to Maude)* It just goes on and on like this.

KAT: "Angel! You were s'posed to be here!"

ROBIN: Like a catalogue. Frequency, locality, number of participants.

KAT: I can't hear myself. Their laughing. I can't breathe.

MAUDE: Where did you get that?

ROBIN: From her pad. An accidental—

MAUDE: You brought me over to your place so you could show me someone's diary?

ROBIN: It's a checklist. Like a purity test.

MAUDE: A what?

ROBIN: You know. Those lists that horny frat boys download off the Internet.

MAUDE: Sounds lovely.

ROBIN: This is better, though. It's real.

MAUDE: It's all so pointless, checklists, you may as well count somebody's teeth, or eyelashes. You'd learn as much.

ROBIN: Okay, you know what? Never mind. I figured, show you something carnal and depraved, it might heat up that blood of yours. But you're not even curious. You're ice. And you are clearly not my target audience.

Pause. He takes out a joint and lights it.

MAUDE: I used to hear my parents through the walls. Fucking. They were so predictable, I knew what nights they do it, how long, everything. One night, I sneak out of my room to go around and look in through the window.

ROBIN: Curious.

MAUDE: Except I run into my mother, smoking on the porch.

ROBIN: I don't get it.

MAUDE: He would bring home prostitutes. Every month! And she would let him.

ROBIN: You're shitting me.

MAUDE: No, Robin. It's the truth.

ROBIN: *(out)* What a great back story.

MAUDE: So "fucking" does not always just mean "hot." Sometimes it's colder.

ROBIN: So that was ugly, what your parents did? Cold-blooded?

MAUDE: It was wrong, yes.

ROBIN: Maybe it was perfect. Daddy gets his nookie, Mom gets cigarettes and doesn't have to ride the hobby horse.

MAUDE: Shut up! You don't know anything about it.

ROBIN: Neither do you. See, this is your whole problem. Everything seems bad until you *live* it. Marijuana seems like Satan's bubble gum until you smoke some. Then it's no big deal.

MAUDE: I... *(out) Merde.* He's right.

ROBIN: *(referring to the diary)* And all this stuff, well, sure, to, like, a virgin—

MAUDE: *(out)* Not be somebody else. Just not be me.

ROBIN: Not *you*, I didn't mean that you were one—

MAUDE: No, no, I am.

ROBIN: *(out)* She is. The cherry-flavoured jelly bean.

MAUDE: *(out)* Just try things. Let them happen.

ROBIN: *(out)* Rafal was right.

MAUDE: *(out)* And then they will be *real.*

ROBIN: *(out)* The Last Virgin in Montreal.

MAUDE: What are you looking at?

ROBIN: I'm...counting your eyelashes.

MAUDE: What? Why?

ROBIN: Scientific research. *(he touches her eyelashes)*

MAUDE: *(out)* He's counting my eyelashes.

ROBIN: *(out)* I'm counting her eyelashes...but really what I'm looking at is something flashing into life inside her eyes. It's like she's hungry.

Maude puts her hand on Robin's mouth.

Hey!

MAUDE: Open up. I'm going to count your teeth.

ROBIN: *(out, with his mouth full of Maude's hand)* She's counting my teeth.

MAUDE: *Vingt-et-un, vingt-deux, vingt-trois, vingt-quatre. (stops) Merci.*

ROBIN: Learn anything?

MAUDE: Your breath smells like pot.

ROBIN: Yeah, well. *(impulsively, she takes his joint from him)* Hey! What—? *(she tokes deeply on the joint. Robin speaks out)* And suddenly the Virgin Mary's drinking up my jay like nectar, and my world stops cold in cherry-flavored awe.

Maude turns around and has a coughing fit.

In the grey light, I can see the shape of her spine through the fabric of her shirt. It looks like a stairway to Heaven. *(pats her lightly on her back, touching her spine)* One, two, three, four, five...

MAUDE: *De l'eau...*

ROBIN: *(closing in to an embrace)* Six, seven, eight, nine, ten...

MAUDE: Robin, stop...

ROBIN: *(turning Maude's head for a kiss)* Eleven, twelve, thirteen...

He tries to kiss her but she pulls away.

Hang on, no.

MAUDE: I have to go.

ROBIN: I was just—just counting—look out! Houdini...

She trips.

MAUDE: I'm sorry. *Au revoir.*

Lights change. Slow fade until the end of the act.

KAT: It's over.

ROBIN: Blew it.

KAT: I'm outside. It's dark and scuddy and the sun is gone, I don't know what time it is, I've been in there for days. I have to *run,* I know they're after me, cock zombies, compasses, and fish-bug eyes and empty faces. My feet are skating, pins-and-needles rain against my face.

ROBIN: And now my article is fucked.

KAT: Thérèse! Where are you? Why didn't you save me?

ROBIN: Slut and virgin both rejected me.

KAT: I think I see the mountain, so I plow towards it.

ROBIN: If I want to write something, I'll have to make it up. And isn't that a drag.

KAT: Everybody's staring.

MAUDE: The school. My interview.

KAT: Across the street. Cocks turn to follow me.

MAUDE: Their faces all are empty.

KAT: Want to scream at them to *fuck off,* I am *not* a whore, I want to make love to an angel…

MAUDE: I don't have a chance.

KAT: To love...to make an angel...to get carried off...

MAUDE: I talk because I have to, but it's pointless. "I want to stay. I want to be an actress. And I know the things I need to fix, to get outside myself. To try new things, to be somebody else..."

"You have potential, but at this point, your experience, your work in *class,* we do not *think,* to keep you *on,* it would not be of use to *you,*" la la la *la,* and so and *so,* and fuck you too.

ROBIN: Houdini's still out sulking somewhere, so I lean out on the fire escape and call his name.

MAUDE: I have to go.

ROBIN: And what the hell—?

MAUDE: Before they see me cry.

ROBIN: The balcony. It's ice.

MAUDE: But on the street my tears are freezing.

ROBIN: Like a little ski hill, only glistening with ultra-slick transparent ice. It's on my bike, expanding like a parasite. Some kind of freezing rain has laminated everything.

Houdini's there, the icy slope. Yikes, don't take a tumble, cat. I drag him back inside. I put one hand down on the hill of ice.

MAUDE: It makes me numb.

ROBIN: *(looking up)* What is this?

MAUDE: Everything is ice but I am burning mad.

ROBIN: Some kind of freaky stealth-storm?

KAT: The mountain. Mount Royal.

MAUDE: Everyone keeps looking up. Fucking freezing rain.

KAT: Something some voice said, back there, inside.

ROBIN: It's gathering on everything. The cars. The trees...

KAT: I asked about Thérèse, and he was laughing like, "She has been gone a long time now, that one."

ROBIN: Power lines...

KAT: "She has a little home beneath the mountain."

ROBIN: A bright orange flash outside the window, and a bang like fireworks, and the lights are out.

MAUDE: I get home and it's dark and cold, like everywhere. I want to make tea, but my stove will not work, and the water comes out grey. The news says we should all stay put, until our power comes back on.

ROBIN: I wonder how long this can last.

MAUDE: But I'm sick of doing what they tell me to.

ROBIN: Maybe I should call up Maude, apologize.

MAUDE: I should not have run out on Robin like that.

ROBIN: No. I got nothing to be sorry for.

MAUDE: He was only being Robin.

ROBIN: She used you, man. Pure research.

MAUDE: He probably likes all this.

ROBIN: I bet she loves this blackout shit. More "observationing" material.

MAUDE: I should call him, maybe. No.

ROBIN: Who needs her, anyway?

MAUDE: If he can make it on his own, then so can I.

KAT: Keep moving.

ROBIN: Jesus, though. It's crazy out.

KAT: Keep looking up.

MAUDE: You know what? Fuck it.

ROBIN: Branches hitting people. People hitting pavement.

MAUDE: I am going out.

KAT: Beneath the mountain. Move towards the mountain.

MAUDE: If you want to drop a tree on me, then do it. Then at least it would be real.

KAT: No sun. No time. The world is black.

ROBIN: I bet it's Rafal's revolution out there.

KAT: Up above me. On the mountain. There's the cross.

MAUDE: On the street, it's quiet.

ROBIN: Riots, looting. Madness and debauchery.

KAT: Climb up. She'll find me.

MAUDE: Faces. Frozen.

ROBIN: I'm supposed to dig this kind of shit.

KAT: Keep climbing.

MAUDE: No one knows what's happening. Now everyone's a virgin.

ROBIN: It's so cold.

KAT: She isn't here. The cross is gone.

ROBIN: The world is ending and I'm all alone.

MAUDE: If everybody stood here, looking up, then we would freeze, like statues, like a city full of tiny baby birds that want to cling together but can never, ever fly.

The lights are out.

ACT TWO

As the lights slowly fade up.

MAUDE: I reach out in the darkness.

KAT: Angel.

MAUDE: It's unlocked.

KAT: I was waiting for you. On the mountain.

MAUDE: *(calls) Âllo?* Is anybody here?

KAT: And it was cold.

MAUDE: No power. But at least it's shelter. Come.

KAT: Where are we?

MAUDE: At the club, the big, the pit place. *Purgatoire.*

KAT: Purgatory. Angel.

MAUDE: I thought somebody would be here, maybe. But—

KAT: There's no one left.

MAUDE: Lay down.

KAT: No one but you.

MAUDE: I'll find a blanket, maybe. *Quelque chose.*

KAT: And me, and you. You found me.

MAUDE: Candles! Good. But now I need a lighter. *(looks around)*

KAT: *(muttering)* Like it was, the things I had to do, they did, to test me. That was all, the test, and stupid frozen soul, I should have known, I should have seen, I should have *faith*—

Maude digs in Kat's pocket for a lighter.

Are we starting now? I'm ready.

MAUDE: Try to rest, okay?

Maude lights candles, while Kat, having misinterpreted Maude's actions, begins removing her clothes. These next two speeches overlap.

KAT: I'm ready, we can go. I didn't doubt. It was the ice, and how they looked, they made me see you wrong, but I can do it, I can go, we'll go together. 'cause it's pure. It's perfect like a diamond and if something's pure, you have to sin, and sin, and sin—

MAUDE: *(out)* This is crazy. *Maudit verglas.* All of this. But where was I supposed to take her? I thought, maybe, people from the club, here, somebody maybe knows her name, or where she lives. And then she started shivering, she felt like she was going to break.

Sees that Kat is down to her underwear.

What are you doing? We have to keep warm!

KAT: I'm ready. We can go.

Maude tries to put Kat's clothes back on her, and eventually gives up and holds her instead.

MAUDE: You will get sick.

KAT: That's what I was. God, I was so so sick and dirty but you're here. You'll make me pure. My Angel. *(laughs)*

MAUDE: *Oh la la.*

ROBIN: *(out)* I see a light.

MAUDE: What am I going to do with you?

ROBIN: *(out)* Like a star that snuck beneath the clouds and found its way inside.

MAUDE: You should not have been up there, like that. Without a coat.

KAT: I knew you'd come. I always, always knew.

ROBIN: *(out)* Crawl across the dance floor.

MAUDE: On the mountain, why? Why me?

KAT: Where angels live. Silly.

Maude laughs.

ROBIN: *(out)* It can't be. Holy fuck. It is.

KAT: Kiss me.

ROBIN: *(out)* Dreaming. Or insane. I've lost my shit, I've gone around the bend and...found...her spine...just like I left it.

MAUDE: New Year's kiss.

They kiss. Robin moves up behind them and puts his hands on Maude's back.

ROBIN: *(out)* One, two, three, four...

MAUDE: *(out)* Hands.

KAT: *(out)* It's happening.

ROBIN: *(out)* Eight, nine, ten, gimme somethin'—

MAUDE: *(out)* Hands on hands on hands.

KAT: *(out)* I leave my body.

MAUDE: Who is there? *(turns around)*

ROBIN: *(seeing Kat)* The fuck?

KAT: *(seeing Robin)* They found us!

They separate.

MAUDE: Robin?

ROBIN: You! It's you and you.

KAT: Make him, no! He has to go! He has to go!

MAUDE: She is fevering. I found her on the mountain.

ROBIN: What, like that? *(referring to her state of undress)*

KAT: He'll bring others. All the cocks. They'll take me back.

MAUDE: Shh. Get dressed.

KAT: First make him go!

MAUDE: He's not going to hurt you.

KAT: You were s'posed to save me!

MAUDE: Well, I have. You're safe.

KAT: And make me pure. That's why we're here. That's why you came.

ROBIN: Y'know, I think I'll just...

MAUDE: No, Robin, wait.

ROBIN: I see the writing.

KAT: Angel!

MAUDE: Robin! *(to Kat)* Stay. Be calm. I will come back.

This next exchange is played on different levels, with Maude calling down to Robin as he climbs down to the exit.

ROBIN: I got a schedule, see? Food to scavenge, trees to dodge...

MAUDE: But I have things I want to tell you.

KAT: *(calling)* Angel!

ROBIN: Tell your bosom buddy.

MAUDE: It's not what you think.

KAT: *(calling)* I love you!

ROBIN: Riiight.

MAUDE: You cannot go back out there.

ROBIN: Why not?

MAUDE: It is a disaster!

ROBIN: Yeah, well, so is she. That girl eats virgins like they're jelly beans.

KAT: *(calling)* Angel!

ROBIN: And what is that, "on the mountain"? I mean, talk about disaster, that's the heart of darkness. *Nobody* is going there!

MAUDE: I know. That's why I went. *(pause. She digs in her bag)* I promised to look after her. So if you have to go, then go. But here. *(she drops a coffee card down to him)*

ROBIN: A relationship of holes.

MAUDE: Come to the café when this all gets better.

She goes back to Kat.

ROBIN: Better. Huh.

Maude finds Kat crying.

KAT: You came back.

MAUDE: I came back.

Lights change.

ROBIN: Stonedate: January Fifth. Or Sixth? Hard to mark time when the sun's blocked out and the clocks don't work. On the rooftops, men with axes dissect giant slabs of ice. Army trucks coagulate the streets. The city's trying to shock itself alive, like some mad doctor bashing paddles on his chest.

"When it gets better," she says. What does she know? "Better." How far off the edge can you go, before you can't come back?

At home, the air is rancid, dust and sour weed. The water in my bong is frozen. Where's my cat? I check the fire escape. "Houdini?" Little ski hill, like before. "Don't take a tumble, cat." *(looks over the fire escape)* Oh. Oh no. Ohhh no.

There, between the chunks and fissures of the ice. Curled up, paws out, reaching for kitty salvation. God damn it. Poor Houdini. I pick his little body up and carry it upstairs. I put him in my freezer, which isn't any colder than the rest of Montreal, but which is easier to open than the ground.

Lights on Kat and Maude. Maude has several bottles of liquor.

MAUDE: I found a sink, but I don't trust the water.

KAT: I trust you.

MAUDE: I heard the treatment plants were down. It could be dirty, and there is no way to test.

KAT: A test. It's what I thought. A leap of faith.

MAUDE: But there is liquor, from the bar. But maybe that will make us thirsty? I am not very good at this.

KAT: You're perfect. And it's just the way I pictured, even though I closed my eyes, and you were floating, like a bird, a rainbow—

MAUDE: Stop. You have mistaken me again.

KAT: Don't say that.

MAUDE: Like before, you saw me, New Year's Eve, you thought I was—who did you say?

KAT: Don't do that, that was then, when I was drunk and sick and ugly.

MAUDE: You were never ugly.

KAT: I just never want to look. We're here, we're through, we're leaving. Let's not look.

MAUDE: We can't leave yet.

KAT: Why not? Did I do something wrong?

MAUDE: No, but outside. It's dangerous. Where would we go?

KAT: L.A.

MAUDE: What?

KAT: It was a sick dumb joke, before—Melania. It was a dream. But you could take us there, right? City of Angels.

MAUDE: I think the airports all are closed.

KAT: Then float, like snowflakes in reverse. We'll just rise up until we fly, and all the moisture in the clouds will wash us pure, because that's what it's like up there. It's—right?

MAUDE: I guess so. I don't know.

KAT: Leap of faith.

MAUDE: It's like everything is backwards. Like I am helpless, and it's danger all around us, and you I do not think are very sane, but still I feel safe.

KAT: It's the spark.

MAUDE: At New Year's Eve. You tried to take me home...

KAT: It's dark now, it's forgotten.

MAUDE: No, I want to tell you. When you whispered...what you wanted to be doing, with me.

KAT: Stop it! Don't remember, ugly bug-eyed catcalls, I did *everything*, and why you make me hear—

MAUDE: I'm sorry.

KAT: I was rotten, I was shit, I know, I know it.

MAUDE: No!

KAT: Because I wanted it, and you and them, and there was so much ugly hunger I could never even tell if it was them or me, or if we, none of us were even real and it was only darkness fucking darkness, on the couches and behind the screens—

MAUDE: Shh, shh, not now. Just calm, now. You are here. You're not back there, wherever, you're with me.

KAT: Don't make me look back. If I go back again, I'll die.

MAUDE: You won't go back.

KAT: You have to take me, make me go, you have to make me into someone—

MAUDE: Someone else.

KAT: To someone else.

MAUDE: It's all right. I am here. Your angel, she is here.

KAT: It's why you came?

MAUDE: It's why I came.

KAT: So I can go?

MAUDE: We'll go together. Okay? *(they kiss)* Starting over.

They keep kissing. Lights change.

ROBIN: *(out)* Cryogenic Limbo City. Try to walk, the ice chunks clutch your ankles. Nighttime streets are clogged with zombies, stumbling in circles, nowhere to go. Facing west on Sherbrooke, you can make out lights, still, here and there. But east, the whole old city, the South Shore, it's like it all just fell into a pit.

I lurch to the foot of the mountain. Fuck. I can't believe she went up there. Pathways, deathtraps, cracks and cave-ins and collapses. Branches shattering like chandeliers.

He prepares to cross the threshold into the park.

I can't do it. I can't enter Hell.

Watching all these ghostly faces flicker by, I wanna grab them, wanna shake them, shouting, "This is nuts! Is this not nuts?

Are we not trapped in here, together? Wait!" But when I reach out... Little kitty paws stretched out, grasping at darkness. Fuck! *(covers his eyes)*

MAUDE: *(out)* She's sleeping, finally. Her skin is not so grey. I still don't remember her name. Little shivers. She is dreaming. Inside her head, I don't know what, some kind of hurt, a wound that keeps on opening. She tries to hide, it hunts her. How could I ever imagine to know what someone else is thinking? It's a stupid joke.

Becoming someone new. And not the man…who paid women to fuck him, or the wife who made the bed when they were through. Not Robin, who counts everything, or Maude who counts for nothing. Do something you thought you never would. Something you think is wrong.

Her hand hovers over Kat's body.

Very, very wrong.

She begins to move her hand along Kat's body.

Can hardly feel. My hand is numb.

Her hand moves down her torso, towards her thighs.

Her name is Kat.

Suddenly, Kat startles awake, slapping Maude's hand away from her and jerking across the floor. They stare at each other for several beats.

It's only me.

KAT: You.

MAUDE: Yes. Your angel.

KAT: You. Oh, God. I have to go.

Kat begins getting dressed. She tries not to take her eyes off Maude.

MAUDE: Go where? You can't—

KAT: Away.

MAUDE: Well, then, together. That is what you said, before—

KAT: Not anymore.

MAUDE: L.A., you said. Or up, like snowflakes—

KAT: If you knew me, then you'd know that's bullshit.

MAUDE: You cannot just go home. I mean—you can, but you will have no power.

KAT: Story of my life.

MAUDE: Then let me walk with you, at least—

KAT: DON'T touch me.

MAUDE: Sorry.

KAT: Everybody's sorry.

MAUDE: It was bad of me to—

KAT: Everything is bad.

MAUDE: What will you do?

KAT: What was I doing, before you came to "save" me?

MAUDE: Freezing to death.

KAT: *Voilà.*

Kat exits. Light change. Robin sits, writing.

ROBIN: *(out)* Squatting in a powerless café. And now I'm sure, the girl was wrong. Our Winter Wonderland is here to stay, and so I'm writing, but I know that when my pen runs dry, I can't just buy another one. And now I know that when the last biscotti's taken from the tin, there won't be more. At home, there's nothing left to eat but canned corn. My opener's electric. *(beat)* I know I'm going to have to eat my cat.

MAUDE: *Salut.*

ROBIN: Hey, hi, *salut.*

MAUDE: What are you doing?

ROBIN: Contemplating supper. You?

MAUDE: I thought I was supposed to work today. But it was yesterday. So now I'm fired.

ROBIN: They fired you in an ice storm? Fuckers.

MAUDE: *Oui.*

ROBIN: Want me to piss on their frother?

MAUDE: Just forget it. *(sits)* I'm too tired to be mad.

ROBIN: I bet you're tired.

MAUDE: Is this your article?

ROBIN: There is no article. I don't think there ever really was. It was a ruse, a poor excuse for writing mordant crap. Now the excuse has expired, and mordancy is moribund. So I guess that just leaves crap.

He crumples up the paper and tosses it on the floor.

MAUDE: What about your girl, the nasty poster girl? You are not still writing her?

ROBIN: On that subject, I defer to your new sexpertise. I'm sure by now you've got enough to write a book.

MAUDE: What are you talking about?

ROBIN: My poster girl. Your Sapphic snow queen. *(he pulls Kat's diary out of his bag)* You didn't know?

MAUDE: *(reads)* "The Sordid Diary of Kat Champagne."

ROBIN: I tried to warn you. But, one taste of catnip...

MAUDE: This belongs to her. You stole it from her place.

ROBIN: You see, I knew it. Loyalties and everything. But fine, I won't be bitter. You're with her now, I'll respect that.

MAUDE: I'm not "with" anybody. I am with myself.

ROBIN: See, *that's* why this whole thing is so fucked up. When I was young, they taught me evil things have weak points: a precise blast to the exhaust port will penetrate the Death Star, blah blah blah. And when the lights go out, all it takes is teamwork, stick-together-ness, and... "Band of brothers, marching together, heads held high in all kinds of weather..."

MAUDE: So? We're trying to stick together.

ROBIN: We're alone. If it were real, if it were like a circuit, we could touch, and the electric current would start up again, and things would come to life.

Maude reaches out and touches Robin's face.

MAUDE: I guess it doesn't work that way.

ROBIN: Give it a minute. *(beat)* I killed someone last night.

Maude tries to pull her hand away. Robin holds onto it.

Maybe it's not quite a mortal sin, because I only *let* him die through negligence. Or maybe since he's got four legs instead of two, but fuck, who's counting, 'cause the point is, I was s'posed to be there. To hang on to him. And maybe, if I'd learned that touching isn't always taking, if I'd tried to share a bit of body heat instead of hoarding it...and you have no idea what I'm talking about. *(drops his hand)*

MAUDE: *(still touching his face)* I know exactly what you're talking about.

Their eyes lock. Beat, and then the lights and power come back on in the café.

ROBIN: Holy Genesis. Did we do that?

MAUDE: I have to go.

ROBIN: What, after that? Come on!

MAUDE: I'm taking this. *(the diary)*

ROBIN: But we just had something. We shared, we can't just—

MAUDE: *Merde.* I do not know her address.

ROBIN: Oh. Oh no. Not her.

MAUDE: *(pulling him up)* You'll have to show me.

ROBIN: If you let her into this, she'll fuck it up. It's what she does.

MAUDE: I thought you liked to share now, Robin. Right?

Lights change. Kat in her apartment, hunkered down, staring into space.

Âllo?

ROBIN: No answer. She's not here, come on.

MAUDE: *Âllo?* Kat?

ROBIN: Tell me why we're here again?

Maude opens the fire escape door and steps inside.

MAUDE: Are you okay?

ROBIN: You see, she's in her happy place.

MAUDE: I came to bring this back. *(hands her the diary)* And to apologize.

Maude sets it down beside Kat. Kat glances at it, then shoves it away.

ROBIN: See, she doesn't even want it. Let's just—

MAUDE: Robin is apologizing, too.

ROBIN: I am?

MAUDE: For stealing from you.

ROBIN: Right. It was a shitty thing to do. I'm slime.

MAUDE: That is enough.

ROBIN: I'm serious.

KAT: *(to Maude)* You promised.

MAUDE: What?

KAT: You promised. You would make me pure.

MAUDE: I never—

KAT: We would leave together. Starting over. Faces, names.

MAUDE: I wanted to. I mean, I still—but Kat, you cannot just—

KAT: And now you bring me *that*? *(the diary)*

ROBIN: C'mon, let's go.

KAT: You know, I thought before that you were all together, laughing, planning ways to make me sick and suck me dry. But now, of course, there's no conspiracy. You're all just running round and fucking things and hurting people. And you know? I think that's worse.

ROBIN: Whoa, point of order. "Running round and fucking things?" That sounds like you, Champagne.

KAT: Fuck you.

ROBIN: And maybe, on a good night, me? But don't pick on the virgin, here.

MAUDE: I'm not a virgin.

ROBIN: What? You're not?

KAT: She molested me.

MAUDE: I was afraid.

KAT: You think I'm that naïve?

MAUDE: It's not just me. It's why we're so messed up. It's fear.

KAT: You're not an angel.

MAUDE: We are scared, and when we try, like this—

KAT: You're not Thérèse à Trois.

MAUDE: We try to reach out, to connect—and then—

KAT: You're nothing. Worse than nothing. You're an ugly nothing.

ROBIN: Thérèse à Trois?

MAUDE: You are right. I am; alone, we have no *personnage.* But with you, together, you and me, you *gave me*—

KAT: No. You took.

ROBIN: *(to Maude)* She thought you were Thérèse à Trois? The porn star? *(laughs)*

KAT: You think that's fucking funny?

ROBIN: Well, it's just, she's dead, is all.

MAUDE: Kat.

ROBIN: Some kind of AIDS-related yuckiness.

MAUDE: I'm sorry.

ROBIN: And she wasn't even Québécoise, she was from Newfoundland. I think she's buried in that cemetery by the mountain.

Kat is trembling, as if she is about to explode.

MAUDE: Kat?

A split second before she starts to move, Maude senses her intention...

Robin!

And then, with a cry, Kat is off and running towards the fire escape, gathering momentum for a leap. Robin intercepts her, pulling her back from the edge. He and Maude both hold her while she cries. After a pause, Robin speaks.

ROBIN: *(out)* Don't take a tumble, Kat. Not this time. This time, I hold on. She cries until the whole world trembles, till a flood of tears rush, Alice-like, out, down the fire escape, and wash across the ice, which hisses and shrinks from the heat and the salt. We hold on until the crying dies away, and there's no sound, except the city slowly coming back to life.

Lights change. Maude finds Robin at the café.

MAUDE: *Salut.*

ROBIN: *Salut.* Hi. Wow, I thought they fired you from this place.

MAUDE: I came to get my cheque.

ROBIN: Good timing.

MAUDE: Here. I ripped this off for you. *(gives him a coffee card puncher)* A lifetime of freebies.

ROBIN: Naughty girl.

MAUDE: I tried to call.

ROBIN: I'm still a drifter. Last guy in Montreal without his power back.

Kat appears in a separate space.

KAT: *(out)* At the airport. Point of no return.

ROBIN: Have you heard from...?

MAUDE: I don't think she wants to talk to me.

ROBIN: Don't beat yourself up.

KAT: *(out)* Ticket in hand. Heart in mouth.

ROBIN: She seemed hell-bent on self-destruction.

MAUDE: I think you're wrong.

KAT: *(out)* But then I step through the detector thing, and suddenly this Junior G-Man airport guard is all like, "What's inside your bag?" and so I dump my purse out on the counter, makeup, condoms, pills, and there it is. A ziplock baggie with my last few clumps of Zombie Orgy weed.

"It's medicinal?" I say.

ROBIN: One thing I gotta know. Just for the record. The whole "virgin" thing...

MAUDE: Are you still trying to measure people?

ROBIN: Well, I just, you, first you said you were, and then you said—

MAUDE: I'm not. I never was. I've fucked a million times, men, women, Catholics, Protestants. And I'm not really from Trois-Rivières. I am from Newfoundland.

ROBIN: Touché.

KAT: *(out)* The G-Man looks me up and down and smiles a cryptic little smile. "I'm going to have to confiscate this." he says. His accent is pure Montreal. I tell him he can keep the rest of my shit. I plan on never needing it. He lets me go. Calls after me: "Have a nice trip." "You too!" I say.

Inside my body I already feel the altitude, the tugging up and up and out. I see the moisture on the outside of the airplane's window, little rivers, pure and cold as birth. Flying west until I find the sun. *(exits)*

ROBIN: I don't suppose you could pretend to be a virgin, for me. For a...no, no, I don't mean—just hear me out. I kind of wrote something. But it needs a pure perspective, if you get my drift.

MAUDE: I don't...

ROBIN: Okay. Remember, "What's the worst thing that you've ever done?" Well, when I found myself, just recently, standing frozen at the gates of Hell, I realized...I guess I owe myself an answer to that question. So, instead of listing someone else's sins, you know...

MAUDE: Are you trying to confess to me?

ROBIN: Just read it. I...I want to know how damned I am.

MAUDE: I'm not a priest.

ROBIN: But you're an actor, right? You can pretend.

MAUDE: It doesn't work that way.

ROBIN: Well, try. Remember observationing? This is your final exam.

MAUDE: You are crazy.

ROBIN: True. But am I evil?

MAUDE: Apparently.

ROBIN: Well, that's the question.

MAUDE: Fine. *(out)* I read the list.

ROBIN: *(out)* I watch her read the list. Her eyes, like bunnies, darting.

MAUDE: *(out)* Most of it is...pretty weak.

ROBIN: *(out)* And I can tell, she's horrified.

MAUDE: *(out)* And what is really bad, he probably made up.

ROBIN: *(out)* But she believes it.

MAUDE: *(out)* He is too sweet to laugh at.

ROBIN: *(out)* Is she—Zoinks, I think she's gonna cry.

MAUDE: *(out)* I know what he wants from me. Or what he needs.

Maude sets the paper down and looks at him.

ROBIN: So...was that...I mean, do you, when you, like, you look at me...?

Pause. Then Maude gesticulates, as if she's going to bless him. Instead, she punches him twice, on the shoulders—just hard enough to hurt.

MAUDE: Don't be a stranger.

She kisses him on the head and exits.

ROBIN: *(out)* And so, our relationship ends as it began: with two unauthorized punches. I limp home, where my bong is thawed, the rent is late, my power's back at last. Which prob'ly means it's time to clean my freezer out.

I struggle up the mountain, which is scarred and tree-bald, like a chemo patient getting back its strength. I hammer out a hole, between the porn star cemetery and the huge electric cross. As I'm lowering Houdini into that from which he never will escape, I hear a weird-ass screeching overhead.

I watch it bank and spiral down towards the ice-thick cross. It's bright yellow, and green, with white wings. It starts to land, and I expect the extra weight to send the whole cross crashing down, on top of me, no doubt.

But it holds. The bird stays there, and so do I, until the street lights all come on. Then I go home.

Blackout.

The End